To my Gilly, our Lily,
and those many generations of Gunn women before them:
foresight has many forms.

COPING WITH FACTS

A SKEPTIC'S GUIDE TO THE PROBLEM OF DEVELOPMENT

Adam Fforde

Kumarian Press
An Imprint of Stylus Publishing

Coping with Facts
Published in 2009 in the United States of America by Kumarian Press
22883 Quicksilver Drive, Sterling, VA 20166-2012 USA

Copyright © 2009 Kumarian Press

The text of this book is set in 10/12.5 New Baskerville

Proofread by Publication Services, Inc.
Index by Publication Services, Inc.

Production and design by Publication Services, Inc.

Printed in the United States of America by IBT Global
Text printed with vegetable oil-based ink.

∞ The paper used in this publication meets the minimum requirements
of the American National Standard for Information Sciences-Permanence of
Paper for printed Library Materials, ANSI Z39.48-1984

Library of Congress Cataloging-in-Publication Data
Fforde, Adam.
    Coping with facts: a skeptic's guide to the problem of development /
Adam Fforde.
        p. cm.
    Includes bibliographical references and index.
    ISBN 978-1-56549-268-4 (pbk. : alk. paper) — ISBN 978-1-56549-274-5
(cloth : alk. paper)
    1. Economic development. 2. Developing countries—Economic policy.
I. Title.
    HD75.F49 2009
    338.9—dc22   2008040103

COPING WITH FACTS

A SKEPTIC'S GUIDE TO THE PROBLEM OF DEVELOPMENT

The five colors make man's eyes blind;
The five notes make his ears deaf;
The five tastes injure his palate;

(Lao Tzu, Tao te ching)

But it is different with commodities. There, the existence of the things *qua* commodities, and the value relation between the products of labor which stamps them as commodities, has absolutely no connection with their physical properties and with the material relations arising therefrom. There it is a definite social relation between men, that assumes, in their eyes, the fantastic form of a relation between things."

(Karl Marx, Das Kapital)

Contents

Boxes

Abbreviations

BOI	board of investment
DRV	Democratic Republic of Vietnam
EOG	export-oriented growth
EPZ	export processing zone
FAO	Food and Agriculture Organization
FDI	foreign direct investment
FYP	Five-Year Plan
GAD	gender and development
GDP	gross domestic product
IMF	International Monetary Fund
IRD	integrated rural development
ISI	import-substituting industrialization
JV	joint venture
NESDB	National Economic and Social Development Board
NGO	nongovernmental organization
NIC	newly industrializing countries
NIEO	New International Economic Order
PHC	primary health care
PPA	participatory poverty assessment
PRA	participatory rural appraisal
PWC	post-Washington Consensus
RIDF	Rural Infrastructure Development Fund
RRA	rapid rural appraisal
SAL	structural adjustment loan
SEA	Southeast Asia
SMEs	small and medium enterprises
SOE	state-owned enterprise
UNCDF	United National Capital Development Fund

VAT	value-added tax
VCP	Vietnamese Communist Party
WC	Washington Consensus
WB	World Bank
WID	Women in Development

Glossary of Terms

In the text I use a number of terms in ways that readers may find unfamiliar or particular. Often, these words are explained within boxes in the text. Here I attempt to explain how I use some of the others and their importance.

Absolutization: A making absolute of something more persuasively thought of as relative. The quote from Lao Tzu can be interpreted to mean that a model is not what it models and written accounts of history are not history. A core issue is the stability of views taken as positions change over time and space. Unlike, say, the knowledge associated with bridge building, what can be studied and learned about development varies over time and between authors. Attempts to deny this, then, implies that the student should experience a stability of views, when, I argue, they do not.

Comparative advantage: This is a technical term in economics. I discuss and define it in the section on globalization, in Chapter 7.

Cyclicality: In histories of policy ideas, this is the idea that patterns of ideas go through cycles related to their internal structure. If thought stresses concepts of centralization and decentralization, then ideas would cycle as they go from support for one pole through to support for the other, and back again. This way of seeing policy ideas is discussed in the section "Policy as doctrine and the return of cyclicality," in Chapter 3.

Instrumental rationality: Within economics, this is a term used to point out what is being done when the standard analytical framework of algebra and models is selected. It can be thought of as coming down to the idea that it is not necessary to think of humans, within economics, as any different from machines. I discuss and define it in the section "Market Failure," in Chapter 6.

Market failure: Within economics, this is a term used to refer to situations in which markets will not, for various reasons, lead to good outcomes. I discuss it in the section "Economists' arguments for state intervention revisited," in Chapter 6.

Positive deviation: This term stems originally from observation of change processes in Vietnam, where varied application of central orders was often the norm, rather than the exception. Under such conditions *viola-*

tions of central norms could be interpreted positively, and so referred to as "positive deviations" (*vi pham tich cuc*, in Vietnamese).

Realization problem: In many discussions of change, if reference is made to some set of ideas that are to be implemented, such as a blueprinted reform plan, then there will arise the issue of how to conceptualize what happens as those ideas influence observed reality. The common phrase is how they are implemented. I discuss this term in the section "Policy as part of development policy: economics as an 'ideal type,'" in Chapter 2.

Preface

The Issue

This book argues that it is wise to be skeptical about claims found in the study and practice of development—of intentional social change. Many thinkers have pointed to what they, like me, see as a peculiar yet common practice of assuming that important things are knowable and experienced as such, when facts point to the contrary.

Consider the two quotes at the start of this book. Lao Tzu, or at least the work attributed to a man of that name, seems to be pointing out that whatever music is, it is different from that written down to be played—the "five notes." Similarly, the categories used to discuss tastes and colors are not the tastes and the colors themselves; history, in this sense, is not *written* history. This does not say what history is but what it is not, and what therefore should not be said about it. And his argument is not presented in terms of facts but based upon rhetoric and persuasion.

More radically, with profound effects upon a wide range of modern thinkers, Marx's quote shows him arguing that a most characteristic aspect of capitalism, which nowadays dominates humankind in many ways, is its production of *commodities*—things produced for profit that appear not as the concrete and specific outputs of a given set of workers in a certain factory, but rather as abstractions: "just another $3 item." That Marx, unlike Lao Tzu, also thought that his theory could establish exactly what reality was, should not obscure the similarity of his point: that in various ways we seem to believe in generalities, in universalities, in categories, and that there are good arguments that this practice, if it asserts that it is consistent with facts, is very unwise, especially in situations in which cause and effect relations are posited.

Both Lau Tzu and Marx, therefore, agree that skepticism is a good thing, although usually not something that most people have adopted. So what about the real meaning of what these two critics of mainstream thought are discussing? This is not something I would dare attempt to answer. But, in this book, I do look at one aspect of such arguments: the problem of facts, and how these relate to issues of *development*.

I address this because it seems to have turned out that, having begun from different starting-points that shared assertions of the existence of knowable development processes, many important positions in the development literature now appear to have to cope with entanglements caused by their facts (and by these I mean their own "contingent" empirics, as I do not at all assert that there exist "objective" facts). The core puzzle is that, if these approaches are consistent, their empirics *deny* the existence of knowable development processes. This is incongruous and contradictory and means that, among many other people, Lao Tzu and Marx were wise. And in turn this has important implications for what we think when we watch these positions interact with intentionalities—with the need to argue that *if* this is done *then* that will happen. For that is not what their facts suggest.

It seems clear that development issues contrast with much of modern social sciences. This is because development is related to practice, with doing things. And this brings in the tricky issue of prediction and the associated puzzle of facts. The book, from a skeptical position, discusses important instances of how this happens and the inconsistencies it raises. From a Daoist perspective, a chimera is obvious; for Marxists and their descendants, it is far trickier. Yet, in a world increasingly subject to a powerful and globalizing capitalism, it seems an obvious consequence of Marx's position that the data required for a predictive analysis will be lacking, for it will necessarily be obscured by the very nature of capitalism itself. Commodities, the characteristic and predominant product of capitalism, appear as they are not. Analysis may demonstrate what they are, but it cannot, necessarily, obtain the data needed to predict consequences. Therefore, hopes for intentionality in social change, if based upon some analytical framework comparable in power to natural sciences, are an illusion. What, then, of development? What, then, of developers and those subject to development?

This is where things start to become fascinating. It is not a matter of any particular explanation, but their shared facts—the stuff collected to buttress the prediction that characterizes the most common policy logics that we find. And in most instances, the facts of approaches need to be coped with precisely because they do not exhibit those perceived regularities that would underpin prediction in terms that make sense to the relevant practices and discourses. We therefore observe, in watching how facts are coped with, tensions and inconsistencies. This is not, then, a theoretical critique of existing positions, but an observation of their empirical troubles. I stress that I understand facts in terms specific to explanatory frameworks, rather than "given."

In contemporary advanced capitalism, these issues seem to generate both tensions and opportunities. Some of us are heavily conditioned, whether by lifestyle or social position. Others experience weak conditioning, or perhaps are better placed to combat it, and so sensitive to similar puzzles this book confronts. So what happens next? That is another project, but what is striking to me is how issues of intentionality in social change encourage coping with facts (in the above sense), and that this generates strong apprehensions of inconsistency. And to get at this, I need to explore that particular area of human intellectual outputs and practice that tends to be called "development thinking" and "development policy." For this is very strange.

From a geographical perspective, it is obvious that developmental ideas are usually exotic in that they come from somewhere else. I use the term in its literal sense, as referring to the distant and different origins of something. In this sense, something that is exotic need not be exciting or novel. A theme that runs through this book is that the exotic aspect of development ideas is strongly related to arguments about why facts are a problem. This will turn out to be related to ways in which "one size fits all" solutions fail to fit persuasively and the degree to which it is wise to assume that the world is homogeneous.

From a radical perspective, it can be said to come down to an illusion that capitalism can be known in ways that allow it to be directed predictably through some simple intentionality—such as policy. Rather, progress now seems to depend upon a diverse range of perceptions and interactions that may add up to something that looks like mass action but contains no clear, realized intentionality. Rather than "thinking globally and acting locally," therefore, progress may thus appear to take the form of "thinking locally and acting globally." Such reflections may push for change in notions of action and intentionality. Notions of global thinking may entail inconsistencies and so they are easily confused by a range of possibilities: "spin," commoditization, and confusion of measurable but abstract form with contingent content, Daoist confrontations of perception with pipes and apples, or whatever. One consequence of inconsistency is a vast freedom to generate spurious belief. Capitalism, it seems, is like that. And then what historians may see as global acts will need to be interpreted as embodying something very different from the simple and egoistic notions of intentionality that permeate development policy.

The Book

This book is thus designed as an extended essay on the nature of development thinking and development policy. It may also be used as a textbook, but it does not aim to present a thorough study of all the relevant literature, which would be boring, not least because the literature is vast. There is, however, another reason, which is that such a literature survey would lack meaning: What is the point of recapitulation? Why do it? My point here is to illuminate the ways in which dominant approaches fail to cope with facts (in the above sense), and how these tensions are related to issues of intentionality and predictability. Through these I also discuss questions of knowledge and its usually exotic character in a development context.

The book may be useful as a classroom manual—a guide to how to manage the literature. And the rather rapid pace with which it covers a large amount of ground may show readers how far they might themselves travel if they were to adopt a similar approach. Its immediate goal, then, is to help make sense of comparisons of development policies, and it uses three countries of Southeast Asia as case studies. This brings out the importance of the ways in which development studies seeks to employ languages that *assume* much: that ideas derived from one context may, without too much concern, be used in another. The exotic nature of much development thinking when applied to poor people is important to the issue. And central to the notion of "exotic" here is the way that the use of exotic ideas *assumes* that the facts used will support the belief that "what works there, also works here." We will see that it usually does not. The book proceeds as follows.

Structure

Chapter 1 begins with an overview and contextualization. The book then divides into three parts. Part I, The Problem of Development, covers Chapters 2 through 6. It starts in Chapter 2, which raises some fundamental questions: How do we present exotic ideas as useful in addressing specific local issues? What are the most important characteristic elements of classic notions of policy? How do these relate to development thinking? How have they changed over time, and why? And how do we usefully select an empirical basis for case studies? This discussion aims to provide a basis for my argument about classic views of policy, and that the related issues of intentionality, the agency of that intention, and assumptions of knowability are illuminated through examination of the development literature. My opinion is that classic views of policy are unpersuasive in many ways. Examples of developmental success may challenge these views by presenting heterodox explanations to make up for deficiencies. The tensions created by the assumptions can then be observed. The rest of Part I examines development literature across two dimensions. In Chapters 3 and 4, I look at histories of development as an idea. Chapters 5 and 6 then review literature thematically, looking at particular approaches and puzzles.

Chapters 3 through 6 are organized as follows. I discuss issues, usually with reference to interesting positions, and I examine particular examples in terms of texts. I do not actually argue that the positions I examine are important, though I believe that many of them are; rather, I present discussion of them as useful for the development of relevant strategies on how to advance. Thus, I do not present an exhaustive survey of either the development studies literature or development practice; rather, I use texts to support my arguments about inconsistencies common to classic views of policy. Such views cope with facts by being inconsistent.

Part II, Exotic Doctrine—Its Local Fates, covers Chapters 7 through 11, and takes development experiences as its main empiric, building on Part I to examine how development policies have been compared. It starts in Chapter 8 by reviewing Part I and its conclusions. These conclusions emphasize the problems posed by the need to cope with facts, and specifically the lack of robust relationships between policies and consequences across different contexts already discussed in Part I. It then examines case studies from Southeast Asia: Vietnam, Thailand, and the Philippines (Chapters 9 through 11). Two of these countries are widely seen as successes (Vietnam and Thailand) and the other (the Philippines) as in many ways a failure.

I am meant to be a Vietnam expert. I speak some Vietnamese, have lived there for a number of years, and have contributed to the scholarly and development literatures. But I access the two other case study countries through secondary sources. The reader may find this contrast between author as producer and as critical consumer useful. One element of this is the way in which expertise so often copes with facts by assertion of successful explanation, thus avoiding tests of prediction.

These case studies enable me to further develop my arguments about development policy. I emphasize issues of intentionality and knowability, leading to questions such as the implications and meanings of knowledge-based practices in policy work. Underlying this is a highlighting of ways in which apparent development success energizes production of *heterodox* approaches, for anomalies in the wider literature reveal issues of consistency and encourage greater attention to criteria that focus upon subsequent events—Chapter 1—rather than intervention logics stressing cause and effect.

Part II presents reasons why the case studies should (but perhaps now with caution) inform such discussions and alert the reader to the importance of the question does policy matter? How? What makes you think that it does? And, crucially but so often ignored in the face of compelling (but why?) authority, just how did you reach this judgment?

Part III, Conclusions, starts in Chapter 12 by reviewing implications of what has gone before, attempting to draw some general conclusions. Before doing so, it broaches issues of *heuristics*—learning by doing. It then examines discussions of mainstream failure that help extend my argument. Chapter 13 then finishes with some implications for changes to practice and ideas on how these might already be observable.

Origins

This book is based upon a career that has lasted more than three decades. About two-thirds of this has been spent in consultancy and the rest in academia involving both research and teaching. This was marked by a change in 1999–2000 when I prepared to teach full-time at the Southeast Asian Studies Program of the National University of Singapore (NUS) and so had to develop subjects in ways that drew upon both my own experiences and the available literature.

Much of my experience in consultancy stemmed from an interest in Third World socialism, which led me to study Vietnamese in Hanoi during 1978–79, to write a PhD thesis, and to various other works. Much of this arose originally from a desire to secure a more rational and civil social change process, and the belief (largely I now think a delusion) that then existing socialism was capable of attaining that. It is also noteworthy that a large part of my published academic work on Vietnam, and indeed consultancy work, was closely associated with the country's transition from plan to market through the 1980s. Through the 1990s it became increasingly evident to me that the emergence of a capitalism in Vietnam was posing hard questions, as corruption and social differentiation accompanied improvements in material standards and steep falls in measured poverty rates. Yet I have reached an important conclusion in my work: that these consequences were *not* in the main the product of policy but rather, in terms of plausible explanation, resulted from other forces.

I found when I prepared my teaching for NUS that what I discovered needed explanation. Further, that in explaining the tensions that I found there seemed to be opportunities for learning and reflection. This book is the result. It owes much to students who have helped me present the ideas. It is also indebted to a number of colleagues in academia and consultancy, as well as to some path-breaking and illuminating studies, whose influence will be clear from citations in the text.[i] I should add that I have learned much over the years from losing arguments with a wide range of laypeople—farmers, drivers, and others.

I hope the book confronts the reader in ways that encourage active response with what I find the most fantastical of all aspects of the development literature: the notion that the reader's own subjectivity can be closely identified with that of powerful politicians and officials (and others) with significant power. Is it reasonable for them to imagine that they are in a position to reply to the question, what is to be done? And that the reader finds in this confrontation a need to confront a puzzle: Why

---

[i] For support of my skepticism, see especially Cowen and Shenton (1996), Dunn (2000), Levine and Zervos (1993), and Winch (1958).

should we think that human social change could be—as it often is—persuasively put in terms of some predictable process, when assuming this can (once we realize it) make it very hard to cope with facts?

But there is more to this than just an intellectual position. To think and act as a politician (or other politically powerful person) is and rightly so different from being an intellectual or analyst (Joll 1965). More importantly, I believe that political decision-making and political responsibility are closely linked, so that seeking to treat fundamentally political decisions as technical is (among other things) to seek power without responsibility, which is for many reasons a precarious moral position.

If I were making a speech, I would say that if you want political power, then create the conditions for getting yourself properly elected. That is, position yourself at a place where you mediate between subsequent events and questions of their acceptability and value.

Finally, the reader will note that I avoid, except when dealing with them as terms, words such as *development* and *developing country*. This is to clarify. I prefer to refer to poor countries as being poor, and, if they appear to be getting less poor, then to say so. Readers may judge for themselves whether they agree with my use of the word in the particular instance.

Thanks

This has been a long road, and I regret that I cannot recall all those who have contributed. I owe particular thanks to various people who shared with me either their own teaching outlines or pointed me toward particular readings. For the former I need to thank Hal Hill, Peter Larmour, Bob Smith, and Christine Sylvester. In particular, I thank the inimitable Regina Abrami for directing me to Cowen and Shenton's work

I express my profound thanks to Nguyen Dinh Huan, Anthony Marcus, Michael Webber, Catherine Earl, Ron Cullen, Greg Thompson, Craig Thorburn, Joerg Wischermann, and Bob Smith, and far too many Vietnamese to mention, for collegial tussling over ideas and practice. I am indebted to Haroon Akram-Lodhi for a discussion that reminded me of Marx's position on commodity production. Bob Smith and Michael Webber were both kind enough to read an earlier manuscript in its entirety, and I owe them special thanks. I thank editorial input from Kumarian.

I also note my thanks in particular to students who have attended my courses on comparative development policy and development economics, and the SEA Studies Program at NUS for hiring me and getting me to put the former together.

I am, of course, responsible for mistakes that remain.

Adam Fforde
Melbourne, 2008

Overview, Puzzles, and Contextualization

The white man's burden
The savage wars of peace—
Fill full the mouth of Famine,
And bid the sickness cease;
And when your goal is nearest
(The end for others sought)
Watch sloth and heathen folly
Bring all your hopes to nought

(Kipling 1899)

Empires of the mind . . .
"Let us go forward in malice to none and good will to all. Such plans offer far better prizes than taking away other people's provinces or lands or grinding them down in exploitation. The empires of the future are the empires of the mind."

(Churchill 1943)

A nineteenth-century Foucault?
"Few ideas are correct ones, and which they are none can tell, but with words we govern men"

(Disraeli 1832 Part 1 ch xxi 33)

Truth?
"There is truth but no finite mortal has it . . ."
Bill Clinton, agreeing with his Georgetown teacher
Carroll Quigley (Clinton 2004, 78)

Development: Policy and Practice

The Puzzle of Policy

Defining Policy

For various reasons I have come to worry that the practice of development suffers from unhealthy tendencies. These I attribute in part to the prevalence of assumptions that appear in many ways implausible and that project confusion and tension into the field of development with a number of negative results.

I have come to believe that these assumptions are conveyed through the ways in which ideas associated with policy are taught, used, and construed. If this is the case, then this author faces the need to make arguments within intellectual contexts whose beliefs and premises he is challenging. This poses considerable problems of exposition, because many of the terms this book uses carry with them the very beliefs and assumptions that the author intends to confront. I trust the reader will bear with me, and perhaps conclude that if an argument appears obviously wrong, this may be because it is challenging unquestioned assumptions. A certain amount of repetition is needed to cope with this, and I use much cross-referencing in the text to identify how certain terms should be used.

This book, then, attempts to clarify issues set deep within ideas of policy and development. Let us start with a discussion of the term *policy*. The *Australian Oxford Dictionary* defines *policy* as a

> course or principle of action adopted or proposed by a government, political party, business, individual etc. (Moore 1996)

This definition can be taken to mean that the term *policy* says something about certain actions: the idea that actions may have certain features—a "course or principle"—associated with them and that these are important because they then give that proposed act its particular meaning as an act of policy. It follows that policy is to be understood as an attribute of certain actions, differentiating them from others.

Ideas of Cause and Effect

Many but not all ideas about policy tend to follow from this definition, adding to it by construing policy in terms of cause and effect: actions as policies lead in some manner to particular consequences. In this way policy as the "course or principle of action" says something about what will happen and why. Policy is thus connected to intentionality and in this way characterizes the action. But the question then arises—how exactly to use the term *intentionality*? The issue may seem clear, but in many ways it is not.

This is where trouble seems to start. An uncritical use of language may mean that sets of ideas met when looking at policy (I call these "policy ideologies") contain much that should be questioned but is not. For example, many of us assume the existence of intentionality within whatever we are looking at—an accompanying, identifiable intention to attain certain consequences and, for me most heroically, an *agency* as something that can adopt and embody that intention.

If, as is common, these assumptions exist, it is then relatively easy (or so it may appear) to link development policy to actions through ideas of cause and effect. To do so requires two things: First, it requires some relationship between them, in other words an *intervention logic*, which tells what happens and what should happen in terms of causes and their consequences (see Box 1.1—*Intervention logics*). Second, it requires *facts*, or some way of dealing with causes and effects empirically, perhaps *observed*. This is self-evident, for it is hard to conceive of situations in which things referred to in discussions of policy would be accepted as explicitly having no empirical reference.

Neither of these requirements, I fear, is as risk-free as may first appear. For example, there is the distinction between intervention logics *before* action (what could be called "ex ante") and intervention logics *after* action (what could be called "ex post"). The first may be found, for example, in aid project documents signed and agreed upon but not yet implemented; the second can be found in accounts (such as evaluations) of what happened. Yet such documents may have multiple interpretations and may be involved with different assessment criteria. Here it is possible to see how troubles start, for questions concerning what such criteria amount to are energized by the ease with which it is possible to see them differing between various organizations and over time for particular organizations. Such examples are easy to find, indeed are demonstrated by many accounts of the history of development ideas and their instability (for an example see Box 1.7—*Pragmatism and contingency*).

Criteria for assessing intervention logics are very interesting. A donor may, for example, give great attention to monitoring plans ex ante, caring deeply whether their intervention logics are correct in terms of vertical consistency (see Box 1.2—*Meanings of consistency—horizontal or vertical?*). Or they may not, and vertically inconsistent ex ante and ex post plans and reports are tolerated so long as they are thought to produce acceptable consequences.

To give an illustrative example, donors may care whether projects they fund are correct in terms of their treatment of the role of participation in securing "subsequent events" that are here seen as outcomes. If so, then donors will expect projects to contain participation, and so project staff, and/or others, should be able to report on this. To do so there will be some understanding of what "correct" participation is. On the other hand, if donors do not care, then they may well argue that there are a variety of options, and the presence or absence of participation is of no great importance. In either case, there is always the question of what happens when there is "positive deviation"—when something is wrong but seems to have positive effects upon "subsequent events." Again, donors vary in their views.

Such tolerance, or its absence, is a social act, and as such usually appears to members of the organization concerned as a normal practice. For them, this is how development occurs. Change, therefore, may

---

Box 1.1
Intervention logics

Intervention logics are a fundamental element to development practice, especially aid, and are discussed in various normative texts, especially evaluation manuals.

They express what is to be done in terms of cause and effect. As such, they are then necessarily central to the design of interventions such as projects, and to their evaluation. Guidance of design and evaluation is normative, and prescriptions can thus be observed through the relevant documents of responsible organizations.

A good example is that of the Swedish bilateral Sida, whose manual *Looking Backward, Moving Forward* (Molund and Schill 2004), can be downloaded from www.sida.se. See Chapter 5 for their comments on the role of experts in determining the acceptability of an intervention logic.

A central issue is the criteria that are said to determine whether any particular intervention logic is accepted or not. For me, what is accepted as logical depends upon acceptance criteria, which may differ (Kline 1980; Winch 1958): there are no knowable "absolutes."

---

require acceptance of something earlier viewed as an unacceptable mistake. But how is it decided what is a mistake? For example, project documents ex ante may mean different things to different people: consultants, radical critics, donor agencies, and so on; project evaluations ex post can be accepted or rejected, and criticized or praised, in many different but recognizable ways. In these ways meanings are valorized: they are made more or less acceptable. Ideas of cause and effect associated with intervention logics are, therefore, wisely treated with caution. Though practices vary, the facts associated with intervention logics are not as simple as they may first appear.

The reader may have noted that my argument so far, despite its references to empirics and facts, has not appeared to require discussion of—or any assertion that there is—an objective reality (whatever that might mean). But, if classic statements about policy are to be accepted in the ways just outlined, they will usually be associated with some basis in an "experienced real"—with facts. This poses the questions of how this should happen and how statements are to be accepted, rejected, or otherwise dealt with. To ask "what are the facts" is to invite, if the answer is

Box 1.2
Meanings of consistency—horizontal or vertical?

I am trying to address two sorts of inconsistency.

There is the internal inconsistency of a document; for example, if it says X and Y at the same time and these positions are usually accepted within that practice as contradictory. More generally, the position is inconsistent with the standards it is meant to follow.

I call this a *vertical* inconsistency. An example might be an aid project proposal that suggests that male and female children are essentially different, which contradicts the donor's requirement for gender equity and belief among its experts that this is the case.

There may also be a rather different sort of inconsistency between two positions that are vertically consistent: both meet the standards required of them but suggest things that are incompatible in terms of some other (external) set of criteria.

I call this a *horizontal* inconsistency: a proposal from an aid project that meets donor requirements but contains incompatible positions in the eyes of an outsider (perhaps somebody who believes that there are innate gender differences). Of course, I am treating the donor as a metaphor to illustrate ways in which positions are valorized.

My point, following Winch (1958), is that to accept a proposition as logical and consistent is to do something.

---

serious, explanation of how they are constructed and what meanings are given to them. And these explanations differ according to contexts. Caution is advisable.

The Issue of Knowability

Lurking behind such puzzles is another. It is, I believe, common for mainstream development policy not to confront the issue of whether intervention logics are reasonably thought to be *knowable*. The familiar assumption is that they are—the belief that, whatever criteria are used (and these may differ), it is possible to construct or arrive at situations in which debate ceases as participants are persuaded that they know enough, either about the power of the argument—perhaps its logic—or its empirics, or perhaps both. Another way of putting this is that the issue of knowability may be thought of as the issue of the possibility of shared belief: what is said to be known does not differ as perspectives change. But this is usually expressed in terms of rather different ideas—usually that something may be said to be right or wrong, or that statements about what happened may be said to be right or wrong.

The assumption of knowability is often associated with the view that knowledge is something that develops in a progressive direction, and this accompanies the ways just mentioned of dealing with mismatches between assumptions and empirics. It tends to see these mismatches as having to do with errors, or correctable mistakes.

The assumption that something is knowable regularly accompanies the habit of concluding that if two positions about it differ then one at least is wrong. Conversely, not to believe in knowability is to avoid concluding from disagreement that at least one side is in error. It appears to me that a significant part (but not all) of the development literature assumes knowability in this sense, and I argue that this assumption is awry: intervention logics are not so reasonably to be assumed knowable, at least not in the same way as the effects of the application of fertilizer to seedlings are knowable.

Two important elements of language are associated with the issue of knowability. First is the idea that a historical process, say of development, is "immanent"—predetermined. Second is the idea that change can be "done"—development is a "transitive" rather than a transitive process, and so it does not simply happen, but results from some action or set of actions. I discuss these further in Chapter 2 (see also Box 1.3—*Development as an immanent process and the issue of "transitivity"*).[i]

Box 1.3
Development as an imminent process and the issue of "transitivity"

Development can be called immanent.

Such a process is thought to contain a working out, over time, of some logic of change that existed before the process itself, thus enabling us to think that we can, for example, know cause-effect relationships ex ante—before they happen. For what seems to me to be an example of this approach applied to technology, see Heidigger (1977, 3–35).

Development can also be called transitive or intransitive.

A verb is transitive if it may take a direct object ("I ate the cake") and intransitive if it may not ("Change happens"). But can we say "Change killed the radio show"?

---

[i] Note the confidence with which I assert knowability in discussing Vietnam in Chapter 9.

Classic Views of Policy—Possible Political Implications

This discussion suggests that mainstream views of aspects of policy as an attribute of actions are problematic, yet familiar. Let me call them *classic views of policy*. They are characterized by various assumptions—of intentionality, of intention located in an agency, and of the knowability of intervention logics.

This use is part of familiar development practice. For example, a given development project is assumed to possess intentionality, to site this on an implementing agency, which acts thus as a location of intention, to embody known cause-effect relationships in its planning (ex ante) and its actions (ex post): that, we are told, is what the project is aiming to do, and this is how its actions will achieve those aims. In this way the project is seen as an example of actions that express policy following the discussion above in that policy has become an attribute of actions through the presence of intentionality, agency, and a knowable or known intervention logic. And these are puzzling ideas. That they should be involved in the use of the word policy in this sense (and so accompany associated development practices) does not seem to be widely appreciated.

Classic views in this sense would exclude alternative conceptions. An example is a view that there is no such simple intentionality at all, rather a range of differing perceptions and activities of various degrees of consistency that come together in various ways. A language that would cope with this would need to be able to discuss intentionality without an assumption of knowability. Pragmatic approaches that avoid blueprints and similar predictive ex ante positions point in this direction. But my main concern here is the familiar, classic views of policy. There is nothing a priori wrong with them, but in practice such approaches too often appear inconsistent. Lest I be misunderstood, I do not mean by consistent anything transcendental or objectively true; rather, following Winch (1958) and many others, I simply mean that statements within the classic approaches often fail to meet certain criteria. Such judgments are best thought of as subjective acts. My concern, though, is not simply that there is inconsistency. There are also, and this is probably more important, political effects that influence how and where power lies in debates.

If cause-effect relations are thought knowable, then this seems likely to give—or try to give—authority to those said to know. Authority is believed to give power to those who hold it. Search for this power may encourage justification of political actions through policy discussions that emphasize the rightness (or not) of certain intervention logics. An alternative, among many, is justification through something else, perhaps outcomes, or more consistently the acceptability of "subsequent events." Note that the latter phrase need not, unlike *outcome* or *consequence*, imply causality. This encourages discussion that avoids the assumption of knowability, and so the common rhetoric that asserts that successful critics should themselves be believed. If we use a term that implies causality, then this encourages debate as to what that is, and this may be at the expense of other alternatives.

I have watched too much developmental effort put into resourcing discussions of "what works"—the search for a known cause-effect relationship. I have seen far too few comparable examples of development efforts put into the politics required to ensure that key, subjective facts associated with development interventions—the subsequent events—were widely acceptable.

The classic views of policy discussed here are fundamental to much political activity. Yet emphasis upon the rightness of intervention logics may easily lead to attempts to impose a view of intentional change within which "subsequent events" are construed as necessarily being known solutions to familiar problems. This normally assumes the existence of a right answer and tends too often to accept spurious references to posited cause-effect relations (see Box 1.4—*Spurious results*). A theme that runs through Part II of this book is that there is a strong tendency for theory to run ahead of reality.

I argue that these habits are strongly associated with classic views of policy. One common consequence of these views is that more resources and attention are focused upon analysis of intervention logics rather than upon ways of gauging the acceptability of subsequent events. In development practice, while many argue for the value of participatory ex post evaluation, such exercises often receive less attention and resources than hunts for plausibly correct intervention logics (see the discussion of the story told by Robert Chambers in Chapter 2).

Box 1.4
Spurious results

By *spurious* I do not mean *wrong*, but rather *meaningless*.

If we measure something with a ruler and report the results, but we start to believe that the ruler is incorrect (in some unknown way), then the results may still be right, but we have little basis for saying that they are. In this sense, they are spurious.

In such practices, people are held responsible, not for "subsequent events," but for their knowledge of what was said to be going to happen (ex ante): "the policy was right." The legitimizing effects are as obvious as the risks.

Correct Policy?

Two Main Examples of Classic Policy Ideology: Introduction

To develop and ground these ideas, the book confronts two classes of what I call "development policy ideology"—two groups of ideas that, through policy, offer meaningful and intentional social change. Both rely heavily, but in different ways, upon cause-effect metaphors and express, despite their frequent mutual distrust, classic views of policy.

The confrontation in both cases focuses upon internal inconsistencies: that both classes present judgments inconsistent with their own criteria for what should be accepted. Both classes primarily seek to justify action by reference to intention. Policy is thus primarily to be assessed in terms of intentionality, and the main issue as a result is whether the analysis of cause and effect embedded in policy is correct.

Explanation Masquerading as Prediction

Pretended predictive power as a prop to explanation characterizes the first class of policy ideologies. It tends to valorize positions based on their purported predictive power. A typical position within this class is: "We know enough about economies to be certain that export-oriented growth (EOG) policies will lead to better outcomes." The quote below is simply one example. "Because labour is the main asset of the poor, making it more productive is the best way to reduce poverty" (World Bank 2007, 2). This quote contains ideas both of knowability and of predictivity, both linked in a classic statement of what should be done and why.

The class contains a range of methods and approaches, but most obvious are methods of analysis derived from social sciences (including contemporary mainstream economics) that advocate and present formal modeling, which inherently suggests predictability because of the nature of such approaches and their use of algebra. For example, in economic models, the role of time is such that different results are linked directly to different settings of a variable referring to time (t), so that cause and effect relations between variables are immediately apparent. Acceptance validates the assumption of knowability of cause-effect relationships, which should then be legitimately embedded in intentional social change as policy. Many assume that contention between positions implies that at

---

Box 1.5
Economics—prediction and empirics

To quote Friedman:

> "The ultimate goal of a positive science is the develop-
> ment of a 'theory' or 'hypothesis' that yields valid and mean-
> ingful (that is, not truistic) predictions about phenomena
> not yet observed" (1953, 7).

For a softer and earlier statement that is very similar, see Stigler:

> "Since economics is a science, it is appropriate to begin
> with an examination of the nature of science . . . The impor-
> tant purpose of a scientific law is to permit prediction"
> (1947, 3).

Intriguingly, a textbook such as Jehle and Reny, in their Part I,
"Language and Methods," presents little that allows a reader to
see how the models exposited in the text link to any observed real
(1998, 1–107).

Unless otherwise stated, when I refer to economics throughout this book, I mean neoclassical economics.

---

least one is false. Intentionality here is clearly linked to outcomes through
the purportedly known cause-effect relationship.

However, I will argue (Chapter 3) that the internal empirics of these
approaches do *not* suggest that they have generated predictability. The
assumption of the knowability of such intervention logics thus loses an
essential prop. What is left, therefore, is explanation (this is the main
thrust of the second class), which is not usually how the arguments are
formally presented. This class, then, produces tensions between an experienced real and a pretended knowledge of that real.

An illustrative example would be that of a mainstream policy-set, such
as export-oriented growth. Advocates argue that this policy-set will generate growth for countries that open their economies to foreign trade and
investment. Many research studies support the idea that such policies lead
to better economic performance with the passing of time. These studies
estimate economic relations that express the analysts' ideas of cause-effect
relationships in formal terms. The approach thus appears predictive, but
there are reasons to judge that research results *within* this class show a failure to predict outcomes.

This is only one example within this class of policy ideologies. What
it often replaced—import-substituting industrialization (ISI)—was also

couched in terms of a knowable development process (Chenery et al. 1974). In contrast to EOG, ISI argued for a relatively closed economy, obtained by protection through tariffs imposed upon imports and controls over capital movements. It relied upon arguments such as those about "infant industries" that required such protection for them to grow and become competitive. The discussion in Chapter 3 suggests that this position also fails to predict.

Prediction Masquerading as Explanation

The second class is characterized as prediction masquerading as explanation. This class tends to self-valorize by combining explanation with a critique of other positions. A typical position within this class is: "Neo-liberal ideas are inherently disempowering, and only through increased participation by the poor will we get better development."

Robert Chambers is an important figure, and he was instrumental in the creation of now-authoritative developmental techniques that valorized various sorts of knowledge, including rapid rural appraisal and participatory rural appraisal (Chambers 1983). He has consistently emphasized the importance of nonprofessional knowledge. It is Chambers' conceptual understanding of knowledge that is most interesting. He believes in finding a "true" knowledge, that is, a removal of bias: "The problem is how . . . to put people first and poor people first of all . . . The thesis of this book is that solutions can be sought in a new paradigm and a new professionalism" (Chambers 1997, 14).

Note that he refers to "paradigm" and "professionalism" in the singular, not the plural. Further, the second chapter of Chambers' book is entitled "Normal Error." It refers to mistakes in forecasting and ". . . errors and myths [that] have persisted through decades, reinforced and reasserted by intelligent, highly educated people across the range of disciplines and professional occupations" (Chambers 1997, 29).

Chambers seems to believe in knowability, and for him the central issue is to replace incorrect with correct knowledge. Yet he does not argue in terms of predictive facts. His and other positions within this second class share an emphasis upon explanation: the idea that the meaning of whatever is under discussion be constructed intelligibly in a way that meets criteria of acceptability. This does not explicitly present as predictive. This appeals to consumers who are not attracted to the formal rigor of the first class and may reject the possible implication that people are as predictable as machines.

A contemporary example is the common view that insufficient participation in projects by poor people explains much of what goes wrong, and that more participation will lead to better development. Participatory rural appraisal is one expression of this view. Yet what is going on here?

This is an intervention logic containing a cause-effect metaphor. It advocates policy in the sense that it advocates a course of action; it entails intentionality.

This class develops ideas to support policy as "courses or principles of action"—ideas presented as valuable and worth accepting—from a critique of other ideas (often those of the first class), as the quotes from Chambers show. Then it presents other ideas—its own—as better by contrast. However, by presenting its own ideas as a valid basis for intentional change but not subjecting them to criteria of prediction, the class becomes inconsistent. While an attack is usually made upon the predictability assumption, when the explanation itself is presented as a valuable guide to intentionality, this critique is absent.

Alternatives

Classic approaches are by no means universal. There are policy handbooks that emphasize ways in which policy may, without inconsistency, rest upon foundations that do not include the assumption of knowable cause-effect relationships (for example, Bridgman and Davis 1998). Important strands in policy studies assert the absence of any reliable, predictive "policy science," and these sit with difficulty beside policy languages that assert the contrary. An example is Lindblom and Woodhouse (1993). Famous economists have challenged the assumption of "instrumental rationality" (see section "Economists' arguments for state intervention revisited," in Chapter 6) that links to these policy science concerns (Simon 1986). Famous political scientists have argued that policy only has consistent meaning ex post, that is, in implementation. One might conjecture, though, that consistent meaning is imposed by the observer's standards of what constitutes an acceptable explanation (Pressman and Wildavsky 1973). Indeed, one of the puzzles of mainstream policy studies is the presence of such arguments, backed by accounts of policy in practice that tend to support them, beside continued tendencies to instruct students and practitioners to seek cause-effect relations and support their findings with evidence.

It is quite possible to recognize that acceptable "subsequent events" may be defined as resulting from various plausible explanations, with quite different policy ethnographies. In other words, there may not only exist different plausible ways in which cat-skinners say they will skin a cat (ex ante), but any particular cat skinner may be found in many different ways to have been acceptably successful (ex post). But this is not the mainstream, especially in development matters.

Evaluation methodology is very relevant here and has already been mentioned in the context of aid projects (see Box 1.1—*Intervention logics*).

Practices associated with large scientific research programs have in some accounts failed to evolve in ways that produce agreement upon a known-to-be-correct evaluation methodology. By the late 1990s, both the US and the UK had seemingly abandoned attempts to apply standard evaluation methodologies to large natural science research programs, though in some ways these appear to have continued (at least in the attempt) in social sciences.[ii]

Van Eijndhoven (1997) gives a clear interpretation:

> Technology assessment was originally conceived of as an analytic activity, aimed at providing decision makers with an objective analysis of effects of a technology. Early in the history of technology assessment, it became clear that assessment projects must involve multiple perspectives. In the United States, this led to stakeholder involvement in the analysis. In a number of European countries, however, forms of technology assessment developed in which the analytic product became of relatively minor importance compared to the interactive process: consensus conferences and constructive technology assessment developed as alternative forms. (269)

Striking differences in approach associated with the knowability assumption are discussed below in the context of changes in the Thai health sector (see sub-section "The Thai health sector—two approaches to policy analysis," in Chapter 10).

Many practitioners tend to ignore these issues. Practice may reflect beliefs based upon a mixture of factors, including experience that, while informal, seeks to integrate contingent approaches to intervention logics (what works where) with sensitivity to the acceptability of "subsequent events." Yet such approaches may be vulnerable to unwanted pressure from classic policy ideologies, whose advocates have powerful beliefs regarding cause-effect relations and the correctness of policy.

One way of approaching this tangle is through consistency: How are statements ordered? What is acceptable and accepted? What is rejected? Answers to these questions can be studied; they are, in a sense, empirical issues.

[ii]Contrast Baker 2000 with the collection of articles introduced by Bimber and Guston (1997) in *Technological Forecasting and Social Change*, especially those by Norton (1997), on the UK Parliamentary Office of Science and Technology and Hill (1997) on the demise of the Congressional Office of Technological Assessment (OTA). Hoos (1999) discusses a more discursive if not ethnographic approach to such work, moving away from the idea of objective assessments.

Conclusions

Prediction is inherent in the two dominant classes of development policy ideology. This is consistent with ideas of knowability discussed in the previous section and is, as expected, problematic. I personally prefer participation to alternatives. What worries me is why. Does increased participation truly lead to better development? What is persuasive about developmental ideas such as EOG, ISI, or even traditional socialism as attempted by the Vietnamese Communist Party prior to the emergence of a market economy in the early 1990s? These questions need to be considered.

Development in Practice: Policy and the Role of Solutions

Who Knows? Judging Exotic Solutions

In the second part of this book, I have chosen to use Vietnam, Thailand, and the Philippines as case studies because the relevant literatures about them usefully illustrate my arguments. They are situated within a region where developmental success is commonly reported (World Bank 1993) but which generates heterodox analyses of what happened. These are relatively hard to ignore: unlike some other regions, success gives voice. Two of the three countries have also experienced strong efforts to impose apparently well-defined and confident exotic development policies: Stalinism in Vietnam, neo-liberalism in the Philippines. There are accessible accounts of what happened in each case.

If my criticisms of the two classic policy ideologies are correct, then development is not simply an analytical problem. Poverty is not the same as a river without a bridge over it. Development is not a set of validly predictive solutions to known problems.

Therefore, ways of assessing judgments that avoid spuriously and/or hastily labeling approaches as wrong must be discovered. I tackle this issue in two ways. First, I discuss approaches taken by various texts. Second, I select several examples of these approaches and examine them in some detail.

To start with, most of these texts are written within Western intellectual contexts. Indeed, for most poor countries, this is what is widely taught, and so much of this literature is by definition exotic for them (thus the title of Part II of this book): it comes from a foreign and different reality, typically Western, and its terminology and texts are usually expressed in foreign languages, most commonly English (Rigg et al. 1999; Heryanto 1990 and 1995). Thus Gerald Meier, in an important study of the origins of development ideas, can state, with perhaps deliberate irony, that: "Rather oddly, in retrospect, most of those who began theorising about

> ## Box 1.6
> ## Variation in doctrine over time
>
> A particularly relevant instance is the position of the IMF regarding the value of controls over international capital flows: liberalization of the capital account of the balance of payments.
>
> Such controls were approved in the 1960s, then anathema through the 1980s and 1990s, yet viewed pragmatically from around 2002–2003—a useful example of doctrinal change: the world did not alter, but the chosen interpretation of it did.
>
> For more details see Chapter 2, especially the subsection "Doctrine in limbo? The IMF and the liberalization of capital flows."

underdeveloped countries were citizens of the developed countries" (Meier 1984, 19). But it is through such sources that most people access a literature on development.

It follows that we need to study the nature of this exotic knowledge and what it assumes. In short, it assumes much. Essentially, this is a problem of judgment: how do we assess positions that advocate certain actions, construed in certain ways? How do we assess the mass of development literature that purports to compare development policies?

A major problem this literature generates stems from a combination of great certainty with great differences of opinion. This is a body of literature characterized by disputes between authorities and by major differences in positions taken by particular authorities over time (see Box 1.6—*Variation in doctrine over time*).

A literature marked by instability and continued dispute provokes judgments advisedly different from others, such as most of the natural sciences, characterized by a strong capacity for convergence. When people learn the basis for such judgments (perhaps in high school), they learn to focus upon logical consistency and empirical reference. More is required to handle a literature that lacks such pressures for convergence yet presents itself at the level of the particular text as correct. One element of the expanded toolkit is confidence in the use of skepticism in the face of inconsistency.

It follows that a strategy for handling warring authorities is not to ask who is right but to focus upon the characteristics of approaches. In learning to cope with the how, we are better prepared to exercise judgment than in learning different and competing ways in which positions are in error. It is more useful to discuss how a developmental position has been constructed, what its logical tone is, and what (if any) its empirics are than it is to present judgments as to whether a position is correct. This of itself is an interesting conclusion.

Politics and Belief

What might be the attraction of seeing judgments about alternative development policies as matters of belief? When economists cannot predict what the GDP will be in six months time, when nobody has a clue how to value a share unambiguously and uncontentiously, and when disputable theory (Fforde 1995) is an apparently inherent element of much social science, a wise observer may judge it better to start by assuming that belief rather than knowledge guides practice. And such behavior (and the literature associated with it) is best approached differently from that of engineers setting out to construct a bridge, an airplane design, or so forth.

The quotations at the start of this chapter from men who all played important political roles are revealing. Disraeli, the nineteenth-century

---

Box 1.7
Pragmatism and contingency

In this book, I have found that I need a term to describe approaches that seem to avoid pitfalls I have outlined and which adopt frameworks that combine relative disengagement from theoretical disputation and are best referred to as contingent explanations. These I term *pragmatic,* exploiting the convention that the precise antonym of the word is *idealist:* That is, such approaches do not engage directly with the categorical and universalistic aspects of many others. Rather they try, practically, to see what works in terms of the generation of persuasive arguments in the particular context: such pragmatism can then help negotiate between the general and the particular. Examples of these approaches are discussed and compared in the case studies.

I understand *contingent relationships* as those said to hold under certain circumstances: for example, as the IMF now dogmatically puts it (see Chapter 7), liberalization of the capital account is good under X conditions and bad under Y conditions; it is said to depend, rather than always being true.

British prime minister, is arguing here that words are used by politicians and others to govern people, even if the ideas they contain are not reliably known to be correct. Bill Clinton, US president, learned, in his period at Columbia, that truth was not knowable, though he was happy to assume that it existed. Churchill, wartime leader, confronting the loss of the British Empire just after WWII, looked for new ways of securing political goals through the use of ideas. And Kipling, in his famous poem, offers the classic explanation of failure to those who try (in a modern language) to achieve development: "heathen folly"—the failure of exotic ideas to gain adequate local power. In Disraeli's terms, the white man's words may fail to govern men and in this sense remain no more than exotic. It is perhaps ironic that Kipling was writing about the US conquest of the Philippines, a country that had long been not heathen but Christian.

Conclusions: Thinking about Developmental Ideologies

Although people examine development and development policy for a range of reasons, concern for intentional social change is usually central to such efforts. So development work typically involves doing something. But examination of the two classic approaches shows that this turns out to be a puzzling thing—how do we "do" a historical process that is assumed to be knowable, especially when the future does not seem to be reliably known? This will be discussed in the next chapter. From these considerations come fundamental questions to ask (but often are not) of an argument that purports to assess development policy.

First, is the notion taken of development one of a known or knowable process, and/or of something possessing intentionality? That is, is development said to be process and/or product? Second, if development is said to be something that is done, to be "transitive," is there actually intentionality? Who or what can persuasively be said to intentionally produce development? Then, is the view one that argues that intentionality actually exists, or that it should, and then discusses how and why? In other words, what is the purported intention to develop? What is its nature? Third, what agency hosts this intentionality? Again, does it actually exist, or, if it does not, why not? Finally, what is the intervention logic: how is the combination of intentionality and agency understood to "do" development? This is often related to cause-effect metaphors associated with assuming knowability. It seems clear that these questions are not often enough posed, especially within the two primary classes of policy ideology. Instead, many are implicitly answered in ways that assume much that is questionable.

Chapter 1 Questions

1. Imagine and discuss a situation in which participants in a project have inconsistent views of intervention logic but still manage to accept the project's "subsequent events." Role play may be useful.

2. Consider a village-level infrastructure project. Divide into two groups, each of which separately prepares a list of possible sites for intentionality and agency. Compare these lists, and see whether it is possible to agree on which is the best site without agreeing on an intervention logic (what will work and why).

3. Set up a role play in which different stakeholders associated with a project seek to find ways of agreeing on allocation of resources. Discuss the effects of agreement and disagreement about intervention logics on the ease of generating agreement on that resource allocation.

PART I

The Problem of Development

CHAPTER 2

Choosing Case Studies

"It should not be essential and ideally not even normal that good
outcomes be seen as solutions to problems"

(Overheard, personal recollection)

Introduction

Development, Agency, and the State—Southeast Asia

From a development policy perspective, Asia presently seems very unlike
Africa or Latin America. It seems to be a good place to "do development."
This has happened for at least two good reasons. First, Asia seems to offer
examples of success, especially of economic advance, to levels comparable
with those in the West. Second, Asia contains examples of cultures and view-
points generally accepted as not only different from the West but robust in
the face of interaction with it.

Examples come from both North Asia (for example, Japan) and
Southeast Asia (for example, Singapore). In the early 2000s, Malaysia's
GDP per capita was comparable to that of Poland. Rapid economic
growth after World War II, as in Western Europe, had effects referred to
as miraculous (World Bank 1993).

From these observations come two apparently simple questions: what
were these successes, and why did they happen? Underlying these questions
is the fundamental question of the criteria applied to judge the persuasiveness of the answers—that is, how should such answers be assessed?

Many respond that success came from the adoption of correct policies.
However, this begs the questions of how judgments are made about success, about the correctness of policies, and about how we attribute success
to policy.

From this perspective, parts of Southeast Asia (SEA) are particularly
interesting. As we will see in Part II, there are persuasive arguments that a
frequent characteristic of change in the region has been either "success
without intention" or "intention without success"; that is, it is often hard to
attribute advance to development policy and that the expected effects of
development policies have often not been forthcoming. Such puzzles tend
to confound classic views of policy. Before we come to examine these issues

in detail, however, we need to discuss how development and development policy have been treated in various literatures, so we can see what consistent answers are meant to be. This issue will be examined in Chapters 4 through 7.

Before looking at the literature in detail, however, we need to look at how words are used and how they relate to experienced realities. A central issue in the literature is how the state's role in development may be expressed. This, we will see, is a significant crosscutting question, behind which are many assumptions, and an understanding of the different roles attributed to the state in development will help us in grasping particular positions on the nature of development and development policy.

The state is indeed often granted a role in development—in articulating and embracing an intention to develop that is presented as natural and unchallengeable. This invites us to believe in positions that need evaluation, especially in terms of ideas and their histories. The positions authoritative sources take seem to change significantly and often. The ways in which they change often contrast starkly with their alleged origins, such as in objective research.

To return to the posited knowable cause-effect relationship between policy and outcome fundamental to classic views of policy, we should note that, for there to be development policy, discussion often assumes the existence (or perhaps possibility) of a state to devise and implement policy, as well as a process of development upon which that policy can operate. Yet if policy (as part of what the state does) is part of an ongoing historical process, then how does the state, as an agent, operate upon itself? Is the posited unidirectional cause-effect relationship of classic views of policy a reasonable way of viewing the world?

If it is not reasonable but still informs much of what an intentional use of state power entails, then what might be the consequences? Consider the likely consequences of operating under assumptions that turn out to be false, in which case judgments usually turn out to be spurious. We will examine the econometric work of Levine and Zervos (1993; see Chapter 9) and reflect upon the likely consequences of the common assumption, which largely contradicts their empirical findings, that development policy-settings are indeed robustly correlated with outcomes.

These broad issues are usefully accessed through the contrast (discussed in greater detail in the next chapter) between Cowen and Shenton (1996) and Grindle and Thomas (1991). The latter assume many things that the former place into historically contingent context, most importantly the nature and characteristics of the often assumed-correct development policy-set referred to as the Washington Consensus (see Chapter 4). This articulated development policy mainly in economic terms and so, given the determinate nature of much economic thinking, was vividly linked to the posited notion of knowable cause-effect relationships under-pinning classic policy studies.

This brings us to possible implications of empirics. Kenny and Williams (2001; see Chapter 3) alert the reader to positions asserting the weak foundations of much policy derived from modern economics. Is it rea-sonable to assume that people are the same and can be understood in the same way, everywhere? What can we learn from the reminder that eco-nomics draws much from assumptions of ontological and epistemological universalism—that is, homogeneity?

Ontological universalism usually means to assume that things are the same everywhere: inflation, peasants, consumers, and so forth. Epistemo-logical universalism usually means to assume that things should be under-stood by the same methods everywhere. A natural science analogy would be to assume that rocks on Mars are the same as rocks on Earth, and then to assume that the same laws of motion may apply to both; they may be studied in the same way. These are assumptions.

Knowability and the Politics of Change

Knowability has remarkable effects. For example, coming at the argu-ment from the direction of the political rationality of economic policy reform, Rodrik (1996) points to certain basic problems, for who would support change? Articulating a common position, he argues that the future nature of benefits, compared with the immediate nature of costs, will make reform hard to accept. Therefore, to be consistent with many value systems, reformers who believe that reform will benefit others should act on this belief.

But Rodrik assumes, like many, not only that a set of changes can be viewed and valued similarly by different people but also that they can be known to lead to certain outcomes. Such assumptions may be challenged. For example, see the discussion of assumptions in an analysis of impacts of import tariffs in the section "Globalization" in Chapter 7. Such analy-ses may be used for or against policy-sets such as ISI (Import Substituting Industrialization) or EOG (Export Oriented Growth). Indeed, it is because of problems securing objective measures of welfare that I stress the *acceptability* of "subsequent events."

Knowability assumptions tend to use a revelation of error on the part of a competitor as support for the protagonist's own position. This relies in part on the consumer assuming that contention implies that one party is wrong. The 1997 Asian crisis, like other events that surprised many, may be interpreted as a confirmation of or a challenge to various positions. For example, Baer, Miles and Moran (1999) discuss the Asian crisis through various ways in which development and development policy have been analyzed. They are critical of what they see as conventional views but are instructive in that they, like many, assert the existence of objective ways (theirs) of understanding economies. Is this reasonable? Is it persuasive to argue that many conventional views of the situation in Asia before the 1997 crisis were errors that could be corrected?

The reader may easily find a wide range of intriguing examples. Pomerleano (1998), showing the views of a senior World Bank analyst about the Asian crisis and its origins, is instructive here. Is it credible to conclude, as Pomerleano does, that his ignorance of commercial conditions in Southeast Asia, specifically their departure from the apparent norms of developed countries, was a mistake?

In coping with many views, it is more useful to seek to grasp the "how" of arguments—how they are constructed, how they work as arguments— rather than to identify contradictions and mistakes as pointing to factors that would and should lead to correction. Grasping the how may help us avoid being pushed into taking sides. Rather, an important part of coping with the how is believing that the origins of such views are to be found not so much in mistakes but in habits of thought and practices better seen as normal and perhaps characteristic. The passage of time does not seem to see these practices replaced.

To give an example, two articles were published in the issue of the *Economist* for December 2, 2000. These discussed the situation in SEA, development problems, and the observation that foreign direct investment (FDI) was increasingly, compared with the early 1990s, going to China and not SEA.

One article pointed to this as an objective reason to explain why economic growth would be slower in SEA than before. The other argued that better policies were needed and sufficient to cause better economic performance. Note the tension between *belief* that policies are crucial (implying that they both exist *and* play an important role) and the *argument* that, *because* of the context, policies are not very important. It is more useful to be aware of and familiar with such tensions than it is to view them as mistakes, which may push us toward assuming knowability. This is a useful example of vertical consistency (assuming that the *Economist*'s editors were happy with the contrast between these two articles) combined with horizontal inconsistency (see Box 1.2—*Meanings of consistency—horizontal or vertical?*).

Such a tension between the asserted potential of intentionality, through policy, and the asserted impotence of intentionality, due to the situation, is for Cowen and Shenton a fundamental characteristic of how development is understood and how the term is used. Awareness of this tension clarifies the how of such positions more than simply pointing to the apparent contradiction. And, as we will see, awareness may then open a way to thinking about how and possibly why development may have become and still largely remains conventionally defined through reference to authority, or doctrinally.

From another point of view, informed by arguments that may point us toward ways in which apparently important issues may be highlighted or ignored, it is useful to examine a central question: How important is policy? This question, intriguingly, is often ignored. It would seem plausible that persuasive accounts could see change as caused by a range of factors and constituted by interactions between various sets of effects. Change, whether positive or negative, could then happen in isolation from policy. When we come to the case studies, we will find that this is the point made in de Vylder and Fforde (1997) with regard to Vietnam and by Pasuk and Baker (1996) for Thailand. Such views embody an intentionality challenging for classic views of policy that require an agency to act as a site for that intentionality. But even if this issue is somehow dealt with, policy must act upon a changing object. After all, development is change. A practical set of questions would then be, does policy matter, and how do we judge its effects? Unfortunately, these questions are often given little emphasis, as progress is deliberately or unconsciously attributed to correct policy. I call this "policy fetishism."

The reader should now start to see how classic views of policy are easily linked to the idea of a state "doing development" and so seek accounts that appear to show this. This is one reason why the relevant literatures on SEA are so appealing and why I now discuss how parts of SEA may appear as sites where a type of development familiar to classic views of policy could occur, and why there may be problems with this perspective. I then expand on these issues before presenting the two sets of contrasting views of the problem of development.

Choosing Case Studies

Development as a Problem, and Solutions to It

Let me start with a quote from a very different context, that of pre-Industrial Revolution England. Describing the reflections and deliberations of the Tudor dynasty in England, a historian commented as follows:

> One of the most delicate tasks that faced the Tudors, therefore, was the creation and education of a new ruling class and the retention of its loyalty. The new men had to be prevented from moving up too fast or too far. The drive and efficiency in economic matters which brought them their wealth and power also made them harsh to their tenants and contemptuous of the common people. (Morris 1955, 25–26)

A problem of development is here stated as a political set of issues posed for a ruler by a dialectic of development and underdevelopment. Note that some historians will tell us that the very creation of the modern English state dates from the Tudors (after the Wars of the Roses). The dynasty started its rule over a country devastated by decades of civil war that had at the same time lost most of England's claims to France, and was under intense pressure from continental powers and later Catholicism (Carpenter 1997). England, when the dynasty ended, was a country with the potential to construct the British Empire. Our focus is upon the interaction between ruler and change, upon the politics of a situation in which judgments entail balancing trend assessments with both positive and negative characteristics and in which political options are discussed under the assumption that rulers, while having scope for action, also face considerable risks. This is obvious—but what about "here and now"?

When we examine contemporary issues in terms of classic views of policy and how to "do development," the basic questions are now obvious. The alleged requirements of development policy apparently familiar from accounts of Western European development exist in SEA. These categories are familiar. They should refer persuasively to states, countries, languages, histories, and policies, and so on. Can they? The answer could be yes.

From some European perspectives, in SEA we may see nation-states and multinational states that evoke a sense of familiarity. Perhaps Austro-Hungary, Britain, Belgium, Poland, and the Netherlands compare with Indonesia, Burma, Laos, Thailand, and Vietnam. But how persuasive are such accounts? Will these lines of thought persuade us that issues of intentionality and agency, apparently clear in modern developed countries, are present in an equivalent way in parts of SEA?

Perhaps, dependent on the particular context in terms of the region's modern history? It is not hard to find arguments that appear to reduce the scope for agency within the region. We should look for studies that refer to context—factors such as Japanese capital and technology, Chinese entrepreneurship and trading capacity, Cold War confrontation, and unusual access to US markets, capital, and technology (unusual, for example, in that India was not given it).

An example of such arguments, downplaying local agency, is an article by the economic historian Chalmers Johnson (see the section "Coping with failure" in Chapter 12) in which he argues that contextual factors should be the core elements of persuasive histories of SEA, and so local intentions given little role to play in the analysis. In such explanations, historical and other factors push issues of agency—of states and development policy—away from the forefront of discussion. Classic views of policy may thus be associated with particular views of how change should be analyzed and presented.

Conundrums: Intention and Success

There are other grounds for concern, even without bringing the exotic nature of mainstream development doctrines into the argument. Consider these three case studies—Vietnam, Thailand, and the Philippines. Do they seem familiar from a classic policy studies perspective? If we consider criteria that we might use to answer this question, we could ask whether there has been a centralization of power comparable to what is widely thought to have occurred in metropolitan countries in modern times (in passing, a central element of the Tudor political project) and expressed in terms equivalent to development policy. We can argue that this centralization of power has not happened, and that efforts to do so have led to odd results. It may take longer than expected to go from the presumption of sovereignty associated with a UN seat to the adoption of the analytical assumptions classically associated with viewing a country as being on the way to development.

Southeast Asian historians have had their debates about the extent to which the region contains examples of "autonomous" history (Smail 1972; Sears 1972). These debates can be linked to the degree to which the region offers heterodox explanations and the links between these explanations and deeper issues in thinking about development.

Such arguments emerge in the political economy literature also. For example, Macintyre (1994) stresses the contrasts in the literature between Northeast and Southeast Asia. These literatures can be interpreted as suggesting far less "intentionality" in the latter, but Macintyre, a political scientist, does not develop his discussion to a consideration of the wider implications of this reduced intentionality for the development literature.

The Philippines. There are strong views that the Philippines lacks prerequisites for its inclusion in a conventional discussion of development policy. According to Mulder (1996), "When the neo-colonial successor elite took over from the Americans, they had long forgotten their fathers' ideas about nationalism, and there has never been any attempt at nation-building." (198) That is, the ways in which sovereignty was received from the Americans led to values, desires, and attitudes that produced negativism and a lack of nationalistic desire to develop the country (and adopt potentially painful change, such as land reform). Thus, we can ask, if development is identified as something that occurs intentionally, rather than something that just happens, to what extent can intentional development be applied here, in post–WWII history? Where is the agency? If no agency is found, then classic views of policy must refer to the possibilities of agency—in a different language, to the creation of executive power. We will see in

Chapter 11 accounts that squarely address this. This apparent lack of agency suggests thinking of the Philippines as "intention without success," which leads observers to a search for agency.

Thailand. Similar issues come up in the literature on Thai development. For example, Unger (1998) implies that Thai politics and society are not usefully seen in the way classic policy studies suggest. Unger argues that, in the absence of adequate Thai capacity to form social associations, standard theory breaks down as the state should then fail to act as a site for intentionality, leading to chaos. To cope with this, he argues that the otherwise anomalous rapid economic expansion should be explained through the notion that Chinese social capability offsets this weakness.

Another example from the Thai development literature is the notion of competitive clientelism (Doner and Ramsay 1997). Here the anomaly was the observation of rapid growth concurrent with high levels of corruption. The literature addressed the anomaly by arguing that the specific type of clientelism seen in Thailand did not matter. The assumed causal relationship between corruption and bad economic performance could then be dealt with. This was seen as a social phenomenon not associated with policy in any simple way.

In both the Unger and the Doner and Ramsay cases, anomalies are addressed through recourse to social arguments rather than by reference to arguments about the state. Cause could then be said to be found, not in a siting of intentionality upon the state, but in something else. In this way Thailand can be presented as an example of "success without intention" and literature finding cause beyond the state. I discuss these issues further in Chapter 10.

Vietnam. There are debates in the literature, but one pragmatic strand (for example, de Vylder and Fforde 1997) argues that policy has tended to *follow* reality. An example of this view is the history of the Vietnamese transition from plan to market in the 1980s. This came from an endogenous process, it is argued, in which the extent of marketization reflected a range of factors, of which policy was but one. Further, at times the power behind marketization proved sufficient to overcome policy hostile to it (Fforde 2007). Such ideas of an endogenous process of transition that is not policy-driven can also be found in the China literature (for example, Naughton 1995).

These studies challenge classic views of policy. Examples that embody classic positions are easy to find, supporting the argument that change was indeed the consequence of policy (for example, Mallon and Van Arkadie 2003). To judge properly between these and other views, it is useful to realize the nature of the arguments and to be aware of the different core assumptions about the role of policy in change, which is discussed in detail in Chapter 9. Vietnam may also be seen as an example of "success without intention, but within a theatre of agency." In other words, heterodox views here confront the common practice of presenting regimes as authors of development—correct change—with arguments that present accounts of change where there is no clear agency and therefore no need to adopt a knowability assumption.

This discussion suggests that the relevance of SEA may not be at all because of the presence of normal states doing normal development, but rather due to the significance for the wider literature about the possible nature of development and the meanings of development policy. The literature pertinent to comparative development policy that refers to parts of SEA is thus particularly useful because lessons learned are valuable for coping with the wider development literature, and so appreciating—and hopefully avoiding—the pitfalls of classic policy ideologies.

Success, thus, speaks: unlike many other parts of the world, the case studies come from a context of rapid economic growth and frequent attributions of developmental success. But this should not be taken too far. The reader may well share my suspicion that similar issues of knowability and heterodoxy are specific to widespread habits of thought, expressed in terms of classic views of policy. If so, these issues will also be present in contexts where attributions of failure tend to greatly weaken interest in local experiences, whether explained in orthodox or heterodox terms. Allegations of failure may encourage readers to believe that the implications of these experiences are "obvious."

We should add that for these SEA countries, Western development thinking can easily be called exotic doctrine (like other external ideas) and identified as such. Whatever they are, the cultures of Thailand and Vietnam are clearly not Western.

Development as a Global Issue

Let us return to thinking about the context. If development policy is considered a global issue bound up in states and societies with a strong focus upon economic growth and visions of "catching up" with a developed world, then what can be said? To start with, are we dealing with facts or political propositions? Dunn (2000) stresses a fundamental distinction between viewing the state as a fact and viewing it as an idea: "Each of these two conceptions (the state as sociological fact and the state as normative political proposal) must relate in some way to most of the entities which we now call states, but neither makes quite clear how to apply it in practice" (69). Similar things might be said about development: is it a sociological fact or a political proposition?

One immediate puzzle is the deceptively simple way in which development, as a policy issue, first appeared. A range of authorities date this to after WWII (for example, Arndt 1987) but others disagree (for example, Cowen and Shenton 1996). The latter point to ways of discussing issues in relation to richer countries' own experiences, thus linking them to discussions about how change is to be discussed, which seems to be a wider topic than accounts of development that start with issues of post–WWII decolonization. Central to such accounts is the apparent acquisition of newly sovereign states by many poorer areas. Given classic views of policy, this appeared to grant a combination of intention and agency with which they could now "do development," given the core assumed prerequisites of development policy. And this policy, and their success or failure, was to be assessed with reference to assumed knowable intervention logics.

But these could not be entirely new ideas. Thus, not only Cowen and Shenton but other writers, such as Waterbury (1999), argue for the importance of understanding the situation before WWII, either in colonies or in other regions coping with the negative aspects of change (or capitalism). While Cowen and Shenton focus upon the UK, France, and the British Dominions, Waterbury points to countries such as Turkey.

This discussion centers on the creation of both intentionality and a site for it. It is noteworthy that we find in studies such as Waterbury and in the earlier discussions of development little attention to questions of knowability. As we will see in the next four chapters, assumptions of knowability permeate the development literature. In Chapter 7 we will discuss in detail evidence from the cross-country regression literature presented by Levine and Zervos that assumptions of knowability are unwise. We will also see that in many ways knowability is a greater source of tensions than the associated issues of intentionality and agency. The persuasive conclusion is the central importance of the assumption of knowability and its projection into exotic doctrine.

The Role of the State and the Meaning of Development Policy

The discussion so far has pointed to the existence of fundamental and intriguing puzzles in notions of development policy. A perceptive reader may have recognized how substitution of the standard developmental terminology by others, such as change associated with intentionality and specific beliefs about agency and the knowability of cause-effect relationships, may clarify the discussion by reducing the extent to which it carries implicit assumptions. Core questions can usefully be asked.

Because we are dealing with contextualized human actions, one major puzzle is that of volition and values. Why should this be a central issue, and why so often is it not? How may this be related to the issue of whether development is immanent or volitional?

Cowen and Shenton pose the question, if development is *volitional*, something that is done, then what values drive intention and where do they come from? Why are values only rarely discussed? This will lead us to discuss ways in which, according to some authors, policy is inescapably bound to ordering and legitimizing. An intriguing aspect of such conceptualizations of policy is the importance of belief and the frequent weakness of empirical support for common beliefs about cause-effect relationships. Strategies to cope with development policy usefully pay due attention to this (see the discussion of the texts of Escobar, Ferguson, and Shore and Wright in Chapter 6).

At a popular level, as well as in terms of what is taught, there are at any given time, various cookbooks—"ask the World Bank" (or AusAID, DFID, CIDA, Sida, etc.). Variants of different normative orientations can be found. And the cookbooks coming from any given authority change over time. Here again we can note a persistence of fault lines within common positions. Rodrik (1996) can be interpreted as arguing about, though perhaps not for, a fundamentally undemocratic side to economists' reform practices. But is this not simply a corollary of habits of thinking in terms of knowable deviation from some ideal state? Because people articulate such beliefs, is it not inevitable that they argue that actions can and should be taken in the name of the welfare of the population? And how can this sit with ideals of empowerment?

We will soon confront arguments that such perceptions, far from being specific to economics, are founded upon a particular resolution of the problem of development. In any case, it would seem obvious that Rodrik may not simply be arguing for an economists' dictatorship but perhaps also, more subtly, seeking to bring debate to a focus upon values and politics. Yet, as we will see, they are so often not part of the discussion.

I conclude that strategies for coping with comparison of development policies need to start by posing fundamental and challenging questions. It is not likely to be just politics, or just economics, or just ideas. There is a need to take a wide-ranging tour of basic concepts to assess policy analyses and policy proposals with any degree of confidence. Treating policy as doctrinally based makes it easier to compare, and so to cope.

Development as Part of Development Policy

I leave it to the reader to search the many available development textbooks and to see whether they find clear and uncontentious definitions of development.[i] Most readers will conclude that the term *development* is

---

[i]Ray 1998 and Todaro and Smith 2006 dominate the US market for development economics textbooks at the tertiary level and are a good place to start. See http://chnm.gmu.edu/tools/syllabi.

itself puzzling and problematic. Why? The tensions among various ideas associated with the term appear to be central.

I am arguing here that these tensions are connected to the issue of knowability, which is itself closely linked to problems of intention and agency. It is these puzzles that link development to development policy and that underpin the classic views of policy associated with much development practice. The assumption of knowability suggests that development is an immanent process, expressing an unfolding of some predetermined logic. Yet how, we might ask, can this be, given that nobody has been able to predict the future?

Despite this, development is typically established on empirical grounds, so it can be related to an experienced real. Vast effort is expended. Does this suggest though that we can recognize it? Apparently not, at least uncontentiously. Most textbooks stress a distinction between economic growth and development. Growth may be identified with simple increases in GDP per capita or with levels of urbanization, of the size of a so-called modern sector, of a so-called formal sector, and so forth. Such indicators may all be said to be consistent or inconsistent with development, depending upon other criteria. Yet there is no convergence to an agreed definition of the term *development*.

Why? This takes us into deep water. For me, the reasons for disagreement on the term are related to matters of perception and persuasion. I am reminded of an early result in what is called welfare economics, which itself drew upon earlier lines of thinking, to the effect that authority is required to stop argument about interpersonal and intertemporal comparisons of welfare because there are no objective measures available to do so. As Lewis Carroll (1895) put it, logic cannot take you by throat and force agreement. The point, it seems, is that nobody has to accept a proposition; to accept is to chose, and choice, being subjective, is in part hidden. Or, as was put in a very different context: "I would not open windows into men's souls" (Elizabeth I, attributed to her by Francis Bacon).

I am also reminded of a story told by Robert Chambers. Apparently, a researcher had examined welfare levels in a South Asian rural community and returned some twenty years later to repeat his investigations. When he presented his results to the village, he reported they were worse off. Villagers replied that they disagreed: when he had carried out his earlier work, they had been subject to violent repression from local landlords, and, since their removal, villagers felt far better off, no matter what his data showed. It seems silly to ask who was right. What is interesting here is how a discourse of development should on the one hand treat development as something measurable but on the other be unable to link that to any agreed and undisputed measure.

This suggests again that it is the acceptability of "subsequent events," rather than outcomes themselves, whatever they may be, that should concern us in discussions of "development." In this sense, development is not best seen as an analytical question with stable empirics, but rather as something for which any relevant definition is part of the process, and so best assumed contentious, at least at the start.

Policy as Part of Development Policy: Economics as an "Ideal Type"

If such unsettling considerations emerge from a short discussion of development, then what may come from a quick discussion of policy? Coherent use of the term *policy* turns out to be similarly fraught with difficulties. As we have seen, in classic views the term is presented as referring to interventions designed to produce certain knowable outcomes. This may be considered technical, so the correctness of policy may be discussed in isolation from, for example, the political. Yet this may be challenged. One authoritative discussion of policy studies, for example, makes the point that the studies of policy and of politics are inseparable. An attempt to present a policy as having an objective base (perhaps evidential) would then be seen as a political act as well as an expression of known cause-effect relations (McLean Ed. 1996, 378–379). Yet if an attempt is made to assert that the discussion is not about prediction but about explanation, it is also puzzling to know how then to assess statements about what is to be done.

Mainstream economic methods are extremely interesting. Despite logical and empirical problems associated with these methods, or perhaps because of them, development policy as classically understood is well suited to contemporary economics with its analytical separation of the economy from the rest of human affairs and its construction of an apparently clear model of cause-effect relationships.[ii] Within mainstream economics, this method is marked by use of the concept of exogeneity, the idea that certain causes can be thought as absolutely distinct from others. Logically, policy change is identified with this category of causes.

Thinking about what this identification means illuminates what is going on. Logically, policy is identified with things that cause change, for within an economy itself, upon which policy acts, there is simultaneity of determination, which means that for variables other than the exogenous ones there is no clear distinction between cause and effect: there is simply a solution of an algebraic model. A simple model of supply and demand is

---

[ii]See, for example, the discussion of economic growth as the central element of change in Ray 1998, Chapter 3.

thus one in which price and the quantities bought and sold are simultaneously determined; they are at the same time both cause and effect.

In such approaches, only by stepping outside of the box may exogenous causes be found. The direction of vision is thus *toward* the economy and upon that which can operate upon it, rather than the reverse. Mainstream economists should and do focus upon the impact of policy, not upon what impacts policy. The vision is toward the economy. This is the conventional view, no matter that bond dealers and others playing poker against the central bank typically spend much time thinking about where policy is coming from in terms of the values and subjectivity of the people involved. But they are not mainstream economists.

An idea of policy common to economists, then, is premised upon the existence of a knowable, external reality where change is exogenously derived. Economists, clearly, are active participants in debates about development and development policy. But in this view, to restate what has been stated before, the reader should note the absence of significant discussion of where policy comes from, or of policymakers and their values. This corresponds to the knowability assumption, for, if reality can be known, then the context or perspective of whoever possesses that knowledge is not a useful thing to consider. It becomes natural to assume that policy is the central issue to explaining change—"policy fetishism"—because policy is based on knowledge that entails a separation of analysts from what they are studying. Yet if the state is thought of as an agent that both knows what correct policy is and does development through policy, how can it be a part of the historical process of development and act upon itself?

It is not hard to think of change processes that exhibit different logics. One example is the bottom-up argument, in which policy as observed adapts to society and derives meaning through practice and implementation. As we will see in Chapters 9 and 10, the Thai and Vietnamese case studies point in this direction. And this view is not uncommon in part of the policy studies literature in rich countries (for example, Pressman and Wildavsky 1973; Lindblom and Woodhouse 1993).

Development thus poses conceptual puzzles for classic notions of policy. An idea to consider is that of implementation, another issue associated with assumptions behind the economists' approach to exogeneity—the idea that policy can be based upon knowledge of change processes of which it is not a part. This frequently leads to a realization problem, a mechanism for relating an idealized construct to the facts—some apparent reality. As a Vietnamese mathematician once put it to me, this process may be seen as an absolutization: a making absolute of something relative. This idea may be linked to something already mentioned—the point that a model is not what it models, and written accounts of history are not history (see the discussion of Lao Tzu in the preface).

In the next four chapters I examine various development ideas. Often the idealized construct is what is said to be known, and the problem then becomes how to ensure that facts fit it. This accompanies a tendency to marry categorical thinking to classic views of policy—for example, arguments that one of the main responsibilities of the Vietnamese state in the 1990s was to create a "proper" market economy. In this way, discussions of policy within development juxtapose an ideal with efforts to implement it. This also offers relatively fruitful grounds for explaining unacceptable "subsequent events," in that it can be said that the policy (which conceptually is linked to the ideal) is correct but implementation was inadequate.

As we will see, focus upon implementation may also limit the ways in which factors external to the adopted approach may be brought into the discussion. We will stress matters of capacity and power, and, more importantly, why they are so often inadequate to ensure implementation of allegedly known-correct policy; views of politics risk too readily associating political problems with how they influence policy implementation. In this way of thinking, democratically supported impediments to implementing correct policies are wrong. As Rodrik pointed out, it may encourage undemocratic politics. The case study of the Philippines in Chapter 11 shows this clearly, as donors saw a chance to push through what they saw as correct policies in the hoped-for opportunities accompanying marshal law under Marcos.

Such situations seem inescapably linked to the specific ways in which classic views of policy, in a development context, deal with issues of agency, intention, and knowability. I argue that these too easily lead to a focus upon implementability issues and therefore a vision of political power as simply something that ensures implementation.

There are good reasons for appreciating what is happening when such ideas dominate development thinking. We will see commentaries that point to the risks involved, arguing that the realization issue is not simply one of power and capacity. One reason is that these terms are problematic (see Chapter 5). It turns out that treating power in a simple "more gives you more" sense is risky. Another reason is the tension between the generally high level of attention paid to debating cause-effect relations compared with managing implementation processes. This will come up in the case studies. Failure to implement easily becomes an excuse to protect a policy-set defined in terms of purportedly known cause-effect relationships.

To add to the puzzle, what is implied by situations in which policy and practice seem different? When trying to think consistently, even the empirics of such situations are far from simple. What is the state, and how may we arrive at a judgment as to what it is doing and what policy is?

Valuable contributions to the political science literature argue that the boundary between state and society usually appears blurred (Mitchell 1991). If observing a state presents problems, similar things would seem to hold for policy itself. What if we see no clear policy regarding a sector, but to discuss change in that sector we read literature that keeps referring to the state?

There may be good reasons for thinking that state practice differs from state policy. In one interview in the mid-1990s, I recall the prime minister of Vietnam, Phan Van Khai, remarking that while in their program of public administration reform they had made considerable progress in eliminating opportunities to extract resources from the public, as they did so, other opportunities seemed to become apparent and seemed to be used by these same officials to maintain the level of extraction. This could be called "Khai's law," in which state practice and state policy are very different.

As we will see, there are alternatives to classic approaches to policy. But the influence of classic approaches remains powerful, and understanding them helps to explain apparently inconsistent behavior. An example in the development literature can be found in Easterly (1999). He refers to two-gap models and the behavior of the World Bank. Two-gap models had authority in much of development economics until the late 1970s. They stemmed in part from views that saw development as mainly economic and input-driven, with a focus on investment (Ray 1998, Chapters 3 and 4). This implied a problem of development and a knowable policy solution that included a supply of capital from overseas to meet "gaps" in the availability of capital in the developing country.

The bank's behavior, according to Easterly, showed the existence of powerful incentive structures within it that encourage lending. They were linked to gap models through the tendency to relate aspirations for certain GDP increases to stated shortages of external resources, part of which bank lending would provide. In this logic, supply of those resources will cause predictable increases in GDP by meeting the gaps.

Easterly shows that this relationship does not hold in terms of his empirics (see Chapter 7). There is no evidence here that increased supplies of aid capital are correlated with higher GDP. But, Easterly argues, country economic reports by the bank as well as other international lending institutions (such as the International Monetary Fund) typically continue with this practice, based upon gap models, as they have done since perhaps the 1960s.

The question then is what to make of this. In Easterly's view, the bank is wrong, and it is irrationally and inconsistently continuing with such practices. Yet clearly the bank does not agree. The bank, thus, is only wrong if certain perspectives and views are adopted.

I recall a story told by a colleague who had prepared many macroeconomic reports for a range of countries. Sitting in the lobby room to a minister of finance, he watched an IMF delegation leave in anger at the failure of the government to do what they wanted. On entering to meet the minister, he expressed concern but was told not worry as "they would be back." Within a few months they were, keen to maintain the support program.

Conclusions

These two chapters have started to explore what this book is about. Several arguments should start to be clear. I will develop them throughout the rest of the book. The first argument is that established development doctrines are insecure empirically. So doctrine changes and in prevalent current forms is supported by authority rather than evidence. The next chapter takes a big step to developing this further. In Chapters 4 through 7 we will explore various ways in which development ideas deal with the tensions created by the need to cope with the facts.

The second argument is that established development doctrines tend to assume intentionality on the part of some agency. (What agency, acting on what authority, and with what logic in mind?) But we may also consider that development is an ongoing process of social change (to which intentional development agents are peripheral). Tensions between these two alternatives and evidence that doctrine seems to assert development is both underpin much of what we have discussed in the first two chapters, and they are the platform for the rest of the book.

The third argument is that much established doctrine is exotic, derived from the assumption that everywhere is the same. Part II looks at the experiences of the three case studies as examples of the effects of exotic doctrine. This will also show the tendency in the literature for heterodox accounts to push forward and challenge the mainstream.

The fourth argument, which so far is only weakly developed, is that this situation appears likely to change. We can see the declining authority of classic views. Another possible change is a shift toward social practices that worry less about doctrine and what it has to say about causes and effects. Instead, people may be more concerned about "subsequent events" and how these events may be associated with social actions in various ways. This could be a shift away from "doing" development and toward various politics of change that have quite different assumptions about intentionality. These arguments develop in the following chapters.

Chapter 2 Questions

1. Why can Southeast Asia provoke questions about the meaning of development and development policy?

2. Can we expect objective analysis of development, meaning that arguments about its correct definition would tend to cease?

3. Does the meaning of development depend upon the will and values of those who enact it?

4. How can we agree upon a definition of policy? Of development policy?

A Challenge to Classic Policy Studies

Introduction

This chapter examines differing views of development problems. The first takes a classic view of policy, siting intentionality squarely upon the state and assuming knowable cause-effect relationships to guide that intentionality. The second takes a different tack, seeing the problem very differently and reporting two different historical responses to it. Grindle and Thomas (1991) illustrate a classic view of policy with a text that is aimed at those interested in "doing development" and playing active roles.

Classic Development Policy and How It Happens—Grindle and Thomas

Grindle and Thomas state that the main historical events of the 1980s were wide-ranging shifts in state development policies away from the interventionist directions brought in earlier (just before and after WWII). They attribute these changes to the ascendancy of neoclassical over Keynesian economics, and external donors supported their adoption in many countries. They ask the question, why did this happen? And their answer, which is what is relevant here, examines the roles decision-makers and policy managers play.

At the root of the analysis is the idea that policymakers have considerable scope for action. They are not simply forced by events, interest group pressures, or external agencies to make particular choices. Thus, the focus is upon how policymakers choose these decisions. This analysis thus appears as an implementation model of development policy, with intentionality identified with reform, and agency sited on reformists as carriers of correct policy ideas.

As is common, opposition to policy change is seen as coming from those who benefit from the status quo (Rodrik 1996). But support comes from those who see that these proposals are wise in the name of efficiency and development and know who they would benefit. Reform is seen as an intentional correction of perceived errors.

Grindle and Thomas base their arguments, they say, upon a range of case studies. They conclude that four main ideas are needed to understand policy change: first, the perceptions and behavior of policymakers and the perceived constraints upon their actions (how they see the world); second, the particular policy context, the circumstances (for example, is there a crisis?); third, the model policymakers adopt when they analyze and discuss proposed changes, the cause-effect relations that permit agency to embrace

Box 3.1
The metaphor of the king and his courtiers

One simplified yet useful way of framing these common approaches in outline (if not caricature) is to see them as a metaphor in which politics is about a sovereign king, his nature and personality, and his environment, focusing upon conditions for securing his agreement to, and then implementation of, some assumed correct doctrine. Intentionality and agency then present relatively clearly.

But, of course, we ask who are the courtiers whose ideas (of correct policy) drive change in this metaphor? And just what are these ideas? Where do they come from? What are they worth? Are they correct?

I think that these rather simple questions are usefully provocative. States are seen as sovereign, taking acts and with intentions, when clearly they are not single actors, unlike a king, who after all is an individual.

It has been argued that there is a tendency for people to treat actions as things that may entail responsibility, viewing discussions of cause and effect as subsequent to this basic sense. Discussions of cause and effect are, in this view, part of social processes to do with the ascription of motives and responsibility entailed by attribution or responsibility through concepts of actions. That is to say that whether causes and/or effects generate predictability is of far less importance than whether they generate judgments of responsibility. See Stoecker (2007).

The metaphor of the king can be usefully thought of as a way of transferring these habits of thought to do with intentionality from thinking about individuals (who have brains and emotions) to thinking about things like states, aid donors, project management committees, and so on (who do not).

intentionality (What will happen? To whom?); last, the particular policy considered and the pattern of costs and benefits.

Given our earlier discussion, a number of points are usefully made. Grindle and Thomas start with an assertion (or more accurately, perhaps, an assumption) that policy matters, and this supports their focus upon decision-makers. Here policy matters because there is choice and because it can lead to change.

Grindle and Thomas then distinguish between explanations that center on ways in which society affects policymakers from those that are more state-centered and focus upon policy elites. They next give the reader a neat summary of different approaches based upon this distinction. Note that Grindle and Thomas are themselves arguing for a more state-centered approach, but bringing in society also. They point out that underlying the variations between approaches are differences in political theory.

Yet fundamental questions of context are not posed. Crucially, the notion of correct policy means that policymakers may—and at times should—be thought of as somehow separate from their context and the society within which they live. In Grindle and Thomas' account, only in this way may reformers access true reformist ideas. Recall that these ideas are *not* local; the issue for Grindle and Thomas is to explain implementation of an exotic policy-set. And this, perhaps, is part of the way in which values are moved from our field of view.

It should be clear that assessing Grindle and Thomas' way of seeing things depends to a great extent upon the assumption of knowability: the idea that universally correct policies exist that need to be implemented for various reasons in different contexts—in other words, whether exotic doctrines will work. After all, given the acceptability of assumptions of ontological and epistemological universalism in, say, girder design, discussion of the exotic nature of a Scottish engineer in, say, Panama would likely be limited.

Reflexivity in Grindle and Thomas: How do They Situate Themselves?

Grindle and Thomas, like others, present a description of various approaches, as they see them, in order to present their self-positioning within this catalog. These are listed as follows.

A. Society-centered approaches—influences on policy makers
Class analytic

These approaches share the idea that political interaction derives from economic conflict. In Marxist theory, a state predominantly acts to maintain capitalist dominance over society. Thus, policy elites act to meet this goal. They have no autonomy. Recent neo-Marxist analyses have moved beyond this, arguing that a state acts to preserve the long-term interests of capitalism and to maintain the capitalist order (rather than just supporting the particular capitalists of the moment). These approaches stress links between state actions and certain interests. But at the end of the day, policymakers' choices are not of great interest.

Pluralist approaches

In these approaches, policy results from conflict, bargaining, and coalition-forming among possible societal groups organized to protect or advance their interests by influencing policy. These interests can vary. The state forms part of the arena within which these conflicts exist. For some it can be neutral, for others, not.

Public choice approaches

These are in some ways a development from pluralist approaches. They apply a cost-benefit metaphor to the behavior of public officials and others, contrasting rational political outcomes with associated irrational economic outcomes (rent-seeking being a good example, as politicians gain support by setting up tariffs that harm growth but get them elected). The state is then far from neutral, because it can create such sources of political benefit to itself, arguably at economic cost.

B. State-centered models—trying to examine what policymakers do

In Grindle and Thomas' view of political science, state-centered models tend simply to assume that the policy process (but in effect understood as policy adoption and implementation) is locally determined and then see how it can be analyzed.

Rational actor models

Here, policymakers are examined to see whether they can be understood as rational actors, choosing among a range of options to suit decisionmakers' preferences. Often, it is argued that their rationality is limited in many ways due to complexity and information limitations.

Bureaucratic politics approach

This approach views policy struggles in terms of the competition between different officials and organizations. Here, of course, policymakers have considerable autonomy.

State interests

This approach focuses upon a notion of the overriding importance of the interests of the state. Societal groups may benefit, but this is not the fundamental cause of state policy.

Issues

The basic position that Grindle and Thomas present themselves as taking (that is, what they judge to be the best reflection of the truth about reality) is a contextualized, state-centered one, with stress upon the perceptions of policymakers and their contexts. This would seem to fit with their initial observation that policy shifts in the 1980s were similar across many countries but that their implementation varied according to situation (which would follow from their case study approach). The gaze thus shifts from the policy-set to implementation issues, preserving the knowability assumption from direct test. How is or was it known, though, that such policies would lead to predictable "subsequent events"? They give no answer and do not seem to need to: exotic doctrine in their eyes is known to be correct.

Empirics—a Reality Check

I discuss the econometrics of relationships between policy and "subsequent events" in developing countries in Chapter 7. Many published articles argue over what works and present contradictory results backed up by statistical analyses. These arguments are usually put in terms of universalistic policies, such as EOG (export-oriented growth) or ISI (import-substituting industrialization), and this reflects wider beliefs in and about a knowable development process. Yet it turns out that so far very few robust relationships exist that can be observed (see also Fforde 2005a). However, I want to bring forward a reality check through the text by Kenny and Williams (2001), which brings certain problems squarely into the open.

Kenny and Williams argue that lurking behind attempts to conduct a variety of econometrics is a combination of epistemological and ontological universalisms, which for them means the assumption that people everywhere are the same and can be understood the same way. Rocks are rocks are rocks: in other words, homogeneity holds—the sample is drawn from a single population. Certainly, contemporary mainstream economics has been said to assume this (see the discussion of Booth 1999 and Dowling and Summers 1998 in Chapter 7). Kenny and Williams point out that:

> Overall, attempts to divine the cause or causes of long-term economic growth, testing a wide range of possible determinants using statistical techniques, have produced results . . . that are frequently contradictory to results reported elsewhere. That is, empirical evidence is hardly unanimous in support of a particular view of the growth process. (Kenny and Williams 2001, 1)

For Kenny and Williams, the observed lack of convergence toward robust agreement implies, profoundly, that basic assumptions are likely to be awry. I postpone detailed discussion of this literature until Chapter 7, but let this rest here as a reality check to positions taken, specifically that it is reasonable to believe in well-known relationships between policy and outcomes, in a development process that can be intentionally directed. This should encourage skepticism in the face of assertions to the contrary and poses questions about the approach taken by Grindle and Thomas.

Development Policy as Doctrine—Cowen and Shenton

The Problem of Development

Cowen and Shenton (1996) offer a very different approach. For them, discussion of development should clarify whether development is seen as an immanent objective process or as something involved with the realization of intentionality—of human creativity and will—through some agency. And to cope with the issue that we ordinarily think, in a somewhat contradictory way, that it is both.

Arndt (1981), nearly half a generation before Cowen and Shenton, had stressed that development, as an idea, was thought of as both transitive and intransitive. In these terms development is both something that is done and something that happens. In one alliterative couple, development is both product and process. Yet he chose, unlike Cowen and Shenton, not to examine how this tension was resolved.

For Cowen and Shenton, this tension is *itself* the problem of development. Mainstream development practice may be viewed as largely determined by how this problem has been resolved, combined with relative ignorance of its conceptual implications. The way in which the conceptualization presents as at the same time both subjective *and* objective is central.

Cowen and Shenton argue that there have been two historical ways of dealing with the "dual nature" of development. The first was to define development as entirely objective by asserting that ideas depend upon (or rather are part of) objective development (Marx); the second was to seek an apparent (but false) objective basis for ideas in some authority.

The reader may well note that neither solution is entirely satisfactory. Yet Cowen and Shenton's argument is extremely useful. It is particularly illuminating to consider that ideas of development usually contain both notions. While this is fundamentally what makes development confusing, Cowen and Shenton point out how this particularly confusing nature seems to strongly influence what we observe in practice.

For Cowen and Shenton, these solutions stem from their historical account rather than some analytical process, which is to say that they do not argue that other solutions are impossible. My references to "subsequent events" indicate where other possible solutions may perhaps be found, as this term deliberately avoids inclusion of ideas of knowable cause-effect relationships and so sidesteps tangles associated with ideas of immanence. I discuss this further in Part III.

The Issue of Empowerment

One way of digesting Cowen and Shenton's point is to consider the view that development, as an immanent process, should also be empowering. This may have powerful implications: the position that "development without freedom is impossible" (Sen 1999). But this is not such a common view. The very term *empowering* can draw us to the conclusion that agents of development, those who carry it out, should, if empowered by it, logically determine its course, or at least to some extent. So this would seem to contradict the initial characterization of development as an immanent process, that is pre-defined, at least in part.

Cowen and Shenton stress the tensions created by their understanding of the problem of development, in which development is seen as both a means and an end, so that certain ends are assumed present beforehand. Choice is needed for development to be subjectively initiated, but how can choice then be created by development? If the political prerequisites existed for people to choose what they wanted their government to do, then surely they would be seen as having been already developed: "Either people have power to exercise choice, in which case there is no cause for empowerment, or they do not and the task of empowerment is that of the logical problem of development." (Cowen and Shenton 1996, 4).

In this sense, development policy cannot be clearly and consistently understood if it is expressed as a solution to a known problem. Thinking in this way leads to a contradictory muddle. And this suggests that, as is the case when thinking is fundamentally contradictory, the ideas generated will be capable of relatively autonomous development: they will neither be grounded in consistency nor robust empirics.

Solutions to the Problem of Development and the Importance of Trusteeship

Now, because living with such tensions is probably inescapable for people who care about issues of power and exploitation and are concerned that their ideas reflect reality, we now need to examine in greater detail the two ways that Cowen and Shenton say have been offered to us to escape from the apparent paradox: how to "do" a historical process.

The first alternative Cowen and Shenton argue is Marx's position that material conditions govern consciousness. Economic advance eventually creates conditions for a true development of mankind as a conscious creative being (for Marx, Communism). Capitalist progress, thus, is not intentional; it is an immanent process, and that process determines consciousness. The second argument, which is somewhat surprising, they derive from the nineteenth-century English Catholic and dogmatist Cardinal Newman: that positive development is to be defined doctrinally. For him, correct development can be found in God's Word as expressed in human doctrine. This logical sleight of hand solves the problem of development—or, as we will see, seems to solve the problem—in that it disconnects ideas of development from other sources of possibly reasonable judgment (that is, from other non-authoritative sources of ideas and opinions).

A reading of Newman will show that his seven criteria for judging whether doctrine has been corrupted are stated in an almost ad hoc manner (Newman 1989, 171 et seq.): preservation of type, continuity of principles, power of assimilation, logical sequence, anticipation of its future, conservative action upon its past, and chronic vigor. This method of argument from a nineteenth-century theologian and priest will become familiar in later chapters. It involves little more than authoritative statement. Once it is spotted and the question of how it should be assessed raised, we can move forward. For another relevant historical comparison, see Armstrong commenting on Plotinus' characteristics of the ordering of ultimate reality—in his case, God (Armstrong 1993, 101–4). Again, these criteria for divinity are simply stated, with authority. As we will see, such habits of argument echo views where the presence of development is known through dogmatically defined characteristics. These positions use familiar but differing terminologies, such as "catching-up," "modernizing," "best practice," and so on. They depend upon belief and authority.

The question now arises as to how such beliefs can become associated with practice. It is one thing to assert that correct development can be known by recourse to authority. It is another to link this to actions. Cowen and Shenton argue that this happens through notions of trusteeship: the idea that those who took (and take) themselves to be developed could act to determine the process of development for those deemed to be less developed. Clearly Cowen and Shenton associate this with much modern development policy, both orthodox and unorthodox. Plenty of authors argue that developers such as the World Bank and the IMF, technocrats, and others are understood as those who attempt the task of developing others who are less developed. Sometimes authors approve these attempts; sometimes they do not. Baer et al. (1999) show the common attempt to assert a professed-correct interpretation of events by juxtaposing it with error on the part of competitors.

What is radically different and useful in Cowen and Shenton is the view that this somewhat peculiar positioning (trusteeship) can be linked to a logical tension, specifically that between development as both product and process. For Cowen and Shenton, this is a tension that continues so long as no other way has been found to cope with this fundamental problem of development. Granted, this dumping the consequences on the heads of the World Bank or some other prominent developer arguably appears unfair, not least because, as Cowen and Shenton argue, this issue is apparent and unresolved in the writings of a far wider range of people.

Intentionality

The modern intention to develop in Cowen and Shenton's account thus emerges historically from awareness—apprehension—of the negative consequences of a process of change: in their account the effects of capitalism. Change, without intention, was seen as disorderly and possessing a destructive dimension. Thus, development is quite different from progress in that it contains notions of intention. It also contains ideas of corruption, meaning a deviation from some ideal state. Thus, it has a subjective element—its approach to intentionality—and is historically a response to the consequences of capitalism. This contrasts with accounts that date underdevelopment from after WWII.

Development, then, may be seen as a conscious response to distorted progress: change should not happen that way, but it does. Intentionality in development is then linked closely to ideas of a potentially correct development, an ideal. According to Cowen and Shenton, the idea of progress emerged initially from older ideas of cyclical change as unfolding the universal potential for human improvement. But it had to confront unhappy evidence that this potential was not necessarily realized, encouraging attempts to create conditions to correct this.

But what of the older idea that destruction is inherent in change? If we reflect again upon Grindle and Thomas, we perhaps start to appreciate the power associated with notions of a true and correct development and a true and correct development policy, in which implementation, rather than consequences ("subsequent events"), is the key issue. Such issues have a history. For example, the risks involved in taking up trusteeship apparently drove Rudyard Kipling to write, for an American audience, his famous poem "The White Man's Burden," quoted above. Morel's polemic "The Black Man's Burden" (Morel 1971) takes Kipling's title and neatly inverts it, but without escaping from his historical context. To quote:

> The purpose of this volume, which was suggested to me by Mr. George Lansbury, is a dual one. It seeks to convey a clear notion of the atrocious wrongs which the white peoples have inflicted upon the black. It seeks to lay down the fundamental principles of a humane and practical policy in the government of Africa by white men. (Morel 1971, Introduction)

The Need for Agency

One valuable aspect of Cowen and Shenton is their historical analysis and the importance they attach to the emergence of markets and capitalism, or rather the apparently shocking effects of rapid social change associated with the capitalism of England and France from the late eighteenth century. How would development arise? Capitalism had posed intellectual puzzles. For example, how could there be negative results if the dominant acts were ones of voluntary exchange?

Adam Smith, in his *Wealth of Nations*, had argued for the positive effects of the latter but also saw negatives. As with the idea of development itself, Cowen and Shenton find Smith in a search for offsetting factors or causes. So the question was asked, what was the moral basis for these exchanges? And the answer Smith gave in his *Theory of Moral Sentiments* was sympathy for others as a counter to self-interest: "Self-interest implants the motion to society and sympathy directs the motion within wholesome constraints" (Cowen and Shenton 1996, 17).

Cowen and Shenton encourage us to think of ways in which the direction of thought sought positives as it found negatives (such as the costs of growth) that seemed to come from something that also generated positives (such as economic growth). In a more modern development jargon: growth creates the wealth that permits a well-governed state to cope with the social and environmental costs of growth.

Malthus, though, and more gloomily, disagreed, arguing that population growth occurred with no reference to moral sentiments. Thus, there would be growth without development, as real wages would stay low. Yet we may see how juxtaposition of Malthus with Smith could and perhaps should energize those wishing to do something about the way things were heading, as well as support not uncommon human sentiments of fatalism.

Thus development arose as a response. As an idea, it did not happen, but was a transformation of society: "Through the active purpose of those who were *entrusted* with the future of society" (Cowen and Shenton 1996, 25). But who? Naturally, various answers came to mind (recall the discussion of Rodrik in Chapter 2). Here we see, with an intentionality now construed, a search for agency to host intentionality. Who would be the developers? Property owners? Hardly. Thus, the early socialists? Or perhaps the banks could do it? Or perhaps a colonial government? The awakened search for intentionality and agency within change is clear, and we may guess where such arguments may head.

Policy as Doctrine and the Return of Cyclicality

My argument is that established development doctrines are insecure empirically. So doctrine changes and in prevalent current forms is supported by authority rather than evidence. The habit of assessing development policy in such terms influences how development policy changes.

Cowen and Shenton argue that an old cyclical movement, earlier seen in the nature of change and removed in the concept of progress, then reappeared in the intention to develop. This intention was "the internal of development, namely the conscious authority of autonomous being to determine and realize its potential" (Cowen and Shenton 1996, 57). So in what way would it be cyclical?

It does not take too much reading to find apparent examples of cyclicality related to the use of dichotomous development categories. Movement between the poles of the dichotomy then appears as cyclical variation between familiar positions—"for," "against," and "unresolved."

One intriguing characteristic of disputable theory in development policy discussions, the persistence of arguments for and against state intervention, has certainly exhibited highly cyclical aspects. One example is the IMF's changing position on capital account liberalization (see Chapter 7). Many views are characterized as pro-state, pro-market, or unresolved (a more earthy term would be *confused;* Lindauer and Pritchett 2002). I have already mentioned the work of Mitchell (1991) on the state, offering a discussion of dichotomous thinking, this time about state and society.

Much understanding of development debates does appear to be presented in terms of who is right and who is wrong, and who is dominant. This is one reflection of the knowability assumption. Yet we see cyclicality. By the start of 2000s, a post-Washington Consensus (PWC) argued for more state intervention in opposition to the Washington Consensus (WC) that dated from the 1980s. While it is useful to see cyclicality as part of how we may obtain a sense of the how of development policy positions, Cowen and Shenton's own framework leads Cowen and Shenton deeper.

For Cowen and Shenton, the cyclical policy sequence relates to a corrupted intention to develop, a consequence of inherent tension that results from attempts to resolve the problem of development (product or process) by linking correct development to authoritative statement. The internal (the idea) of development is "embraced by the intention to develop"; thus, it is not development as an immanent process that is oscillating, but policy. I understand Cowen and Shenton's point here to be that policy debate, once authority determines policy validation and policy becomes doctrine, evolves in ways largely explained in terms of its internal structures—thus the importance of the familiar dichotomies. In this sense Lao Tzu's remark, that history as written is not history as lived, is wise.[i]

It is useful to look for changes to the intellectual inputs of policy discussions. Clearly, economists are important. The fascinating study by Yonay (1998) offers a history of the struggle between mainly North American

---

[i]We may also note that for him, living in a culture where musical notation reflected pentatonic scales, it was quite natural to blame the "five notes" as deafening. Other cultures are accustomed to different music, different scales, and different notations and so deafen themselves in their own ways.

institutional and neoclassical economists in the years before WWII. His account does not proceed in terms of increasing knowledge but rather habits of thought, political contexts, personal and institutional rivalries, and so on. Yonay argues that a central goal of the institutionalists was to use a rapid increase in data availability to seek empirical regularities. By contrast, the neoclassicals held to the value of their models. This shows that belief in the value of models had not been driven primarily by their predictive ability, no matter their form.

The reader advisedly bears this in mind when surveying more modern histories. Accounts of policy evolution often contradict the pretensions of policy, and this seems linked to ways in which policy is part of a solution to the problem of development in Cowen and Shenton's terms that grounds assessment of policy in reference to authority.

Conclusions: The Problem of Development and Different Solutions to It

> A characteristic of propaganda in general is that it ceases to have power over you once you realize that it is propaganda. (Personal communication, ex-security analyst, Singapore, 2001)

The contrasts between the positions of Cowen and Shenton and Grindle and Thomas are very instructive. The two texts give very different but connected answers to the problem of development. Cowen and Shenton argue that the legacy of Newman is the tendency to identify correct development with what proper authority says it is. Grindle and Thomas show this by focusing upon implementation of what they uncritically accept as correct development policy and then by focusing upon reasons for the particular histories of implementation they observe. We can note, for example, in Grindle and Thomas the absence of reference to those values and what could be called the global history of debates that surely underpinned pro-market reforms.

There is also little articulation within Grindle and Thomas of a basic question: to what extent does policy actually matter? Sited upon a state, intentionality and agency are assumed and furthermore presented as essential to positive (good) change. Their position can thus be seen as ignoring a possibility that the positive change could occur without policy change (Ray 1998, 684–698).

For those who wish to argue with Grindle and Thomas (and many others) whether correct policy exists and is the main driver, the apparent developmental success of Thailand and Vietnam thus poses questions. As we shall see, much of the literature that we must use to compare development policy in the case studies has to grapple with issues of intentionality and agency in situations where neither is easy to observe. When intentionality and agency may be seen, success seems to come without intention, and intention does not appear to necessarily lead to success. Recall the central importance of intentionality and agency, linked to development through knowability, to classic policy ideologies. What I called the first class of classic policy ideologies suggests predictability, and—in failing at prediction—reduces to explanation. The second class—presenting as explanation but going beyond the boundaries it says it sets for itself by moving into prediction, so as to become a guide to classic policy—also becomes very exposed. Thus, neither really addresses the Cowen and Shenton critique.

Finally, it may be useful to recall that the origins of the 1980s policy orthodoxy are not something on which Grindle and Thomas spent much time. They do not discuss the issue of whether evidence actually does suggest that the cause-effect relationships they rely upon to construct a notion of correct policy may reasonably be said to exist. We can now see how this is not strange but rather quite normal.

Chapter 3 Questions

1. What is the "problem of development" as Cowen and Shenton understand it, and what, according to them, have been the two main solutions to it?

2. What are the main distinctions between ideas of "'immanent" or "intransitive" development and ideas of "intentional" or "transitive" development?

3. What should we look for if we wish to establish the main historical origins of development as an idea?

Development as an Idea—History

Introduction: From Analysis to History

So far I have used a rather analytical approach to the puzzles development presents. I started with an examination of policy issues and went on to look at ways in which common approaches dealt with them. I argued that these approaches ignore in various ways problems arising from assumptions of intentionality, agency, and the knowability of cause-effect relationships. I then argued that parts of Southeast Asia (SEA) were likely to project, in part because of apparent developmental success, heterodox analyses into the wider literature in that they seemed to offer examples of situations in which these assumptions were met but perhaps often were not. I concluded by contrasting two approaches: Cowen and Shenton, and Grindle and Thomas. I drew from this various points, in particular the view that it was useful to consider definitions of correct development as derived from doctrine, which made questions of knowability less important than authority.

I now turn to examine histories of development as an idea, taking the discussion up to the first decade of the 2000s. Chapters 4 and 5 summarize histories of development as an idea. A central argument of this book concerns the lack of interest in the origins of primary concepts, specifically where developmental ideas came from compared to the focus on post–WWII problems of poor regions. This relates to universalism, which denies the relevance of discussions of possible ontological and epistemological differences between the "there" and the "here." I try to retain a focus upon broad-brush issues, which I then refine in Chapters 6 and 7 by looking at disciplinary approaches and questions of measurement and empirics that add to the discussion of knowability.

This chapter deals with the period up to the mid-1990s, and the next with more contemporary events. The chapter treats Arndt (1987) as an accessible history of development as an idea. Recall that Cowen and Shenton take issue with a common view that Arndt shares (and treats as fundamental)— that this history started just after the end of WWII.

The Exotic Origins of Development as an Idea: Economics as an Example

Many accounts of the history of development as an idea stress development's exotic nature from the perspectives of many poor countries. I have already mentioned remarks by Meier (1984), and these are worth further discussion. In an attempt to define significant pioneers in development economics, we can note the statement in his preface that "when the Second World War ended, economists were challenged by the urgent problems of development" (Meier 1984, ix). We can compare this with the statement only a few pages later by Meier that "the subject matter of development economics is at once among the oldest and the newest branches of economics" (Meier 1984, 3).

The tensions stem from his view that before WWII the static focus of much marginalist analysis combined with the short-period focus of Keynesian economics to deemphasize long-run questions. "Static" here refers to characteristics of economists' models, and contrasts with "dynamic." The former typically compare two states that have different values of t, such as the situation before and after imposition of a tax on imports. This means that there is little if any discussion of process—how the shift between these two states happens.

This meant that mainstream economics was not very concerned with the study of historical change, which Meier confronts as an economist of standing who is deeply interested in change. Thus in his preface to *Leading Issues in Economic Development* (1976), he writes: "Development economists must operate in an imperfect second-best world, away from the simplified premises of neoclassical economics. Their subject matter is therefore not yet a coherent or self-contained discipline" (Meier 1976, vii). Here we find an issue that recurs in a range of contexts: the view that one of the most significant problems facing developing countries and the analysis of their economies is that their markets are weakly developed. This makes it hard for economists to apply standard models, and so to participate in development.

Studies such as Agenor and Montiel (1999) argue that standard macroeconomics textbooks use assumptions that suit developed, not developing, countries. Similar arguments can be found in Bardhan and Udry (1999). Bardhan (1993) argues that early development economists focused upon important issues that have come back into mainstream focus. But Stern, onetime chief economist at the World Bank, reveals (1989) the tensions between a sense that research has been unable to discover regularities and a language that confidently ignores the pitfalls of ontological and epistemological universalism implied by Levine and Zervos (1993). Thus, one of his concluding questions: "How can the productivity of investment be raised and what determines investment?" (Stern 1989, 672). He treats investment as a category ontologically free of tensions (see Kenny and Williams 2001 and the section "Empirics—a reality check" in Chapter 3). Clearly, the issue of the exotic is highlighted here, and the way in which exoticism and universalism interact with trusteeship.

Discussion in this chapter will center upon a puzzle already discussed. If development as an idea necessarily involves trusteeship, then we may ask how development practitioners have argued that they know what to do. How does this relate to the configurations of intentionality, agency, and cause-effect relationships embodied in various approaches? These configurations show how development policy has been construed and explained, as well as different ways in which underdevelopment has been presented within various notions of development policy. The embodiment of agency and the selection of agents upon whom developmental intentionality is to be sited is fundamental.

Ideas of Development "Before Aid"

According to Arndt (1987), almost no economic studies of development as now understood existed prior to WWII. Compare Arndt's position, which is common, with Waterbury (1999) and other histories of poor regions' attempts to develop prior to WWII, as well as Cowen and Shenton. As we have seen, Cowen and Shenton locate the problem of development well before WWII in late nineteenth-century UK and France as they confronted the negative social consequences and underdevelopment that came with a well-established industrial revolution.

Earlier still, Adam Smith had argued in the eighteenth century for positive aspects of capitalism and markets, stressing the role of an invisible hand in allocating resources to good social ends. Self-interest could thus be thought to be a source of order and progress amid the squalor and chaos. Yet we can note that laissez-faire doctrine was conscious intent—policy—and, later in the nineteenth century, metropolitan and colonial progress was viewed as highly state-driven and intentional. The economic historian Polanyi had argued for the historical importance of powerful, though not necessarily intentional, state intervention to create national markets. This is discussed in Chapter 12.

In these and other writings, we can see tensions between development as product and as process. Writers argued that trade and economic enterprise—social practices that by definition could not be of themselves moral agents—were agents of change and development. Adam Smith's "invisible hand" is a clear example of something that acts without having any idea of social intention. How was intentionality to be brought into the discussion?

The references to articles in the *Economist* above suggest common tendencies to treat development issues through exotic ideas and practices. Confronted with such practices, it often took an effort to bring historical issues into the discussion. Ha-joon Chang argues (2003), iconoclastically, that the institutions presented to poor countries by mainstream development as objects of emulation were, if his historical account is believed, the *result*, not the cause, of rich country development. Core institutions of mainstream development, such as avoidance of protection, emerged in rich countries, including the US, only once they were rich. Yet debates that imply that protection and state intervention are both identifiable ontologically and necessarily "good for development" remain risky.

Historical accounts can thus be juxtaposed with the emergence of exotic development theory after WWII. One way to resolve this is to define development as an issue related to specific practices in the increasingly post-imperial world of the United Nations after WWII. Thus, many histories of development start with President Truman's 1949 speech calling for aid.

If nineteenth-century French and British metropolitan experiences are worth noting but often ignored, then so too are other differences between conditions before and after WWII. In histories of development, note the importance of WWII to Latin America, for in the nineteenth century many of these countries had included rich free traders exploiting primary product exports (similar to British Dominions such as Canada and Australia), but then fell to Third World status by the end of WWII (Blomstrom and Meller 1991). For such countries, where wartime import controls had seemed to have positive effects, development after the war often took the form of ISI (import-substituting industrialization). This historical perspective is useful.

Even if at the end of WWII many poor areas still lacked the formally independent states that came with decolonization, the shift in global power away from imperial powers such as Britain, France, and others and toward the US and the Soviet Union meant that typical relations between rich and poor would transform. The change to focus upon development as a central issue after the war seems inseparable from the movement in the field of intentionality offered by statehood granted to or won by ex-colonies. Agency had to be transferred—and so, transformed. Histories of development show a search for comparators, and these could be found in the pre–WWII context.

The USSR and Republican China could be cited. Sun Yat Sen had called for institutional and economic change in China to be energized by foreign investment (Sun Yat Sen 1928). From the 1920s until the fall of the Soviet regime in the early 1990s, planned economic development and interpretations of Soviet experience were part of debates in ways that ceased once the Soviet Union fell. These stressed intentionality and the state. But the USSR was far more significant. Marx himself, to ignore the voluntarism of official Soviet thinking for the moment, believed in immanent development. His theories were full of references to prediction, predictability, and laws of change, and, if we follow Cowen and Shenton, this can be seen as an absolute unintentionality (intransitive development in Arndt's terminology). The economic base determines the superstructure (including ideas). Leaving aside the vast array of literature and debate as to how intentionality would or could be experienced within such a viewpoint, if we move beyond Marx (as Lenin and then Stalin created socialism under quite different conditions from those Marx had envisaged), the Soviet Union can be presented, perhaps ironically, as a striking example of development with extreme intentionality.

After winning the civil war and faced with hostile external forces who had often sided with the Whites, autarkic industrialization was the chosen foundation for Soviet socialism. Expressed in the Five Year Plans and metaphors of economic muscle, autarkic industrialization largely assumed that increasing the stock of fixed capital was a main determinant of growth, and much of the extremely heavy-handed and unpleasant institutional framework arguably followed from this. The reader should note, though, that the core ideas were a combination of institutions "known to work," with a heavy focus upon physical resources, above all capital, to define a problem of development and a correct solution to it. For regions such as communist North Vietnam after 1954, this policy-set was as exotic as any.

We need also to recall the reactive nationalism epitomized by Japan and its success in economic competition with industrialized countries prior to WWII. By the 1930s, if not earlier, Japan was widely seen as an equal of Western countries in terms of economic power. Japan's history since the arrival of the Black Ships was often written as one of institutional adaptation from a good starting point (Smith 1959), with strong protection and state activism (Johnson 1998). Success could be seen as a modernization to preserve national independence and, like that of the USSR, cast a long shadow before and after WWII.

In terms of intentionality, this rapid overview suggests two things. First, it was not too hard to assert the positive potential of the state as a site for intentionality, though there was much debate as to how this should be used. Japan and the USSR both seemed to confirm the value of the state. Second, there is little questioning of the knowability of cause-effect logics; in fact, quite the reverse. A reading of much of the literature suggests great belief in the knowability of answers to questions of what works.

Experiences in poor areas prior to WWII thus seemed to present strong arguments for harnessing state power if development was to happen. Intentionality was linked to the state, rather than society, banks, or some other site. We can recall Cowen and Shenton's points about the origins of development in mid-nineteenth-century responses to nondevelopmental change. Intentionality arose in reactions to unwanted situations yet was philosophically unresolved, or rather resolved spuriously through Newman's logical sleight of hand.

To follow Cowen and Shenton, if the origin of the problem of development was in the negative consequences of capitalism in France and the UK during the mid-nineteenth century, the problem of development arising for poor areas after WWII was also viewed as coping with a negative. Although the problem was construed in different ways, often argued as consequential upon capitalism (or colonialism), it was widely linked to the absence of the presumed mechanism and vehicle for positive development: a formally independent state. Post–WWII energies, or more accurately the expected directions in which energy would and could be channeled, were thus readily associated with the state as a site for intentionality, which tended to require belief in the positive consequences (effects) of interventions (construed as causes).[i] Ideas in the richer countries had been changing to a similar statist direction, though not to extinguish free-market views.

The Great Depression and the 1929 stock market crash are often associated with changes in attitudes to state intervention, most importantly the election of Roosevelt and the Democrats' New Deal in the US. Yonay, in the work already cited (1998), describes links between the institutional economists involved with the various organizations set up by the New Deal and postwar interventionist thinking in multilateral institutions under the UN, such as the Food and Agriculture Organization (FAO). Such accounts also link political support for intervention in the US to wartime planning. In the UK, Beveridge and Keynes could be seen as "saving Capitalism in its confrontation with Fascism and Communism." These trends amounted to an increased acceptance, especially in the UK and the US, of an active role for the state (Shonfield 1965). This accompanied the ideas behind the United Nations, creation of the Bretton Woods institutions (the International Monetary Fund, IMF, and the World Bank), and their harnessing with the UN as co-developers for the postwar world of independent sovereign states.

The international structures that arose thus embodied ideas entailing support for emergent formally independent states as sites for developmental intentionality. These international organizations also offered sites linked

---

[i]The interested reader may wish to research histories of late colonialism that find shifts in patterns of interaction that see colonies often become far more statist in their makeup. See in a large literature, for example, Anderson (1983), Trocki (1999), and Osborne (1997) discussing Southeast Asia. See also Scott (1998).

to earlier expressions of trusteeship that would share that intentionality. As aid programs emerged, development could then start to evolve into now familiar structures, offering their solutions to development. The tensions inherent in colonial trusteeship and identified by Cowen and Shenton may easily be seen as having been only partially transformed—most strikingly, in ways in which tensions arising from assumptions, such as that of knowability, were resolved through recourse to authority.

The optimism of the period after WWII is striking regarding attitudes toward aid recipients. Successful European reconstruction after WWII under the Marshall Plan supplied resources to and through *existing* institutions. That is, there were no projects in a modern developmental sense, and no technical assistance. Postwar reconstruction, for all its focus upon Cold War issues, saw little need to secure appropriate institutional change in a developmental sense, and as a result there was little in the way of any institutional development problem recognizable to today's development professionals.

Thus the trusteeship of late imperialism—progress under foreign tutelage—could be transferred and transformed. Decolonization would be enough. Free of the foreign yoke and supported by capital and technical advice (the tools of modernization), positive development would happen. Yet this assumed much, not least confidence in local states as sites for intentionality and the application of known intervention logics. But this intentionality was to be shared with international developers, such as the World Bank and rich governments' bilateral aid agencies that arose after decolonization. Sovereignty was attained, and aid arose to supplement it. Yet, in that it required an interaction between at least two sovereign powers, aid practice would not find it easy to avoid tensions implied by trusteeship.

Aid-Based Developmentalism and Ideas of Development Immediately after WWII

Arndt argues that immediately after WWII underdevelopment was generally seen as mass poverty. Increasingly discussed in economic terms, development ideas increasingly stressed material change, because development was identified closely with economic growth. And the ideas of the World Bank and other important institutions of global governance charged with development came to be dominated, accordingly, by economics.

Compared with the pessimism of the prewar years, the postwar economic miracle experienced by many countries in Western Europe—which included such very different approaches as the use of economic planning in France and the UK (though the French continued with it longer than the

British) and the more free-market-based German Economic Miracle (the Wirtschaftswunder)—seemed to lead to renewed confidence in liberal democratic government and institutions (Shonfield 1965). A similar sunniness of disposition drew upon US economic experiences after the war, with the rise of an unprecedentedly affluent mass consumer society, increasingly shared by richer areas of Western Europe and elsewhere.

Many poor countries implemented ISI in the 1950s and 1960s with support from multilateral institutions such as the World Bank and IMF. The reader may find it useful to examine the policy prescriptions of such institutions at this time. Import-substituting industrialization was seen as correct policy that would lead to economic growth. The success stories of the 1950s and 1960s may make somewhat startling reading to contemporary eyes and include countries such as Burma, Pakistan, Ghana, and Brazil. Justification for interventions that reduced the freedom of markets was found in various areas, including the idea important to development economics at the time that factor markets (that is, markets for land, labor, and capital) in poor countries were usually weakly developed. Without good market-mediated access to crucial inputs, businesses (for example) could not grow and flourish; the logical argument was that to obtain development the state had to come in, providing credits through state banks, ensuring land access through land reforms, and supporting labor supply through measures such as training, controlled migration, and guidance to trade unions. Protection was also needed. Tariffs and controls on capital movements would ensure that national resources were used well, and infant industries could grow without being destroyed by foreign competition. These were core elements of ISI doctrine.

In many standard narratives, things started to unravel by the 1960s. There were growing complaints that higher investments did not necessarily lead to more growth. Further, the significant growth occurring in some countries did not seem to be leading to or even accompanying higher popular welfare. By the early 1970s, economists at the World Bank could push for strongly interventionist policies that sought to address perceived inequalities said to be accompanying the growth process:

> Recent evidence confirms earlier speculations that in the early stages of development the distribution of income tends to become more concentrated . . . As growth continues, its benefits are more widely spread, but there are a number of obstacles that limit the share received by the poor . . . the bulk of the developing countries in which the poor have shared equitably in income growth—Israel, Yugoslavia, Taiwan, Korea, Sri Lanka, Costa Rica, Tanzania—consists of countries that have taken positive action to this end. (Chenery et al. 1974, xiv–xv)

This statement assumes both a knowable development process and knowably correct policies to influence it. Also, as Arndt puts it, the Third World struck back. We see the rise of positions such as dependency theory and the development of underdevelopment (Frank 1966) and notions of unequal exchange based on earlier work by Prebisch, who had argued that the terms of trade for primary exporters tended over time to worsen. These views challenged assumptions that decolonization and the post–WWII order would lead to progress with economic growth by arguing that the world system itself was creating underdevelopment. These ideas remain attractive to many, not least because of the persistence of poverty. Writers such as Hoogvelt (2001) remain important articulators of these approaches (see also Glassman, below, in the section "Geographers and space" in Chapter 6).

Given the now large number of UN seats held by poor countries and the international politics of the period, the 1970s accompanied calls for a New International Economic Order (NIEO), in which such global inequities would be eased by state intervention at a global level. The rules of international development efforts were thus contested in loud debates about aid and international institutions. These contests were one element of the now often forgotten background to major changes in orthodox development thinking during the late 1970s and 1980s.

It is useful also to note radical political opposition in rich countries during the 1960s and 1970s (Caute 1988). Ideas were changing. The contrasts between rich and poor, between developed and underdeveloped, became starker. With such wealth and abundance in rich countries, many now saw a savage impact from development in the Third World and shrank at its images. In contrast with establishment developers comfortable with official institutions and decolonization, others asserted underdevelopment as disempowering and brutalizing (Sachs 1992; Rahnema and Bawtree Eds 1997).

The Background to 1980s Radicalism

The 1970s saw the end of the postwar boom. The Cold War was still on, as was the war in Indochina (until 1975), and countries saw the US and USSR intervene directly. Decolonization was still recent, but stagflation now gripped many of the richer countries. The events of 1968 and radical social change challenged much.

The orthodox sociology of development as seen in the early 1970s was in many ways very simple: trade and the expected political and social consequences of capitalist development flows would lead eventually to emergence of a middle class, democracy, and Western values (Rostow 1971). But increasingly attention focused upon failure and its consequences, and what to do if things went wrong. If development was seen as a problem with solutions, then how did this logic work its way out?

Initially, in the late 1960s and early 1970s, one answer was basic needs and/or redistribution (Chenery et al. 1974). But what was the implicit role of the state? The center of gravity of discussion, in comparison with what was to come, remained skeptical about the value of free markets and supportive of intervention. Although widely criticized from the Left at the time, this position was far to the left of what was to come with the the growing power of the New Right and the radical nature of the attack on the state in the late 1970s and early 1980s (Toye 1983 and 1987). Views that became orthodox in the 1980s, that the market if left alone would work things out, were highly unorthodox in institutions such as the World Bank and the IMF in the 1950s and 1960s. The simplest and in many ways most revealing way of accessing this information is to read World Bank reports: contrasts between the 1950s, early 1970s, early 1980s, and early 2000s are striking.

Born in the 1960s?

The Rise of Critique

Coming to development writings without awareness of these histories makes them hard to assess. Positions taken in the literature of the late 1990s and early 2000s seem to go back to earlier times. One recurrent allegation is the narrow definition of *underdevelopment* as lack of economic growth. This definition combined with tensions in applying criteria of civilization to the Third World after decolonization. Why should common criteria be applied? And why a single metric sought? Such questions appear reasonable, and their apparent strangeness only makes sense in terms of their historical contexts and the beliefs in posited solutions to the problem of development.

For many, underdevelopment is not only always there, it is created. But what actions should follow? Here various positions seek to replace orthodoxy with alternatives drawn from a critique of orthodoxy, without, in the sense used by Cowen and Shenton, creating any new solution to the problem of development and so failing to deal with its basic conundrums. For me they usually remain within realms where it remains reasonable to speak of known correct development and to base judgments of what constitutes correct development upon familiar grounds: authority. Thus Chenery et al. (1974), a radical critique from within the WB, asserts knowability, nests this in classic policy logic, and is within a few years swept aside by the Washington Consensus (WC). A reading of Frank (1966) also shows little sense that he might be wrong in what he advocates.

Consider generational changes of the 1960s and 1970s. Critique and opposition to the system arose strongly, often with stress on alienation. The development literature shows influences from the New Left, "1968 and all that" (Caute 1988), and growing antistatism. This became institutionalized as people grew up, wrote books and became professors, joined NGOs or official donor agencies, or returned home. Criticism may also be linked to an emerging importance of Third World intellectuals and the later Subaltern literature (Sylvester 1999).

Mainstream thinking was accused of ignoring pain and alienation in poor countries (or at least some of them) and also of disregarding not only apparent consequences of the focus upon economic growth but also allegedly blatant contradictions with dominant political values in rich countries. Naturally, such accusations were strongly rejected and resented. Some poor countries saw rapid economic growth, but far from all. Large populations seemed to live in backwaters—Africa, Latin America, and South Asia increasingly seemed to offer negative examples of the way in which an increasingly mutually aware world was changing. Rapid growth in India did not resume until the 1980s. In the same decade, China (and Vietnam but not Cuba), earlier icons of some on the Left, went through complex transitions from plan to market, to emerge to what appeared as rapid market-based growth around the time of the collapse of the Soviet Union and the Communist regimes of Central and Eastern Europe.

Intentionality and Agency: The Beginnings of Non-Categorical Pragmatism?

It is perhaps not unexpected, if we take on board Cowen and Shenton's arguments, that long-established challengers of authority should have projected new issues into development thinking: gender and non-state organization. Gender studies and feminism were powerful bases for radical development thinking (for example, Marchand 1996; see also the discussion in the section "Discursive orders" in Chapter 5). Note, however, ways in which much of the discussion was underlain by concerns over intentionality and agency: What was the correct position for women's issues in development? Should they be treated as special, and so risk being sidelined, or mainstreamed, and risk co-option? Should women be co-developers? In Cowen and Shenton's terms, belief in Newman's solution to the problem of development could perhaps too easily be seen as a corruption of the intention to develop.

Sylvester (1999) provides a stimulating discussion of different and perhaps contradictory perceptions of gender issues among developers and the developed. Her irony links to the emerging queer and third wave feminist literature that appears to reject categorization and seek what I referred to in Chapter 1 as pragmatic positions. Did opposition to authority and external definition lie beneath this trend?

NGOs started to become increasingly important with their frequent stress upon participation and psychologies of the bottom-up (antistatism from the grassroots). Unlike the 1990s, when NGOs were increasingly funded by governments, in the 1970s and 1980s their access to what appeared as quite different and qualitative sources of information saw them play an increasingly tart role in debates (Edwards 1999). From a Cowen and Shenton perspective, among NGOs we start to see approaches that seem to circumvent classic views of policy and the definition of correct development in terms of doctrine, in part through a rhetoric of participation. Yet as we have seen, Chambers, a central figure in these developments, arguably holds to a knowability assumption.

1980s Radicalism

Central to most accounts of development since the 1980s is the so-called Washington Consensus (WC; Williamson 1990 and 2000). Because it is so clearly pro-market, it seems wise to consider whether the WC of the 1980s was bound up with the rise of Reagan and Thatcher and the nature of their democratic support. In these important, rich countries, a major shift in public opinion toward the free market and away from state intervention occurred (Dunn 2000). In any case, with the shift in mainstream development theory, histories of the internal politics of the World Bank point to powerful actions to effect rapid change in personnel and thinking.[ii] Doctrinally, the bank moved decisively against intervention. Its 1987 World Development Report is cited as a clear expression of the Washington Consensus.

Attention was drawn to the so-called NICs (newly industrializing countries), mainly in East Asia, and how their apparent success was to be integrated into doctrine. An ostensibly clear element of what had been happening to them was export success, combined with confidence and international competitiveness. The starkest contrast was made between ISI (import-substituting industrialization) and EOG (export-oriented growth), and the natural and logical focus of attention was upon how to ensure correct pro-free market and antistate policies. Paradoxically, this had to entail thinking about the state and how and why correct policies did or did not happen, posing questions of the suitability of developing country states as sites for intentionality. What policymakers did or did not do and whether they were insulated from social and other pressures that would prevent them adopting and implementing correct policy (now expressed in pro-market terms, as laid down by the new doctrine) became the central focus. We have seen already how writers such as Rodrik can find themselves arguing that economic reformers may need—in the name of what they "know to be true"—to override democratic expressions of popular will.

Much was made of distributional coalitions and vested interests that would oppose implementation of correct policies. Confidence in the

---

[ii]See the section on Anne Krueger in Rodgers and Cooley (1999).

authority of Third World governments was eroded, while new doctrine was reinforced by practices and research. Histories are extremely contentious. Ray (1998, 684–698) offers an account of interactions between balance of payment crises, the role of the WB and IMF in debt renegotiation, and shifts away from ISI. This suggests that any simple explanation is not plausible. There is a vast discussion of the apparent failure of WC policies to accelerate growth. Easterly (2001) grapples with the possibility that his basic analytical framework may be awry (see Chapter 12; see also Easterly and Montiel 1997). The reader may recall my discussion in Chapter 1 of the problems facing evaluation, which can also be found here in the multiplicity of contesting accounts. My own belief (but why?) is that the main effects of the shifts away from ISI and intervention were political, greatly weakening the authority of both donors and recipient governments in a historical process that continues today.

To enforce compliance, structural adjustment loans (SALs) and imposition of conditionality were mechanisms that were initially proposed. Although these were quickly seen as failures, from a longer historical perspective the core issue seems to be a willingness to take on governments to obtain reform. A generation after decolonization, confidence in poor country governments as reliable trustees (or co-trustees) for the task of development would no longer be taken for granted.

A key issue, though, is the renewed sense of trusteeship issues, although this was not always made explicit. The role of the WB changed. Initially, it had been a source of lending resources, premised upon the belief that the fundamental issue that it should address was a shortage of capital due to problems with markets and the belief that "market failure" was extensive. One interpretation of Washington Consensus ideas was that market failure was far less important. The bank was now presented as a global developer that could negotiate to support the implementation of correct policies. The intellectual context was familiar: belief, supported by much effort to assert doctrine, that there was a way that all governments could and should follow. This combined with a search for empowered technocratic elites as the means to do so: the search for agency to host intentionality. We start to read much about issues of governance.

Challenging State Sovereignty

Juxtaposition of successes and failures changed the literature. In the terms used by Cowen and Shenton, many sought to site an intention to develop in the local state, and debate then focused upon how to do this. Classic policy ideologies and their assumptions drove research and practice that focused upon how to secure states "doing" development. Concern thus shifted to local conditions for implementation of correct policies. Change was increasingly written up as a history within which the state was seen as the central agent, or site for intentionality.

Failure meant that somebody or something had botched his historic task, and postcolonial states were an obvious target. Almond (1988) offers a perceptive and detailed history of the treatment of the state by political science (mainly American political science). In particular, he gives a history of the return of academic interest in the state and includes discussion of what others have called co-developers: those desiring to participate in the intentionality and practice of the exercise of state power. Amsden (1997) is an accessible introduction to the developmental literature.

In the postcolonial world, in which the United Nations defined global governance in terms of sovereign states, the sovereignty issue tended to imply problems once legacies of trusteeship helped reduce confidence in poor country governments as developers. Fine (1999) argues strongly that trusteeship was gaining greater prominence in the apparent decline in respect for the sovereignty of the local state. I think that the 2000s show rather clearly a trend toward greater willingness to violate the principle of sovereignty. It has become, for example, far easier to find staff for aid projects operating in situations where the local armed forces are responsible to external agencies rather than a local state, as "transitional" arrangements become institutionalized (Ashdown 2007).

Two Case Studies of Development Doctrine—ISI and EOG

I now discuss two case studies of major and contending policy-sets: ISI and EOG. These case studies illuminate the more general issues I have been discussing and provide important detail. The first examines what is today largely an anathema, heresy in many quarters—ISI. But supporters of intervention remain. EOG is articulated in doctrinal terms by the World Bank's defining text, the 1993 East Asian Miracle study.

ISI—Import-Substituting Industrialization

Import-substituting industrialization (ISI) is an important element both of histories of development and of ongoing debates. Orthodox doctrine after WWII, ISI was later largely condemned. Central in many histories of doctrine is the notion of ISI as a major error from which students and poor countries should be protected. These views are often strongly held. It is therefore worth looking at ISI in some detail. Waterbury (1999) provides an accessible entry to the issues, but the reader would do well to explore the literature more widely. Waterbury makes two main arguments. First, that ISI is not a pure type, and, second, that it often set conditions for successful export promotion in terms of historical sequence as well as possible cause-effect relations.

Many governments attempt to protect domestic markets for domestic producers. These businesses can be foreign-owned or domestically owned. Protecting their home markets against imports arguably pushes up domestic prices, likely increasing producers' profits. There is, logically, always the option of doing this, perhaps with the intention to encourage investment and business activity. Therefore, it is useful for those who oppose such actions to set up a straw man that can be used in debate to show that these policy options should not be followed.[iii] For this, among

---

[iii]A "straw man" in debate is when an opponent of a position sketches a characterization of that position and then criticizes it. This can be more effective in debate than dealing with the position as outlined by its advocates. See my earlier references (in Chapter 2) to tendencies to argue that errors revealed in a competitor should encourage belief in the position taken by the protagonist. Consider the following exchange from the excellent film *Thank You for Smoking:*

Nick Naylor: That's the beauty of argument: if you argue correctly, you're never wrong.

Joey Naylor: . . . so what happens when you're wrong?

Nick Naylor: Whoa, Joey, I'm never wrong.

Joey Naylor: But you can't always be right . . .

Nick Naylor: Well, if it's your job to be right, then you're never wrong.

Joey Naylor: But what if you are wrong?

Nick Naylor: OK, let's say that you're defending chocolate, and I'm defending vanilla. Now if I were to say to you, "Vanilla is the best flavor ice cream," you'd say . . .

Joey Naylor: No, chocolate is.

Nick Naylor: Exactly, but you can't win that argument . . . so, I'll ask you, "So you think chocolate is the end-all and the be-all of ice-cream, do you?"

Joey Naylor: It's the best ice cream. I wouldn't order any other.

Nick Naylor: Oh! So it's all chocolate for you, is it?

Joey Naylor: Yes, chocolate is all I need.

Nick Naylor: Well, I need more than chocolate, and for that matter I need more than vanilla. I believe that we need freedom and choice when it comes to our ice cream, and that, Joey Naylor, that is the definition of liberty.

Joey Naylor: But that's not what we're talking about

Nick Naylor: Ah! But that's what I'm talking about.

Joey Naylor: . . . But you didn't prove that vanilla was the best . . .

Nick Naylor: I didn't have to. I proved that you're wrong, and if you're wrong, I'm right.

Joey Naylor: But you still didn't convince me

Nick Naylor: It's that I'm not after you. I'm after them. [He points into the crowd.]

(Source: http://www.imdb.com/title/tt0427944/quotes. From *Thank You for Smoking,* 2005)

See also my references to Dunn on the shift away from Keynesian ideas, at the beginning of Chapter 5.

other reasons, ISI is a part of most courses on development, development economics, and development policy.

Waterbury points to commonalities between many historical experiences of ISI: industrialization was usually (but not always) conceived of as heavy industrialization aiming at self-sufficiency; tariffs, quotas, and quantitative trade restrictions were widely used; ISI was often driven by military/strategic aims; the agricultural sector was seen as the major source of surplus for industrial investment; and it was commonly thought that markets could be tamed by substituting plans and policy interventions for markets. He argues also that there was no commonality regarding the following:

- The role of foreign direct investment (FDI)
- The role of the private sector
- The extent and presence of state-owned enterprises (SOEs) in different sectors
- Macroeconomic policies—exchange rate, fiscal and monetary[iv]
- Policies toward agriculture
- Redistributive policies

The thrust of this argument is against tendencies, such as on the part of advocates of other policies (such as EOG), to construct ISI as a "straw man" and to seek to bundle into this straw man a wide range of elements to which the anti-ISI position is also opposed, such as the state sector, pro-agriculture policies, and so on. In a common tactic in argument, the counter is then to seek to "unbundle" by deconstructing "ISI" into elements that can be treated separately, which is what Waterbury is doing above. It would follow, therefore, that ISI, if positive in attitude toward light industry, agriculture, and markets, could return to original arguments in favor of infant industries. Note Stiglitz's willingness to support a correct ISI under certain circumstances (Stiglitz 1998). As in other areas of dispute, deconstruction of straw men may show how a position is developed and advanced.

I turn now to the World Bank's famous 1993 Miracle study, which is thoroughly and doctrinally anti-ISI and pro-EOG: the message is "we know." Like ISI, where EOG is blamed for this and that, it is often used to construct a straw man, and many courses and articles use similar tactics to attack the World Bank, especially this famous study.

[iv]Many accounts of ISI argue that it led to macroeconomic imbalances (inflation, major distortions in key prices such as real interest rates, labor costs, etc) and balance-of-payments problems.

EOG Doctrine: The World Bank's 1993 East Asian Miracle Study

Origins

The East Asian Miracle study reportedly had its origins in Japanese official disagreement with the bank's position on guided credit and SALs. Japanese assistance to poor countries often took the form of two-step credits, whereby the recipient received credits that were then meant to be lent to priority sectors, typically exporters. Japanese interests agreed to fund the study to gain support for their development doctrine (see the discussion of Ohno in the section "State activism—some Japanese views" in Chapter 6).

The World Bank's Eight Lessons from the East Asian Miracle

The East Asian Miracle study focused upon the causes of the developmental success of eight countries—Hong Kong, Singapore, Japan, Taiwan, Republic of Korea, Malaysia, Indonesia, and Thailand. It concludes that eight lessons were to be learned. All relate to implementation of intended activities by government: that is, actual implementation of correct policies. The basic framework is one of knowable cause-effect relations and their use as a platform for trusteeship and intentionality. The language, reflecting its users' ontological and epistemological assumptions, is thoroughly universalistic, as discussed in Chapter 3. Lessons to be learned, therefore, are aimed at policymakers and governments. The thrust is not at the negotiation of acceptable "subsequent events" but at the realization of cause-effect relationships asserted to be known.

Lesson # 1—Maintaining macroeconomic stability

Inflation was kept low, and the exchange rate kept competitive. Success was both in terms of trends and in the management of macroeconomic balance in the face of shocks (for example, oil price hikes). This, they say, resulted from technocratic elites insulated from political pressures.

Lesson # 2—Building human capital

Considerable public and private resources were put into education. Tertiary education tended to be vocational, and female participation was high.

Lesson # 3—Creating effective and secure financial systems

Popular financial savings were mobilized at rather high levels through a shift toward positive real interest rates (though rather late on in the process), and the creation of secure and stable banking systems through protection and regulation (although this reduced the level of competition). Also, state development banks were often used along with commercial banks.

Lesson # 4—Limiting macro price distortions

Wages were kept near "correct" levels through flexible labor markets, and interest rates were (after an initial period where they were kept too low) maintained at levels higher than inflation. This meant that resources flowed toward sectors that reflected changing "comparative advantage" (enhancing the efficiency of growth), affecting labor-intensive and resource sectors early on, then moving into more capital-intensive areas later.

Lesson # 5—Maintaining openness to foreign technology

It was possible, when these successful developers started rapid growth, to obtain technology through licensing, importation of machinery, and reverse engineering.

Lesson # 6—Avoiding more than minimal bias against agriculture

Unlike some other countries, agriculture was not seen as a source of capital for industrialization. Rural incomes benefited from state spending on rural infrastructure, the Green Revolution, and low direct and indirect taxation

Lesson # 7—Creating a secure environment for private investment

Central to success was a core of technocratic managers (relatively insulated from commerce, though less so in Thailand and Indonesia) who created a secure environment. How? There were basically three mechanisms—good pay, rule-governed organizations, and high status that was granted to public employment. Also, institutions were set up that linked bureaucracy to the private sector.

Lesson # 8—Limited market intervention that sometimes had positive effects

Interventions tended to be carried out within limits. There were three types:

- Promotion of specific industries—this was ineffective; the economic structure that emerged resulted from market forces and relative factor prices/comparative advantage.

- Directed credit—this was effective, but brought with it high risks.

- Export promotion—this was effective.

The World Bank's Analysis

The World Bank's analysis shows a classic view of policy, with now-familiar characteristics. Intentionality is sited upon the state and associated with correct policies reflecting contemporary doctrine, stated here as minimal (but not zero) intervention. Some argue that policy had no effect different from the market. This presumes that existing economic structures, in the absence of policy, actually do reflect such an economic logic, which is rather a strong assumption. This assumes that it is possible to know what would have happened in the absence of intervention, a view made far easier by assumptions of ontological and epistemological universalism, for then the argument requires less attention to particular local history and conditions. The assumptions facilitate statistical analysis, because the comparative sample can be assumed to be drawn from a uniform population. The latter point, if invalid, of course makes the results spurious.

What is striking, though, is that, despite general belief at the time in a relatively low incidence of market failure, the bank was led to encourage some state intervention, primarily to support exports. This may, perhaps uncharitably, be viewed as a rationale for measures to push implementation of what was then seen as correct development—EOG; in other words, to assist in solving the realization problem.

Critics of the World Bank's Position

The bank's position has been widely debated. Various points are worth noting. Recall Waterbury's suggestion that these countries may have gone through a period of protection that perhaps allowed infant industries to emerge. This would suggest ISI now, EOG later as doctrine, and debate would then focus on transitioning from ISI to EOG. The bank does not follow this line of argument. Indeed, as we shall see in Part II, some accounts argue that the Southeast Asian export pushes of the 1980s followed removal of import protection as ISI was abandoned, encouraging support to exporters such as giving them duty-free import of inputs. But such accounts of the centrality of state intervention to the export-push histories of the Miracle study (in the early stages) are anathema to core WB doctrine of the time. Policy advice thus continued to push for avoidance of ISI. The reader may see this as an example of the limits imposed by the role of authority in doctrine and its development, leading to a reduced focus on process to secure articulation of an ideal, construed as EOG. Why not argue for ISI now and EOG later?

It is also useful to consider contemporary critics of the study. The two chosen are Rodrik 1994 and Haggard 1994, who can usefully be viewed as doctrinally avant-garde, in that they were ahead in terms of the direction in which mainstream doctrine was heading. They are not as radical as many other critics. They reveal trends in mainstream doctrine toward a renewed pessimism about the extent to which free markets were positive, accompanying assertion of the extent of problems with markets and so increasing justification and rationalization of state intervention (see next chapter). They express classic views of policy and show its cyclicality.

Rodrik (1994) interprets the Miracle study in exactly this way, stating that it puts the positive value of intervention back on the map, and identifies this as major change. Yet he takes issue with the specific cause-effect relationships posited by the study.

Rodrik asserts that much of the success and character of these countries can be explained by the starting point: flat resource allocation, especially land and the corresponding absence of landlords, and high education levels. Further, he contends that high levels of investment and rising labor force participation are the main correlates with high growth, and that these countries have not actually shown high rates of labor productivity growth over and above what increased capital and sectoral shifts explains. The issue is then how to explain high investment—the cause or the result of rapid growth? Rodrik's main position then is that the data shows results contrary to the bank's.

Haggard (1994) argues like Rodrik that income and asset distributions in these countries reflected starting points more than patterns of development. However, he shifts focus to the policy side of the question, for he asks why these policies were adopted. For him, development was driven by reform, which tended to be preceded by a concentration of authority in the executive (in the terms used in Chapter 1, especially the section Conclusions: thinking about developmental ideologies, a "creation of agency"), and then some of that authority was delegated to technocrats. Legitimacy may have come through shared growth, but, as these countries tended not to be democratic, this did not matter.

Unlike Rodrik, Haggard tends to accept the bank's view of export orientation—that as policy it enhances growth. His main concern is politics, and he sees big problems with the arguments about state-business relations and the extent to which institutions can prevent business interests from capturing the bureaucracy. Like many political scientists, he argues that institutions are heavily dependent upon the choices and judgments of the people who occupy and interact with them.

These arguments appear persuasive in different ways, yet they are very different and they lead to very different conclusions, both from each other and from the bank. This may be taken to show that we are perhaps not driven to choose between explanations too readily, if at all. Rather, they mark different aspects of an evolving historical discussion that shares categories and assumptions about the knowability of causes and effects that are deep within their classic notions of policy. If we choose not to take sides in this debate and refuse the invitation to agree with one of the offered positions, then we may start to see possibilities that allow us to escape from the inconsistencies of classic policy ideologies.

Conclusions: The Problem of Development

To cope with these varying and contentious histories, Cowen and Shenton's position is useful: to focus upon the problem of development in ways that stress the doctrinal nature of development and to appreciate this, in its

historical origin, as a solution to tensions between development as immanent process and development as intentionality expressed through state
policy: between process and product. We may then ask what we are to
make of a particular approach to development policy.

As I keep reminding the reader, the data shows little robustness in
global relationships between economic policy and outcomes, and this suggests a level of heterogeneity among human societies that invalidates the
basic ontological and epistemological assumptions that usually underpin
these discussions. After all, the East Asian Miracle study does not say to
countries in Africa and Latin America that Asia's experiences are sui
generis and not for emulation. It conceivably could have, but it did not.

Chapter 4 Questions

1. What do you think are the main elements of the history of development as an idea? What are the main sources of change? Is the
   "scientific" explanation, that knowledge has increased, reasonable?

2. What do you feel about the pace and/or rhythm of change in the history of development ideas? What conclusions do you draw from this
   for the assessment of proposals for current development policies?

3. If, as Cowen and Shenton argue, judgments about "correct" development and development policy tend to rely not upon agreed and
   known cause-effect relations but upon authority, then how does
   one best cope with a literature that does not assume this?

4. How is "trusteeship" fundamental to much thinking about
   development?

Development as an Idea—
Contemporary Issues

Introduction

In this chapter I examine recent shifts in orthodoxy and contentious positions. Coming to a firm conclusion about exactly why these changes occur is a somewhat heroic task, as Dunn aptly put it, noting political shifts in part reflected in the move from ISI (import-substituting industrialization) to EOG (export-oriented growth):

> It is extraordinarily difficult to see clearly and steadily quite what is at stake in this drastic shift . . . Some of the judgments required are essentially causal. . . . [they] are enormously complicated and inherently highly uncertain. (Dunn 2000, 73)

But certain elements of doctrinal shifts are clear, at least in what they are not:

> In the case of the massive impetus towards economic liberalisation of the last two decades of the twentieth century . . . it is natural to see this [as] the discovery of ever clearer and more reliable techniques for fostering economic efficiency . . . This is very much the way in which a whole generation of economists actively engaged in public service have come to view it, just as their Keynesian predecessors a generation or so earlier saw the previous move in a roughly opposite direction. Viewed epistemologically, however, the sequence looks strikingly different. . . . [I]t was the increasingly evident falsity of one set of false beliefs, not the steadily growing epistemic authority of their replacements, which did most of the work. . . . The clear result is the negative result. (Dunn 2000, 184–5)

Dunn is arguing that a growing sense of frustration and failure was associated with the practices that embraced the body of ideas within which ISI could be found. We have seen this in the narrower context of development with the feeling that somehow the combination of prescribed policy and postcolonial independence had failed. This seems best viewed as not so much a failure of the specific policies adopted—call them "ISI"—but a consequence of the assumptions upon which classic policy ideology is constructed. There is too much instability, so hoped-for links between what is thought to "work there" to drive what is intended to "work here" tend to be spurious. In this sense, the apparent failure of EOG is the same as that of ISI and appears at the root of the tension between assumptions of knowability and the failure of prediction.

In this chapter we will focus upon various contemporary policy rationalities: first, the so-called post-Washington Consensus (PWC); then, by contrast, what is labeled "post-development thinking," which often derives from more anthropological analyses, with a focus upon the analysis of discourse. This stark contrast is deliberate. The reader would see from most surveys of contemporary development literature that many of these positions are widely presented as important. The meaning and significance of the PWC is contentious, but the discussion it has generated provides a useful pivot, not least as Washington Consensus (WC) pro-market thinking remains common.

Now-familiar ideas about the correct role of the state, the nature of policy, and so on are central to the discussion. Recall that the knowability assumption projects a major role for implementation arguments into classic views of policy when trouble strikes. Reference to a "realization problem" may help cope with ways in which idealized solutions fail to relate to experiences. More concretely, failure may then be explained as a lack of state capacity to implement policies still asserted as correct. It is common to see this idea, an example of a realization problem, expressed in very simple terms, so that, for example, a powerful state is then said to be one with the capacity to "do" development correctly. Yet, things are not so simple. For example, problems seem to arise with the use of the term *power*, particularly when associated with notions that intentional development occurs predominantly through use of state power and is thus related to ideas of state capacity. Here I will discuss a very accessible text from Hindess (1996), but let me start with the post-Washington Consensus (PWC).

The Post-Washington Consensus of the Late 1990s: What Role for the State?

The previous chapter showed how the question of the role of the state has remained important. Mainstream approaches to securing implementation of correct policy have shifted from structural adjustment loans (SALs) to the wider issue of governance, seeking to influence poor country politics and define roles for states.

Given my tendency to see many issues in terms of doctrine, a suitable point of departure is to examine authoritative shifts in orthodox ideas since the early 1990s. Stiglitz and the notion of the post-Washington Consensus (PWC) provide both a candidate and an entry point for this discussion. The PWC may be viewed as a way to expand the role of the state but in limited ways, asserting that regulation of markets is more complex and more important than had been asserted, and supporting a shift in correct policy from deregulation to reregulation (another dichotomy).

Stiglitz (1998) starts by criticizing the WC: development policy needs more instruments to secure well-operating markets and should include objectives of sustainability, equality, and democracy. How does he argue this? He contends that a basic lesson of the 1997 Asian crisis was that the state often had done too little, not too much. He argues that success in Asia was deeply associated with what the state did and as such was "success with intention." Any survey by the reader will easily provide studies that argue the same point, such as Amsden (1997), Macintyre (1994), Wade (1990), and so on. I have already referred to Almond (1988) as a point of view that puts such statist positions into a perspective. Macintyre further argues that the state was far less important in Southeast Asia (SEA) than in East Asia.

But, perhaps ironically, Stiglitz's main thrust is *not* toward a refinement of intentionality, involving for example policymakers, politicians, or social movements, but toward the economy, or rather the WC's economic framework. Intentionality, for him, must still rest upon correct analysis—an analytical framework that generates *known* cause-effect relationships. For Stiglitz, the weakness of the WC was its tendency, with its emphasis upon trade liberalization and deregulation, to ignore other issues—most importantly competition and using it to get good markets. It also underplayed education and technology. The reason was the rooted belief that these things would happen once the state got out of the way. It therefore tended to believe that macroeconomic stability and liberalization would be sufficient. It was wrong.

After this portrait of a competitor's incorrect characterization of reality (a pointing to the errors of others), he asserts that the PWC instead adds, in its own view of correct policy, other issues. It is correct. He asserts that regulation and competition policies are needed to attain less distorted and more efficient markets, which is what the state has to ensure. Stiglitz gives examples of ways in which privatization created or preserved monopoly, for a classic error of the WC was to liberalize financial systems without enough reregulation. In his view, experience of financial problems and the effects of poor regulation of financial systems are crucial. Stiglitz argues that the WC tended to assume that institutional and cultural aspects could be ignored. In this return to reasserting the importance of the state, he argues that ISI need not necessarily stifle competition, for it depends upon the state of domestic competition and competition policy. With a similar logic, he criticizes the WC's blanket hostility to state-owned enterprises (SOEs).

The question then arises as to why the advance from the WC to the PWC has occurred. His explanation is that the PWC ideas are related to renewed stress among economists on the apparent existence of wide-spread lack of adequate competition in the real world (so competition is usually imperfect—that is, markets fail often).[i] The reader may wish to pause at this point and consider just what such statements may mean: Is reality changing? Is theory changing? What empirics underlie a strong statement such as, "We used to think that markets usually do not fail, and now we think that they do"? One possible interpretation is that the shifts are related to the internal aspects of doctrinal production: economic models have changed, and little else (see the discussion of the effects of the corruption of the intention to develop by Cowen and Shenton in the section "Policy as doctrine and the return of cyclicality" in Chapter 3 and Yonay's study of what happened when far more data became available to economics in the 1930s).

Granted that "we now know" what correct policies are, the discussion then turns to implementation—how to ensure that good policies are devised and implemented. Here Stiglitz is not so clear, yet his practical suggestions are striking. He mentions four areas: reform of government (along Western lines—independent judiciary, separation of powers, reduced scope for arbitrary actions by officials); greater use of markets (for example, in procurement by government departments); better government, such as greater use of participation; and a shift to broader development goals. These are very American prescriptions. The UK, clearly a backward and underdeveloped country, lacks constitutionally both a formal separation of powers and, until recently, a nonpolitical peak to the judicial system. His conditions, according to Chang, did not hold in now-rich countries when they were developing (Chang 2003). Given this skepticism, we should not argue about whether Stiglitz is right, but examine his approach further. Fine (1999) is an accessible entry point.

Fine gives an account of the nature and politics of the PWC. He argues that an attempt to define politics in certain ways, limited in scope, by laying down what the state should and should not do is central to the PWC.

---

[i]Stiglitz won a Nobel Prize in part for his work on asymmetry of information, which economic theory had long accepted as likely to lead to models of the economy within which outcomes were suboptimal. On some views of the nature of human transactions such asymmetry would seem universal, a skepticism that can be read into the conclusions of his very early work on the subject (Rothschild and Stiglitz 1976)—though compare Stiglitz's work from 2000.

He argues that the PWC has little to do with criticisms of the World Bank's (WB) position (as they have been going on and continue), nor of intellectual changes (for example, in economics), as they are two decades old. Rather, they stem from the issues of the day. The conundrum, to which the PWC is an answer, is just how to bring the state back in. Fine states that the developmental state literature (for example, Haggard 1990; Wade 1990; Amsden 1997; see the section "Political science and the developmental state" in Chapter 6) had two strands. First, an economic school that built arguments for intervention, but with little analysis of why it did or did not happen. Second, a political school that examined when, in the abstract, states could or might intervene.

For Fine, the PWC identifies a limited number of areas in which state intervention should take place. The PWC permits economics to explain the social, and institutions are then said to exist to cope with "market failure." His discussion of the PWC thus comes down to the issue of the renewed importance of the state. Fine explains this mainly by the effects of crisis and of globalization, requiring capacity for regulation and support to capital. Fine argues that the PWC is highly selective in how it addresses the role of the non-economic in economic performance; it can therefore choose to ignore other approaches, such as internationalist, class-based, feminist, or so on. Fine's approach is useful here because it points to divisions between competing doctrines. Yet he does not present much evidence to support his assertions as to why the PWC exists.

It seems to me that the texts of both Stiglitz and Fine support the importance of intentionality issues to understanding classic views of policy and can be seen as focusing upon the role of the state in development, though in very different ways. Stiglitz tends to found his view of development upon authoritative statements, whereas Fine argues that Stiglitz's view simply reflects the requirements of capitalist change, articulating his own Marxist attempt to solve the same problem. These authors offer us examples of the two solutions to the problem of development posited by Cowen and Shenton: the one defines development as entirely *objective* by making ideas depend upon (or rather part of) objective development (Marx), whereas the other seeks an apparent objective basis for ideas in some *authority*.

Contemporary Development Doctrines: Science, Power, and Language

Natural Science?

Classic views of policy in many ways show assumptions about the world that were once, but are no longer, common in the natural sciences. These are related to assumptions of knowability. Histories of mathematics and natural science point, perhaps from the early twentieth century, to far less certainty and greater acceptance of skeptical practices (Kline 1980).

We can find pointers to increased self-reflection in natural sciences: their origins and limitations, with frequent reference to scholars such as Kuhn (1962) and Popper (1977), and also Eds. Lakatos and Musgrave (1970), who tend to assert science as contingent. Underpinning this is the evident success of prediction. Here it may be interesting for the reader to note practices that cope with situations in which there is prediction without explanation. For example, engineering, like medicine but unlike, say, physics, is well capable of privileging outcomes (that is prediction) over explanation. For example, until computer software was developed to cope, design of stressed membranes (for example, surrounding an airplane window) was based upon actual simulations rather than any theory. There was no adequate explanation of what was happening, simply observations—prediction without explanation. This stresses something that remains intriguing if not puzzling, which is the failure of social science and economics to possess equivalent predictable regularities.

It is this, I believe, that makes economics so fascinating. It shares with natural science assumptions about the value of axiomatization and the associated use of algebra. Global developers—such as the World Bank and the International Monetary Fund (IMF)—have been dominated by economists from the early 1960s. Yet there is no robust predictive capacity. The tensions that arise are a strong thread running through this book. Economics faces a problem in treating its statements as explanation and, like other social sciences, in buttressing this through reference to the general shift toward subjective truth. Another problem is the frequent siting of economics departments within universities outside of arts faculties. Another is the frequently rather naïve treatment of issues of implementation, typically through ideas of capacity, by development economists as they move outside their disciplinary boundaries.

Strong belief in the correctness of development policy leads to a stress upon implementation issues and related notions of state capacity. Lack of capacity is used as an explanation of failure to implement good policies. Power is then assumed to generate and accompany a capability to implement correct policies. But careless use of ideas of power may be problematic. An accessible discussion is Hindess (1996), to which I now turn.

The Problem of Power and Ideas of Capacity in Development Thinking

Hindess asks why the "view of power as a quantitative and mechanical phenomenon which determines the capacity of actors to realize their will or to secure their interests has been enormously influential" (26) For, while "[i]t appears to promise an easy means of identifying who has power and who has not," (26) appearances may be misleading, for real power may be behind the throne. "[S]uch a conception is itself profoundly flawed" (26).

Why? Hindess argues for a range of issues. First, is the *heterogeneity* of the bases of power, that is, of the attributes and means of action at an individual's disposal. This means that such sources of power are not *commensurable*, for they cannot be measured against each other in terms of quantities. Second, these bases of power are *contingent* in their effectiveness. "Means of action of different kinds will be effective under different conditions . . . [so the] idea of an underlying common substance or essence of power is clearly unsatisfactory" (26).

Third is the unreliability of such ideas of power as predictors of subsequent events; perhaps most importantly, the implication that once the power available to contending parties is known, the outcome of any conflict between them would thus be entirely predictable. Hindess notes that this is dubious. Why?

> The resources available to the parties engaged in a dispute will normally depend upon circumstances outside their control . . . [The] presumption is that quantities of power should be seen as being decisive . . . as if all cases of conflict were really just the working out of their pre-ordained scripts . . . Once the exercise of power is seen as involving the use of definite resources under conditions that are not entirely determined by the persons concerned, then it ceases to be a capacity to secure one's preferred objectives. Instead, and at best, it becomes a capacity to act in pursuit of those objectives. . . . In view of its glaring deficiencies the most interesting question raised by the quantitative conception of power is why it is that so many students of power have been able to take it seriously. (1996, 26)

Hindess does not deny the value of power as an analytical term. But he strongly suggests that the ways in which it is normally used direct attention from important questions about the production of power and the social conditions on which its existence depends. This echoes Cowen and Shenton's concerns (see Chapter 3).

Note that these criticisms concerning the use of the term *power* may also be made against many notions of state capacity. For example, reference to relatively insulated technocrats permits a sweeping aside of problems that arise in discussing how this capacity might be compared with others (its commensurability), when it will be effective (its contingency), and whether it can help predict subsequent events.

It may be now clear that ideas of state capacity may be rather risky. This suggests an interpretation of common statements in the literature—for example, Stiglitz's views (see the section "The post-Washington Consensus of the late 1990s: what role for the state?" in this chapter)—that supports my arguments about the profound influence of the assumptions rooted deep within classic notions of policy. I turn now to a look at critique.

Post-Development

Immanent Development?

In coping with the literature on development policy, we find writings referred to as postdevelopment (Sachs 1992; Rahnema and Bawtree Eds 1997). Pieterse (1998) is a useful introduction. These reflect much modern thinking—often muted, often locally influential and powerful, often deeply influential upon nonprofessionals, and often drawing upon Marxist and other currents of the 1960s. Various ideas seem common. Part of the value of critique here is precisely that it engages with mainstream views and seeks to offer radical and alternative perspectives. It highlights weaknesses and assumptions in orthodox thinking. However, some of this literature has its own problems (see, for example, Sylvester 1999), such as its use of categorical thinking.

Postdevelopment writings often reject things usually thought of as normal and good and enjoyed as products of modern governments and politics. Hostility to development may arise because of its alleged material effects (environmental damage, poverty) or because of its consequences for freedom of thought (the imposition of science as power, as a new religion, etc.). Note rather old but still pointed arguments that it may be impossible for the world, with present technologies, to support middle-class lifestyles for all. And, clearly, life for many in the world is unpleasant.

A common critique stems from a reexamination of poverty that de-links it from the absence of doctrinally defined development and so positions an argument that development itself is pauperizing. Link this to a confrontation with knowledge as power, and a powerful line of attack may take wing.

Pieterse argues that another common view is that development issues should be looked at *discursively*, linking developers' activities to the formation of knowledge and the deployment of forms of power. The reader may wish to be cautious with such notions of power (see the section "The problem of power and ideas of capacity in development thinking" in this chapter for Hindess' comments). They may be better understood as statements about order and may not confer power in the same way as a checkbook or a labor contract.

I find it very useful to read writers such as Ferguson (1997), who point to what seem to be situations in which rationalities of development policy that we find in writings such as the World Bank's East Asian Miracle study appear vividly challenged and in striking contradiction with the intentionality of aid donors and development experts. We may think of these stories as pointing to pervasive anomalies, suggesting deep-rooted problems in mainstream approaches.

Intentionality?

In many postdevelopment writings (unlike socialism/communism) Pieterse (1998) critically stresses an absence of any state program that could replace that which is critiqued. His argument suggests that postdevelopment offers no alternative. This relates to major themes of this book. What Pieterse appears to have in mind is conscious state action. We might pause to consider the possibility, linked to the evident failure of many attempts at intentional development, of a state pessimism in much postdevelopment thinking comparable to that of 1980s neoliberals. Yet this is to assume that the position of the state is crucial. But is it? Pieterse's basic position is that unless we are willing to grant the state a role, then we advocate nothing—political impasse and quietism. Is this persuasive? The reader may consider this for themselves; a point I would make here is that Pieterse's view of the role of the state reveals how his approach tends to a classic view of policy, seeking intentionality and a site for it. The question of action and intentionality is thus solved in familiar ways, though from a heterodox perspective.

Discursive Orders

I turn now to look at the influence of linguistic analysis, often referred to as *discourse analysis*, with reference to text and narrative. Here notions of intentionality are influenced by ideas that what can be articulated limit what can be done. This echoes Disraeli's view that it is "through words that we govern men." But, if this is a political analysis, the question still arises of how a powerful politician such as Disraeli chose what words to use, not to mention whether he created new ones.

Escobar (1995) is a useful introduction to the literature. The approach is different from others discussed so far. For a rare definition of discourse analysis, see Fairclough (1992). A framework of discourse analysis, to use Escobar's terminology, has a number of characteristics. First, a discursive order is rule-governed and will match a development discourse. Some things may change, called, for example, a discursive regime or discursive formation, but others may not—the discursive practice. Second, certain other things are privileged and assumed to have a tendency not to change, such as history. This point is often not made explicit. Third, in an object under study, certain things are structured and ordered *by* the discourse.

Various logics commonly met elsewhere are reversed: development *defines* its actors (for example, farmers) rather than they being situated in reality and studied and apprehended by development's thinkers. This reversal is seen as part of politics and power relations, so that whatever or whoever dominates the discourse is seen as possessing power. Finally, discourses are assumed to have various attributes: they are structured and can be apprehended and discussed, that is, there exists a discursive practice; they tend to be professionalized; and they tend to be institutionalized and resourced.

Escobar looks at three examples: integrated rural development (IRD) and the introduction of small farmers into development with the Green Revolution; Women in Development (WID); and environmental issues and the idea of sustainable development. He argues for each that the discourse may act as a framework for understanding, especially how certain things are made invisible or made visible within the discourse. This clearly resonates with a focus upon doctrine in thinking about development policy. The focus is not upon a reality, but upon a policy ideology, to use an earlier language. It says that some of the basics of development thinking may not alter: that change requires action guided by experts, the use of physicalist ideas,[ii] and so forth. Texts, reports, and other documentation may well omit things that others want to include (Ferguson 1997; Scott 1998). Why does this happen? Escobar argues for various reasons (1995, 162): the ideas may not change for it does not matter, to careers or ideas, if they do not. In this sense ideas have powerful effects of themselves, and they manage to survive contrasts between their visions and those of others. How plausible is this?

For all its insights and frequently energizing impact, there are arguably a number of problems with this approach. Note that Escobar asserts the existence of enormous power exercised by the WB as well as other international and national development agencies through various channels, their financial resources, their coordination activities, research, and so on. Yet is this power discretionary? Are large organizations such as the WB usefully viewed as a success? Or is this reference to an order, a situation? A useful text that discusses the issues involved is Campbell (1997), looking at the question of legal positivism and political power: that is, the argument that, for example, judges cannot make judgments that go beyond what would be thought suited to their particular perceptions and interests. Campbell argues that they can.

Three issues arise when assessing Escobar. First, he takes certain things as external or contextual to his analysis or presentation. For instance, he treats

---

[ii]By this is meant ideas that assert that development is a process of change that requires more capital, more capacity, and so on, and that these terms refer to things that can be measured, such as the weight of a pile of sand.

history as an area where he can refer to "facts" and sources. Second, he asserts his priors, his basic assumptions, as true, for, as he argues, nothing has really changed at the level of the discourse. Finally, note his activism, asserting that we need a new language to speak of such Third World perspectives. Taken together, these may well be persuasive, but they are inherently predictive: accepting this view of the world will lead to something worthwhile. In which case, this is prediction masquerading as explanation.

Such views, combined with developments in other areas, had a strong influence upon judgments of statements about development policy by the 2000s. I would argue that they have greatly eroded the authority of many policy prescriptions and positions and also influence how modern, rich societies may be governed. It is interesting to reflect on likely effects upon those who, in Cowen and Shenton's terms, bear the burden of trusteeship, in other words, development practitioners—aid workers, planners, policymakers, and others. It has been said that such people are mercenaries, madmen, or missionaries. Where, we might ask, are the midwives? At this point, and in stark contrast, I turn to examine economics.

Economics

One of the most difficult problems in comparing development policies is that posed by economics, for a high proportion of the literature is written by economists. Experience suggests that, for those without professional training, it requires considerable effort to be able to cope with the ways in which economists' positions are developed and articulated.

Many also find economics unattractive. My own experience suggests this is a result of the somewhat idiosyncratic nature of economics within social science, combined with frequent lack of empirical support offered for theory when it is presented. Compare, for example, an economics textbook such as Jehle and Reny (1998) with a standard engineering textbook (now rather old) such as Panlilio (1963), and note ways in which the latter explains with reference to the "experienced real" what works where, whereas the former does not. In the annex to this chapter, I present one approach to putting neoclassical economics—the dominant subdiscipline of economics—into perspective.

One reason for the frequently low appeal of economics is the extensive recourse to mathematics. Another is the very particular approach to assessing economic situations, typically in terms of their deviations from a vision of some best state, phrased in terms of distortions to prices, to resource allocations, or to some other observable. A real is thus contrasted with a valorized ideal, or muddle with model in simpler language.

Economics has a number of strongly positive aspects that competitors often dismiss. Behavioral assumptions essentially underpin belief in algebra and confrontation of models with data. A use of naïve scientific method accompanies considerable investment of resources in creation and use of data. Models are fundamentally universalistic in basic assumption: consumers, producers, prices, and so forth are assumed the same ontologically and epistemologically across most imaginable frontiers. As we have touched on already, evidence within economics suggests that there *are* significant regularities across time, space, and culture, but these are very limited in extent. Without economics' naïve scientific methodology, we would not be aware of these judgments.

Based upon this underlying rationality, we will then frequently observe common views. Typically, though this is far from universal, we find a belief that markets can, or at least could, so mediate relations between the core elements of the economy (producers and consumers) that there arises an outcome in which the welfare of no consumer could be improved without making that of another worse off—what is called Pareto optimality (Stiglitz 2000). Much of what economists mean when they refer to efficiency refers to this notion. An economy is efficient when resources are allocated in this way; in an absence of "market failure," models show that using markets leads to this outcome. What is useful for assessing policy judgments is to realize the centrality of this perspective. Thus, the importance to the antistate ideas of the WC that market failure be said not to be extensive.

As we will see, hopes for such outcomes underpin notions of market failure, that is, those attributes or characteristics of particular commodities or production processes that suggest that markets left to their own resources will *not* lead to an optimal outcome. Given that these attributes are, to the layperson, frequent if not (as in the case of so-called information asymmetries) inevitable, it follows that the ideal from which deviations are being imagined may appear hopelessly unattainable.

There is a deeper problem. What reasons are there for thinking that a movement *toward* such an ideal would be as good a thing as actually getting there? This is what is sometimes called the problem of the second best, and it seems inescapable. This is the issue of the value of *partial* reforms which move some things toward the ideal, but not all of them. This again is usefully thought of as part of a realization problem.

We thus often find in the literature a debate that absolutizes and confuses model with muddle. A position develops by comparing purported aspects of a reality, not with some other possible reality, but with an ideal position possessing the characteristics of an economic model, such as one of freely operating markets. Thus if market failure, as in the PWC approach, is said to be relatively widespread (more so when compared with beliefs associated with WC approaches), then idealized models should include much market failure; if not, as in the WC approach, then idealized models should include mainly free markets. All this would be less problematic if economics had persuasive evidence of the existence of known solutions to the problem of development. Internal evidence suggests that this is lacking (see Chapter 7).

Responses to Developmental Thinking: Power and Order

Power or Order?

Hindess, like others such as Escobar and Ferguson, suggests that it may be useful to consider how power or order may be presented as apolitical. I note frequent references in classic views of policy to so-called technical issues and, as we saw clearly in Grindle and Thomas, much attention to issues of implementation. A focus upon implementation suggests a corresponding focus upon some ideal end point, and this is the basis of plans or projects that have blueprints.

But Cowen and Shenton do not take this tack. For them, these tensions derive from inescapable mystery, an inscrutability articulated by the problem of development and the practice of viewing development as simultaneously both immanent process and intention. In this view of the confusion, these tensions are not so much a result of politics but of pretending that we can know our own futures, or those of others, and encouraging practices based upon such beliefs. What, though, may happen if we realize this?

Power and Coping with It

The reader may sense powerful and perhaps contradictory forces associated with the effects of power upon development practitioners. Action appears organized, but in which organization? With what intentionality? Defined by whom?

The center of gravity of development doctrine appears recently to have moved from a strong belief in markets associated with the WC to greater interest in nonmarket institutions. These institutions may be seen as essential to markets, because they are where markets find their social embeddedness (a role that naturally expresses the PWC call for the state to regulate and reregulate). These institutions may also identify boundaries for roles allocated to markets and a sense that broad history can be better understood in terms of how economic efficiency increases through the spread of well-functioning markets. Yet these tend to treat issues of power and politics as external to their approach, though they then seem to return through notions of implementation and state capacity. This risks begging questions more than providing answers (as in the search for an insulated technocracy) once the knowability assumption is highlighted.

We have seen two rather different approaches to this external to economics. Writers such as Escobar and others see power and domination largely in terms of meaning and its determination. Thus Escobar's focus upon discursive orders stresses the disempowering effects of development discourses and practices. Postdevelopment also suggests strong limits to practice, whether we follow Pieterse in taking an optimistic view of the potential for states to play positive roles in development or the more negative conclusions of writers such as Ferguson, Illich, and Sachs. These accounts counsel great caution.

But too ready an acceptance of these ideas of power and domination may also be risky, and these may be explored through Hindess' critique of Foucault. Hindess takes issue with ways in which notions of power become conflated with notions of order, so it is made, perhaps, to appear that those who benefit from a particular order should be seen as those who exercise power within it. There are obviously plausible reasons for doubting this, including Hindess' stress upon the dangers of treating power as too simple or too unambiguous a notion.

Practice—Some Initial Remarks

What is Present-Day Underdevelopment, against Which Intentionality will Operate?

We live in interesting times in terms of solutions to the problem of development. On the one hand, significant numbers of people in many Western democracies appear to have less confidence in poor country states as developers. On the other, internal developments in various approaches that govern and underpin development thinking have tended to weaken the authority of didactic and doctrinaire positions and confident universalistic prescription. Even the shift from the WC toward the PWC, for all the criticisms made, articulates a certain albeit limited openness to the contingent. Recall the IMF's current dogmatic position on liberalization of the capital account of the balance of payments (see "Doctrine in limbo? The IMF and the liberalization of capital flows," in Chapter 7).

And, although often simply rhetorical, we may observe greater discussion of the popular and the value of the local, of spontaneous action, of unprofessionalised knowledge seen and presented as external to development. These may all risk becoming co-opted and/or professionalized, but the point has been made. It is striking, for example, to see the emergence of participatory poverty assessments (PPAs) financed and supported by organizations such as the World Bank (Turk 2001). To assess this, Cowen and Shenton would have us look at the negative side of development itself, expressed by writers such as Ferguson (1997) in truly shocking terms. This is obvious.

Yet what seems to come from teaching as well as research is a sense that reflection on the problem of development leads, in practice, to appreciation of what Foucault and Disraeli seem to mean by rule being the conduct of conduct. People come to believe that they live in contexts characterized by orders, of situations in which people usually want to do what their superiors and peers want them to do. And an obvious question may then be, what happens next?

Development in Practice—a Personal Experience

Evaluation and Subjectivity

Two sets of questions plague us when we seek to compare development policy. First: What is development policy? How can it be accessed? How can it be known? Second: How to judge development policy, to assess it? I turn now to a personal experience in grappling with these two sets of questions. This was associated with the evaluation of a project, in this case the United National Capital Development Fund's (UNCDF) Rural Infrastructure Development Fund (RIDEF) project in Quang Nam province in central Vietnam.

The inherent subjectivity in the evaluation is revealing. Recall the discussion of evaluation in Chapter 1. I mentioned there the Sida Evaluation Manual (Molund and Schill 2004) as an example of normative positions on what a good evaluation is. Molund and Schill argue clearly that even if project documentation is not clear about whether the intervention logic was based (for example) upon a careful analysis of poverty (and so how the project would concretely improve the situation of the poor), the evaluation should seek to reconstruct such an analysis. Further:

> With the help of control groups who have not been exposed to the intervention it is sometimes possible to get a good idea of how the target group would have fared without the intervention. When the counterfactual cannot be estimated in this way—a common situation in development cooperation—statements about impact rest upon weaker foundations. The intervention is often taken to be the cause of the identified changes if such a conclusion appears to be consistent with expert knowledge and there seems to be no better explanation around. Although less compelling than an explanation based on control group methodology in most cases, an argument of this type can be good enough for the purpose of the evaluation. (Molund and Schill 2004, 32)

Note the use of the word *knowledge*. If it is common that counterfactuals cannot be estimated, as they say, and if there is good reason to treat most expert opinion as belief rather than knowledge, then the statement, part of an authoritative operational text, can well be read as an endorsement of the view that correct development is what authority says it is. From this point of view, UNCDF saw the field covered by the authority behind its views extended into parts of Vietnamese society. How did this happen?

Project Outline

This project can usefully be seen as a Stage 2, where a Stage 1 is an add-on to existing investment-driven development thinking, with likely negligible developmental impact and large opportunity costs in terms of reduced potential welfare gains or reduced actual gains. Despite this, or rather likely because of it, Stage 1 of the early 1990s had seen strong local appropriation by officials (with some intense conflicts) and distinctly passive behavior by local community formal leaders, signs of corruption, and no evidence for any ongoing institutional change process associated with it. However, there was then a Stage 2, in which the RIDEF package, or basket of flowers, was introduced, backed by rather large sums of development finance.

This package had three main ideas (the three flowers): decentralized capital budgets, local implementation of infrastructure spending, and community participation. Details can be found in various official documents.[iii]

Technically, Stage 1 amounted to an upgrade of an existing irrigation scheme, with some add-ons, which focused upon wet rice. Stage 2 allocated tranches of UNCDF development finance to targeted poor communities.

When it came to assessing impact, focus groups and other discussions seemed to suggest that "subsequent events" were widely and highly appreciated, and there was considerable agreement that there were large gains in impact compared with ongoing local rural development investments. Furthermore, the project required the local population to participate in decisions, and this was contested in a number of ways, including pressures to localize methods (from some Vietnamese) as well as pressures to ensure global best practice (from foreign consultants). Finally, despite the push for institutional change, there was local resistance. On the whole it appeared as a project worth supporting—but why?

[iii]See http://www.uncdf.org/local_governance/reports/case_studies/vietnam, also http://www.uncdf.org/english/countries/viet_nam/index.html and http://www.uncdf.org/english/countries/evaluation_reports/vie95co1_midterm.html.

This was not a simple project, but it was clear that it would not be possible to present this history as a classic "policy formation and implementation" process. It was more interesting and convincing to be more political and anthropological, but universal economic and organizational logics seemed to be visible. In microcosm, therefore, and this should not be surprising, plausible judgments and comparisons could and were made that gave strong weight to both local and global rationalities and to local perceptions of cause-effect relationships.

Yet development interventions were coming from UNCDF, part of the UN system interacting with official Vietnamese development efforts. We may ask, therefore, what values and ideas were associated with these actions? UNCDF, unlike most of the UN system, could deliver capital. This was due to a historical compromise between the UN system and the World Bank in the 1950s, according to which within the multilateral system only banks may deliver capital; the UN delivers technical assistance and is meant to coordinate interventions. Unlike the bank, then, the UN in general and UNCDF in particular relied upon funds from donors rather than the capital market. UNCDF, though, could supply things like 4WDs, air conditioners, and other capital equipment needed by technical assistance projects.

In the early 1990s UNCDF had had a loose remit. People within it wanted to develop a relationship with Vietnam, adopted somewhat passive tactics, and so ended up providing capital to upgrade a dam and water delivery hardware. This was an area very badly damaged by war. Intervention was top-down and focused upon wet rice production. In implementation, this stage (Stage 1) was driven by a project document that foresaw quantitative gains in welfare through rice output and better market access (bridges built). It also envisaged institutional change through tendering for construction (gaining better efficiency). There were conflicts between the UNCDF adviser and local government, and very little participation by the local people. At this stage, the Vietnamese Communist Party (VCP) largely frowned upon such civil society methods. NGOs instead were developing relations with formal bodies such as the party-dominated mass organizations and local government (McCall 1998). This was to continue well into the 2000s (Fforde 2008).

UNCDF's corporate remit then changed in response to donor criticisms and shifted to a focus upon cooperation with local (rather than national) governments, including community participation and a high priority to institutional development. This could be linked to the wider shifts in development doctrine to a focus upon governance and greater involvement with civil society. The three flowers articulated these changes and entailed decentralization to the commune level of capital allocations, project selection (participation), and implementation. UNCDF had thus effectively maneuvered around the prohibition on UN organizations supplying development capital.

Impact analysis of Stage 1 argued that very little could be plausibly attributed to the project. Partly due to ongoing change processes, it was hard to see what exact difference the project had made. Further, there were signs that its focus upon rice was unwise because rice paid low profits, especially in this region that had effectively to compete with Mekong Delta rice. People reported higher profits for farmers in cash crops, using irrigation, but requiring additional resources. But the project had been designed in a way that made it particularly hard to evaluate because of a lack of relevant data.

RIDEF was then set up to carry on from Stage 1. A special project office was sited within the Vietnamese local government system (but isolated from it). Evaluation showed reasonably certainly that the three flowers were seen as valuable, but with certain caveats:

- Decentralized capital allocation was still very political, reducing commune sense of ownership and responsibility and reducing efficiency.

- Participation was very interesting: first, it was required, so tended to become theatrical, with strong tendency for parties close to the project to go along with the discourse; second, it was seen as positive, with better project choice, but politically difficult (related to rural unrest from 1997 onward and to local infrastructure corruption); third, there was no attempt to build in learning from "positive deviation." Logically, localization of imported social practices would involve the strong likelihood of deviations from the imported models; crucially, how would such positive deviations be tracked and assessed?

- Decentralized implementation was successful, but part of a process of legalization (for example, in contract signing by communal officials), and so change did not happen rapidly or discontinuously.

- Institutional change processes were isolated, partly because of corruption, partly a desire to retain power, and partly because dissemination had not been thought of.

- There was among some officials (centrally and locally) a strong sense that the ideas were good in improving institutions and in raising the development impact of spending that the government was often carrying out.

The natural next step was to treat these ideas as post hoc policy and extend them to other areas. Just as *ad hoc* means activities that derive from the contingent present, so by *post hoc* policy I mean policy that derives from the contingent past—existing practice. If so, UNCDF development doctrine would have extended its reach.

Discussion

This is an exercise in orthodox development practice. In my account, ideas and negotiated meaning are made crucial to understanding what was happening, yet there is a role for what might, with tongue in cheek, be called "universal" institutional logics (that is, areas where there seems little dispute). Institutional change can, for example, seem to improve efficiency, thought of as changes in the ways in which state development funds are allocated. Further, the apparent greater efficiency of particular set-ups is neither necessary nor sufficient for their adoption.

In this assessment RIDEF and other donor ideas are taken as given. The internal intervention logic sees the project as an agent of change. The ambiguity and tension of classic policy ideology is thus maintained: development is thought of as both product and process, and development doctrine driven by authority (negotiated and created) acts as the plate riveted to this tension that keeps it from exploding the organization of activities.

If we reexamine the internal intervention logic, then clearly intentionality is seen to exist in the agreement articulated in the project documentation between the project's stakeholders. The nature of the intention can be seen in the project documentation, which identifies activities, outputs, and outcomes linked to them through the classic project logic and agency can be seen in the project as organization. The combination of intentionality and agency are understood to "do" development through the project, the site where intentionality and agency meet. This exercise shows clearly, therefore, how subjectivity operates to order and organize development at the project level. As I said, we liked it, but I am still not sure exactly why.

Conclusions

We have examined contrasts between the PWC and the WC positions through an exposition of Stiglitz's understanding of the former, amplified by Fine's critique of the PWC. These contrasts were strongly linked to different views of how a common concern should be resolved—the role of the state. We have also looked at aspects of economics and related these to a discussion of how implementation issues often arise and how these are often linked to notions of state capacity.

Because the implementation issue appears so closely related to ideas of capacity, and so to power, we then discussed problems in using a simple notion of power, and how use of the term may be somewhat fraught. The reader was alerted to the character of development policy approaches that do not explicitly address these issues, typically by assuming that state capacity can be compared across contexts and that more of it should lead to a greater ability to implement correct policy. This does not appear to be a reliable, predictive basis for action. Once again, the basic assumptions of classic policy ideologies seem to lead to difficulties.

Central here is the practice of siting agency for intentional development upon a state, and with this focus we also examined views of development that concentrate upon discourse. These amounted to radically different views of the correct relationships between terms in argument, so that development defined its actors (for example, farmers) rather than these actors being in reality, and studied and apprehended by development's thinkers. This is in stark contrast to writers such as Stiglitz, and indeed most orthodox economists, and so is useful. But it also seemed to be the case that these views retained implicit assumptions, possibly confusing issues of order with those of power. Pieterse's arguments could suggest that attempts to resolve this confusion could again lead to classic policy ideology (in hopefully radical guise) and the search for correct policies.

Finally, I considered a personal experience in evaluating an aid project in Vietnam. This, from a limited perspective, confirmed the inherently subjective aspect of development practice and the importance of doctrine, including the ways in which authority was located in experts in formal evaluation techniques. A persuasive account nevertheless contained reference to various different perspectives and rationalities, so that it appeared possible to report and discuss the acceptability of "subsequent events" to various people, including the evaluators (most of whom were Vietnamese).

Annex: Coping with Economics

Introduction

Mainstream economics texts usually give little context within which to develop ways of assessing it. By contrast, this text may be useful for those with little or limited background in economics (Robinson and Eatwell 1973). This annex will take the reader very quickly through some useful issues.

Robinson and Eatwell discuss what they term "a basic puzzle." There are, they say, strong arguments that whoever controls land in rural areas will be politically powerful and so economically important; that whoever controls capital will also have political influence; and that labor, if organized, will also have political clout. Yet they argue that "neoclassical economics" de-links such economic issues from politics. The reader may examine standard development economics textbooks such as Ray (1998) and Todaro and Smith (2006). Note, for example, the problems Ray has in developing an economic analysis of land tenure arrangements, when his conclusions read as though the most important factors determining economic arrangements are non-economic (1998, 457–462). So why de-link economics from politics?

What is "Neoclassical Economics," For They Argue That It Dominates the Profession?

Robinson and Eatwell's answer may help. They argue that the method-ological origins of economics lie in the idea that laws govern economics as well as other areas of life. They note that there have always been com-peting economic doctrines, whose differences are arguably not always resolved (unlike natural science) through intense interaction with exper-iments and data.

They identify a so-called classic political economy associated with Adam Smith and David Ricardo, and also Karl Marx. Fundamental ideas included class analysis—the economic characteristics of social classes (workers, capitalists, and landlords, in Smith's thinking). This linked eco-nomic and political activity.

These analyses, Robinson and Eatwell say, focused primarily upon issues of accumulation: economic change that increased production, per-haps by increasing the division of labor, by institutional change such as the introduction of the factory system, or by technological innovation. This led to questions of how a distribution of surplus between profits and rent took place (workers tended to be paid a wage based upon subsistence needs, or perhaps social factors). Ricardo developed a way of analyzing this. Rents were then seen as an excess return on land, higher than that paid on the poorest land. But problems remained with how to explain prices, though accumulation, not prices and resource allocation, remained the focus of analysis. Marx ignored the issue of price determi-nation and focused his analysis on social relations embodied in com-modities, that is, labor. Again, however, his basic unit of analysis was class, defined economically (workers and capitalists).

All this, Robinson and Eatwell argue, was replaced in the late nine-teenth century by neoclassical approaches, which dominate today. These replaced a focus upon accumulation with one that stressed look-ing at interactions between supply and demand in a steady state (that is, without major changes), thus bringing price determination to center stage.

Why did This Happen?

Robinson and Eatwell offer two reasons: first, because of academic problems that classic economics could not explain; second, because classic economics was politically dangerous—it stressed the economic basis of social classes and conflicts of interest. The focus of economics thus shifted toward individual consumers and producers, primarily interacting through markets. Exchange was stressed above relations between classes. Utility, and its maximization, was the most important facet of social relationships. This required avoiding the likelihood that richer people enjoy good things less than poorer ones (as they have less of them), thus pointing toward egalitarianism. A way was found: Pareto optimality as a criterion of outcomes.

Neoclassical economics was and is far more interested in static analysis of different equilibria. Profits are understood mainly as a reward for waiting. Factors of production need no historical explanation and gain prices through market interactions. How they came to be owned and how they stayed that way are ignored.

Chapter 5 Questions

1. What are the main problems in treating power as a simple capability, and how does this mistake link to the wider issue of implementability in policy studies?

2. What do Kenny and Williams (2001) appear to mean by *epistemological universalism?* What impact might this term have upon development policymaking?

3. How might a critique be mounted of Rodrik's idea that good policies will tend not to be adopted because the benefits do not yet exist, unlike the benefits associated with the current situation?

4. Discuss alternative courses of action for postdevelopment thinkers who are skeptical of development but yet wish to see change.

Disciplines and Viewpoints— Notions of Policy

Introduction

This chapter is intended to help assess issues raised thus far by using relevant disciplines as the entry point. Different disciplines contribute in various ways to what can be said about ideas of intentionality, agency, and knowability.

For instance, Escobar, an anthropologist, characteristically focused upon meanings: how certain things came into and out of discussion and debate. He did not appear to find it necessary to take a view as to whether positions were right or wrong. This contrasted with economics, which is deeply concerned to secure correctness.

This chapter first looks at anthropologists' comments on the nature of policy and then compares them with a discussion of political economy, political science, and some positions taken by geographers. The chapter also examines by comparison non-Western development orthodoxy, in this case some Japanese work that turned out to be related to Vietnam.

Disciplines, Policy, and "Doing" Development

Introduction

Different disciplines seem to provoke the same question: why is the problem of development usually defined in terms of development policy and understood as what states do? One answer may be a tendency to see the state as the best-qualified site for developmental intentionality. Anthropologists seem to stress the importance of meaning, studying how ideas such as the importance of agency are manifest. So that is a good place to start.

Anthropology

Shore and Wright (1997), in their corner of anthropology, pose acute questions:

- How do policies work as instruments of governance? Why do they sometimes fail?

- What language helps to legitimate policy in its participation in the processes of governance?

- How do policies construct their subjects?

- How do changes in discourse become authoritative?

- How is it that claims are made that define a particular problem and its solution, thus closing avenues for other alternative definitions?

Shore and Wright confirm that anthropologists tend to focus upon the generation of meaning:

> Policy increasingly shapes the way individuals construct themselves as subjects. . . . From cradle to the grave, people are classified, shaped, and ordered according to policies, but they may have little consciousness of . . . the processes at work. (1997, 4)

They argue that changing patterns of governance are accompanied both by changing political technology and by export of ideas and practices to the Third World. The reader can easily find accounts that record the backgrounds of key individuals. For an example, see Doshi and Coclanis (1999), which gives us a case study of a key Southeast Asian (SEA) policymaker from Singapore. The story mixes the role of ideas (the origins of intellectual positions and constructions) and the importance of political activities. Such histories are accessible for many countries.

Shore and Wright cite and approve earlier work that concluded that organizations "are continually organizing." For this to happen, policy plays a central role as it is formulated, codified, publicized, and implemented. Policy is the central pivot of meaning, giving sense to the organization and its members. It is the ghost in the machine, breathing life into bureaucratic apparatus. Power in bureaucracies and organizations, Shore and Wright argue, and the power of such bodies, stems from legitimacy and authority, and these derive in large part from policy, which plays a major role in giving answers to questions about what we are doing and why. From this perspective, questions of the truth of claims to prediction and the inconsistencies I have identified are then relevant as they become part of organized meaning. Coping with facts, then, is what is done—simply one part of how things subjectively are.

It is then remarkable to see how Shore and Wright argue that on close examination policy often becomes incoherent. One reason they offer is that policy speaks to a range of interests and perspectives and so works by being inconsistent. This leads to valid comments about empirics—

what, in a particular context, is policy? Reference may be made to speeches, regulations, and records of practice, yet Shore and Wright argue that these usually differ and are often inconsistent. Indeed, they assert that many organizing activities intend to make policy *appear* coherent so it can more easily be claimed that an intention has been realized and a successful result achieved.

In my own experience as a researcher, one value of the examination of policy documents is precisely that construction of a credible, working definition of policy very often seems to result in levels of complexity and dimensionality that do not sit well with more theoretical constructions. If we work with the classic cause-effect logic, it is hard to denote a clear link between the categories of cause and effect and terms found in policy documents. Policy, Shore and Wright argue, is a concept central to our social life and thus as important as ideas such as family and society. Yet, by contrast, policy is viewed as neutral and technical.

Shore and Wright note the contrast between morality and policy. Policy is said to be instrumental and objective, serving to distance policymakers from the objects of policy (those upon whom it acts). This may also assist legitimization by making policy appear based upon universal (and so unchallengeable) goals and reducing scope for disagreement.

In my view Shore and Wright offer us a useful set of ideas. We can platform on these to look at political economy and political science in terms of how they contribute to the various meanings of policy.

Political Economy

A convenient entry to political economy that has the added benefit of focusing upon SEA is Rodan et al. (1997). These authors present three categories of political economy. These can be compared with the typology advanced by Grindle and Thomas.

Neoclassical economics and political economy (the Washington Consensus)

New institutional political economy (the post-Washington Consensus)

Pluralist and Marxist-derived political economy

This last category, Rodan et al. argue, employs social and political theories of markets in which markets and market institutions are seen as products of social and political interests and conflict. This conflict inevitably shapes the course of development, not necessarily to the detriment of a market economy. This is, it appears, where they self-situate, as Grindle and Thomas self-situated as using a *contextualized* state-centered approach. Two matters to puzzle over here are: first, what are interests? Are these bundled with perceptions, values, and beliefs, or viewed in limited material terms? Second, what is meant by "to the detriment of a market economy"?

Their own analysis stresses pluralist views that give the state a relative autonomy, so that it can be captured by political groups based upon interests, and Marxist views that policy is a reflection of the dominant structure in society. They emphasize the conflictual nature of economic development and the importance of the state as an arena for conflict. Compare this with approaches (echoed by Shore and Wright) in which power involves an ordering of activities, typically so that overt conflict is reduced or unimportant. Yet conflict is central. Thus Beresford (1997 and 1993; see the Vietnam case study, below) in analyzing Vietnam, saw the plan as emerging as the outcome of a process of negotiation between groups with differing, often conflicting, interests.

The central basis for analysis, it seems, is interests, or rather perceived material interests. We have seen how common in the development literature it is for developers to blame vested interests for failure to implement correct policies. Recall how Rodrik (1996) referred to essentially unobservable (for they only exist in the future) "subsequent events" and to a corresponding lack of interests "here and now" for whom those "subsequent events" would be important. This led him to argue that reformers had to act. We can then ask what occurs when economists are construed as representing certain interests when they push through policies by stealth. Tensions may arise if the very conceptualization of such situations argues that they are insulated from interests.

Such an interpretation may suggest, not that such carriers of policy-sets (such as the WC) are driven by the interests of certain groups but rather the reverse—the ideas drive the process. Recall that one of Grindle and Thomas' arguments is that the importance of the technocrats' social context is not so much to do with any particular policy but with the implementability of the particular policy that they are assuming to be correct—a realization problem. Recall also the WB's desire, in the East Asian Miracle study, for relatively insulated technocrats with sufficient power to implement correct policies. Why should exotic doctrines be likely to have any clear relationship to local interests?

What seems to be happening is that the assumptions of classic policy are showing their power and influence over this third category of political economy. The reader may contrast arguments for the importance of interests with evidence that encourages skepticism about the knowability of globally correct and known policies of any type that may act "in the interests" of categories such as capital, or indeed labor. Interests, then, in such Marxist perspectives, may be seen as a way to project intentionality into the analysis and link it to an assumed immanence of development: here, the logic of capitalism. Again, as Cowen and Shenton put it, "The paradox is that cyclical movement reappeared, whatever the purpose of progressive development, in the intention to develop. It was the intention to development which embraced the internal [the idea] of development, namely the conscious authority of autonomous being to determine and realise its potential" (54) and the cart placed before the horse. The question of intentionality now brings us to discuss notions of a developmental state.

Political Science and the Developmental State

Ideas of a developmental state are a central and recurring issue in the development literature, although its importance varies over time and intersects with the ebb and flow of ideas as to what the problem of development is. By the late 1990s and early 2000s, thinking in terms of a developmental state had fallen somewhat out of fashion, but the issue articulates deep-rooted desires within classic views of policy about how intentionality and agency should be secured: how a state adopts the right policies—the fundamental issue facing Grindle and Thomas and, it must be said, many if not most development organizations.

Again, there is a vast literature. A useful entry point is Haggard's comparative analysis of *Pathways from the Periphery* (1990). He presents an objective process in somewhat formal terms. His focus is upon just how successful development occurred, and his analysis has mainly to do with the ability of state-based elites to construct and implement national developmental policies. The state, clearly, is for Haggard the natural site of an intention to develop, and he examines how business and other interests, often shaped by earlier ISI (import-substituting industrialization) experiences, constrain this. His account, therefore, adopts categories such as the state and institutional capability and presents, in my opinion, a somewhat deterministic analysis. Politics is analyzed as being constrained by structures of interests, rent-seeking coalitions, and so forth. This suggests that Haggard is using a variant of those familiar analytical frameworks that reflect assumptions of an ontological and epistemological universalism. In other words, he does not question important assumptions behind a comparative approach.

This permits us to pose key questions related to such frameworks, reminiscent of challenges to the instrumental rationality assumption. For example, how would a creative political leadership construct a new technology of governance and find other ways to define the nature and direction of development? How would new "words to govern men" arise? And how would such a project then be seen through the analytical frameworks Haggard uses? In Part II the presence of heterodox analyses specific to particular contexts poses exactly this question. Pragmatic approaches may more easily grasp creative, and thus non-immanent, processes.

Categories suited to comparative analysis generate tensions. The reader may have noted this in other accounts, and here we may note as an example Haggard's analysis of relationships between regime type and level of development. This analysis may create a problem, as it imposes a framework in which the stage of development reached is taken as the central explanatory factor. This can be challenged as tautologous. This does not necessarily make the analysis wrong but simply shows its limitations.

If a developmental state does development and development is taken as an empirical fact, then this suggests that policy is correct in that it matches the laws of development. We find these discussions using ideas of capacity as a central parameter of any particular government. For instance, Haggard argues that development strategy influences the structure of interests. Thus, he argues that the focus upon export-oriented growth (EOG) in the East Asian newly industrializing countries (NICs) required labor costs to remain competitive, encouraging the control and/or political exclusion of the working class. He argues that not until the expansion of the middle class, a by-product of rapid economic development, did new social pressures for democratic rule emerge. Thus, "Democratization will place new constraints upon economic policy" (Haggard 1990, 265). Here we see again the common conclusion that—having started from the idea that there are knowably correct policies—somehow democracy gets in the way. A counterargument could be that by offering a source of political authority democracy expands political options.

His approach is, I think, significant in that it appears to locate policy-making within particular countries and at particular times, but at the same time maintains an idea that success is in part the result of correct policies with knowable cause-effect relations, knowledge of which requires insulation from the immediate environment. This creates an exotic doctrine that purports, like Grindle and Thomas, to deal with local variation.

This clearly adopts ontological and epistemological universalism, with the associated problems of coping with accompanying facts. Also, by continuing to view the state as the intended or hoped-for carrier of correct policies, these approaches will at some point confront issues to do with the ways in which the local state may or may not seem to share the intentionality of development with outsiders—those from some other place.

Geographers and Space

This starts us off on a new set of ideas related to the changing position of the nation-state vis-à-vis other forms of large social organization. This is common in much discussion of globalization, for example the trilemma argument of Summers (1999; see Chapter 7), which argues that the objective nature of the world economy means that states can realize only two of three policy objectives: greater economic integration, proper public economic management, or national sovereignty (Summers 1999). The scope of policy is thus limited, implying inherent limits to sovereignty.

Here the focus is upon the state, and this is something usefully viewed historically. It is not hard to find scholarly discussions of the historical specificity of the state (for example, Spruyt 1994). Glassman (1999) points to ideas about the position of the state in a globalizing world. As in other areas, this discussion leads quickly to reflection on problems with classic views of policy (for example, that in Grindle and Thomas) which, by *assuming* (as it were) a king on the throne and accompanied by his advisers, in effect assumes intentionality and a site for it (see Box 3.1— *The metaphor of the king and his courtiers*).

Glassman argues that the status of states in SEA has to do with their positions within an internationalized system of class and interstate relations rather than local historical processes. He argues that the WC and the PWC, especially the former, have been widely adopted, and that this implies significant reductions in state sovereignty. Globalization for Glassman involves a ceding of power by national governments. States are increasingly internationalized. They act as facilitators for globalization and in so doing establish important relationships with international capital and markets and facilitate capital accumulation for the most internationalized investors.

Such a view resonates with the pluralist and Marxist positions described by Rodan et al. (1997)and has major implications for understanding development policies, for its objects (those who are to be developed) are then most naturally seen as international and the state's role as developer can be found in its participation in and alignment with internationalized processes and structures.

Glassman also posits creation of a like-mined international business elite, and he argues that production, class relations, and so forth are all becoming international in character. Particular fractions of capital act to facilitate those forms of internationalization of capital that are most in their interests, for capital and capitalist classes are seen as inherently geographically expansive, and the state is seen as a set of institutions through which class and other social struggles are worked out. This implies that states, and by implication development policy, should be seen as sites for internationalization in the interests of capitalist development. That is what drives policy, not national interests.

State Activism—Some Japanese Views

We have seen quite different views of the nature of policy. Both tensions and opportunities are created by construing a state as an agent for intentional development. The discussion has, however, so far referred almost entirely to Western texts. In this section we examine a Japanese view that derives from policy advice given to the Vietnamese government in the 1990s and is in some ways very different. We will then spend some time examining economic thinking as it rationalizes state intervention.

Recall the argument in Chapter 2 that Asia is different from other poor regions of the world in that it contains successes and robust cultural bases for disagreement with external ideas. Ohno (1998) is accessible, can be linked to this idea that Asia is different and contains success, and offers different approaches to intentionality. The Ohno presentation asserts that its own definition of the role of aid and two-step lending takes a different position from the WB and is critical of the WB's East Asian Miracle study.

Ohno starts by defining a correct development. He searches for an authoritative position, attaching great importance to the real economy (rather than macroeconomic stability), while real economic stability is to be attained through various measures, most importantly but not solely financial. Therefore, the state must set a long-term orientation and take steps to ensure it is implemented. State intervention and a long-term orientation are important for developing countries so that resources are concentrated, for free markets dissipate limited human and nonhuman resources. This is different from the IMF (International Monetary Fund), with its focus upon the short-term, and the WB, with its avoidance of concentration strategies.

Market and government must be blended: rather than the WC hostility to state intervention, economic success depends upon the quality of government intervention. Nothing happens fast in terms of major change. Marketization is a total social process, and so long-term strategies need to be prepared and should be country-specific.

Yet, for all the contrast made with the WB and IMF, from a Cowen and Shenton perspective the change model appears highly immanent, with development defined (and so pre-known) as shifts of resources between sectors (customary, state, and market) as marketization occurs. For Ohno, progress is the change from a rural to an urbanized and industrialized stage of development.

But then Ohno's argument shifts stance, asserting that change takes place within international structures of power, in the relationships between the center and periphery that Japan experienced also. The core idea here is that of translative adaptation, as each non-Western society interprets and accepts Western culture without cultural discontinuity, so that a successful latecomer will retain its dual character—both outsider and insider, both modern and premodern. Yet, or perhaps thus, government is both the subject and the object of reform. Government must initiate change to implement policies that create the necessary institutions and attitudes for the market economy.

The reasonableness and specific rationality of this position requires thought. If government is to initiate change, how can it be both the subject and the object of reform? The answer here seems to be that by definition a good government knows what is good for development. This seems very close to a Newman position (in Cowen and Shenton terms). And, intriguingly, the policies advocated are in many ways similar to orthodox Western doctrines of the immediate post–WWII period, mainly in the distrust of markets.

Economists' Arguments for State Intervention Revisited

This leads us to a more detailed look at economists' arguments for state intervention. Recall the natural perspective of much economics—toward the economy rather than toward the policymaker. In this view any noneconomic (such as political) impacts of statements about how the world should be (in terms of what policy should be) or any values that underpin them need not be given much importance. One implication of the knowability assumption is that no essential distinction need be made between statements about how a market should be regulated and those about how a bridge should be built; instrumental rationality is assumed.

In this section I simply bring together a list of standard economic explanations of how and why market failure occurs. This is not directly concerned with why actual markets fail to operate, but how and when models of freely operating markets (those without some extra-market intervention) may fail to lead to good outcomes.

Many find the arguments puzzling. One strategy is to bear in mind that market failure is primarily a characteristic of certain algebraic models, and only with additional argument capable of interpretation as being about anything else. Given Stiglitz's work on information asymmetry, it does not seem silly to conclude that all markets fail, all the time. As with all models, there is the risk of absolutization, of confusing model with reality, and of paying too little attention to observation theory (Lakatos and Musgrave Eds. 1970).

Market Failure

As we have already seen, the focus of mainstream economists' arguments is upon the construal of situations in which markets will fail to generate good outcomes, welfare will suffer, and nonmarket forms of organization will enhance welfare. Statements that offer definitions of market failure can be found in any standard economics textbook. Bates (1995) gives an overview:

> *Production externalities.* Benefits or costs accrue to other agents. Response—property rights, which are said to require state-supported legal institutions for them to operate well. The state, then, must come back in.

Public goods. Goods where those who do not pay can obtain benefits without reducing others' benefits. Response—some organization to produce the goods, which need not be publicly owned and managed (for example a private but state-regulated monopoly). Again, the state has to come in.

Imperfect information. Acquiring information is costly. Less well-informed people pay higher prices. Response—leadership, public production of information, opinion leaders, or market makers.

Hidden action. Principal-agent problems[i]—monitoring costs. Response—use of contracts of various forms (sharecropping is a usual example) instead of spot markets.

Hidden type. Markets for lemons, where buyers cannot know what they are buying before they buy it (labor hiring). A "lemon" here is a commodity that is of far lower quality than usual with such commodities, but where this quality is not easily known. Response—one is frequent hiring and regularizing of the employment relationship; another is use of signals.

Moral hazard. Situations in which the behavior of the agent that buys or receives the service changes against the interests of the seller or supplier. For example, where insurers find that those with insurance policies take greater risks, or borrowers who have been bailed out by banks then proceed to take greater risks because they do not expect the bank to foreclose. Here the seller or supplier, and some customers, cannot prevent nondisclosure of information by the bad risks, thus again leading to market failure. The response to moral hazard is not entirely obvious, and at the time of writing the Global Financial Crisis of 2007–08 drives home the issues involved. Arguments center upon matters such as social pressures to reduce greed, and the importance of regulation and of learning processes (Wade 1988 and 1990; Zysman 1983).

Unforeseen contingencies. Especially in investments. Response—development of capital markets, limited liability, and socialization of risk in various forms—stock markets, commercial banking systems underwritten by central banks and states, and business relationships all act to reduce risk.

The argument here is that when markets fail in these senses, other organizational forms can and should arise to exploit the opportunities for

---

[i]Here the principal is, for example, a company that contracts with some other body, such as a salesman, to act on its behalf—its agent.

gain that exist. This means that state intervention may be justified, although other nonmarket solutions may also work. To repeat: discussion of market failure can be found in any standard economics textbook (for example, Jehle and Reny 1998).

A large literature discusses the validity of this approach. Here we need to step back and appreciate the suitability of such arguments for exotic doctrine. The list above works in terms of categories that exist without context and so support arguments that "what works there, works here." "Market failure" arguments thus tend to adopt the assumptions of ontological and epistemological universalism, and they assert that much is knowable. They support algebraic models that claim, because they contain variables that include or imply "time," that the causes and effects of changes from situation A to situation B can be known. This is the basic analytical framework.

In critiquing economic arguments that underpinned the WC, North states (see also Simon 1986) that the central issue confronting economics is the assumption of instrumental rationality, the idea that:

> It is not necessary to distinguish between the real world and the decision-maker's perceptions of it [and] . . . that it is possible to predict the choices that will be made by a rational decision-maker entirely from a knowledge of the real world and without a knowledge of the decision-makers' perceptions or modes of calculation. [Thus] Institutions are unnecessary; ideas and ideologies do not matter; and efficient markets— both economic and political—characterize economics. (1995, 2)

North and Simon both argue that the assumption of instrumental rationality is central to modern economics. Failure to reject it has disciplinary consequences, for statements (such as academic papers) are accepted or not accepted according to whether they make such assumptions. The assumption of instrumental rationality thus tends to perpetuate assumptions that the world is homogeneous in ontological and epistemological terms, made up of a single population in statistical terms. In passing, of course, this sits well with humanistic beliefs about the essentially shared nature of humanity; yet, as we have seen, this generates tensions when the poor are viewed by the rich as those to be developed through application of exotic doctrine.

If instrumental rationality is, by contrast, questioned, the various roles granted by economics to the state may be revisited. North's arguments do not seem to state exactly what the role of the state should be but instead pose questions to which he accepts a wider range of answers than those in the above list of market failures. North stresses politics as far more important than economics:

> It is polities that shape economic performance because they define and enforce the economic rules of the game. Therefore the heart of development policy must be the creation of polities that will create and enforce different property rights. (1995, 25)

It is not wise, however, to deny that meanings, as humans seem to experience them, may certainly be local and contingent as well as universal and ideal. The main tension, it is increasingly clear, is rather between the strongly universalistic nature of much development language and the lack of empirical support for conclusions about cause-effect relationships based upon universalistic assumptions. The puzzles associated with economic ideas of market failure and instrumental rationality show this clearly.

Conclusions

This chapter contrasts the powerful and rigorous naïve scientism of the dominant discipline that informs orthodox development doctrine, economics, and positions taken by others, such as anthropologists. The differences starkly outline the importance and significance of the core assumptions that drive classic approaches to policy. The chapter also shows that other ideas of the role of state in development tend to share these assumptions, whether Japanese, Marxist political economy, or comparative political economy and the idea of the developmental state.

A criticism of many perspectives is their tendency to cope with facts, not by questioning how their assumptions help relate their positions and conclusions to empirical issues, but by stepping around them. Yet we should not ignore debates within economics and the contrasting uses of empirics. Levine and Zervos (1993) were published in the *American Economic Review* (Fforde 2005a). There is nothing, surely, too unreasonable about a search for regularities in human behavior based upon formal models and metrics, and it is not implausible that such a search could actually and convincingly discover such regularities. At least it should be given a chance to try. In my opinion, the issue is that the regularities have not been found and the discipline therefore best construed as explanation masquerading as prediction.

By contrast, many other approaches appear as prediction masquerading as explanation. Classic views of policy push predictability into development thinking, and the issue thus is not so much whether it is reasonable to seek prediction, but what happens when it has not been found. This seems a characteristic of much exotic doctrine.

Chapter 6 Questions

1. According to Shore and Wright, why does policy become more incoherent the closer you get to it?

2. What do neoclassical economists mean by *market failure*?

3. Discuss the idea that, if Levine and Zervos are right, then their own research is meaningless, because the categories that they use assume the very ontological and epistemological universalism that their research suggests is awry.

Empirics—Measurement and "Facts"

Introduction

This chapter completes Part I by assessing "facts" and issues of measurement. Our focus is globalization, as statements about development across contexts drive the assumptions of universalism that in turn power exotic doctrine—"what works there, works here."

First we consider general questions about the sources of economic growth and then move on to arguments about globalization, more specifically the general value of economic openness in policy toward both trade and capital flows, as well as the effects of globalization upon patterns of change, most importantly upon employment. We then look at areas relevant to an empirical perspective: the measurable and measured effects of human capital and how these issues have been dealt with; and gender. Recall my view that what are taken as "facts" in different contexts and practices vary and are dependent upon various things, such as observation theory (Lakatos and Musgrave Eds 1973).

The Sources of Growth

Introduction

A vast literature uses the enormous volume of statistics built up since WWII to look at relationships between developmental variables. Kenny and Williams (2001) discussed this (see Chapter 3). They argued that the *lack* of agreement was worthy of note and reflected the presence of far more heterogeneity in human affairs than was generally assumed. They pointed to the perils of the epistemological and ontological universalisms arguably inherent in common notions of development economics and large parts of development studies.

Are There Regularities?

Much literature examines the sources of growth. Some things may be said about this massive volume of work. First, some suggest that parts of the literature present spurious results (see Box 1.4—*Spurious Results*), and there are reasons for this. This is a more general issue in statistical work. Granger (1990) discusses an earlier experiment (Granger and Newbold 1974) in which regressions were run to see whether they would generate spurious results. Using randomly generated variables—in other words, variables that were unrelated—in 100 cases, statistical relations could be reported using standard criteria (a t-value of 2 or more) in 96 occasions (Granger 1987, 247). Granger argued that this phenomenon, of statistical results that are meaningless—*spurious*, in the strict sense of the term "is most likely to occur when testing relationships between highly auto-correlated series" (246). And of course in human change processes data is usually highly autocorrelated.

Another issue worth bringing up, though I leave it to the interested reader to pursue it in detail, is that the apparatus of statistical testing has allegedly been designed to generate support for theory that can be said to have found regularities. As a social practice, and this fits with the approaches of classic policy ideologies, it is set up to find answers, not their absence. Published results therefore tend to *support* theory. This follows somewhat clearly the assumption of knowability and makes it easier to report that things are known. This is risky. Cohen (1994) is one way into this literature. Such arguments suggest that the standard policy studies advice to policy advisers, which is to search for cause-effect relations, encounters practices that may make it rather too easy to find results, leading to reliance upon spurious relationships.

Levine and Zervos, in an article published in the early 1990s in the *American Economic Review*, showed that there was little *reliably* (robustly) known about global relationships between economic policy and performance (1993). This they argued for two reasons—first, that policy is extremely hard to express quantitatively (another pointer to heterogeneity); second, because if the statistical exercise is protected (by formal techniques to test the robustness of relationships) from simple attempts to find ways to demonstrate relationships, there is usually no clear result. The point is that researchers can create statistical results that are spurious but reported as meaningful by selecting from data and functional forms.[i] If the functional forms are then allowed to vary, to gauge the robustness of the relationship, the apparent statistical relationships will depart. A range of contentious and contradictory—but each statistically justified— results is, likely, an indicator that this is happening.

Levine and Zervos found just two exceptions: long-run growth was robustly related to financial sector developments and to the black market exchange rate premium. This implies that various well-known "facts" are not proven, such as the belief that inflation harms economic growth. They report that: "Inflation is not significantly negatively correlated to long-run growth" (1993, 429). This article was published in the economics

---

[i] See Rodriguez and Rodrik (1999) discussing just how papers by Dollar (1992) and Sachs and Warner (1995) were crafted.

profession's peak journal and concluded that it is extremely difficult to identify believable links between a wide assortment of indicators of individual policies and long-run growth. This is not to say that such links do not exist, but that they are not *known* to exist in terms of the approach's own assessment criteria. This result is useful. Personally, I take it to show that the world is a far more heterogeneous place than is often assumed; assumptions of ontological and epistemological universalism are unwise (Kenny and Williams 2001). Statements located in explanatory theory and based upon the standard categories of development are equivalent to Lao Tzu's "five notes" in making practitioners unaware of the spurious nature of their empirics.

I discuss elsewhere (Fforde 2005a) the profession's response to this article, through an examination of citations data. This analysis showed, among other things, that only a minority saw the implications of Levine and Zervos; in general, these consequences were ignored. The assumptions of knowability and universalism were not questioned. But it is also useful to point to the relativity of Levine and Zervos' results, for they depend, of course, upon the approach's own assessment criteria, which are subjective: specifically, the confidence level required for a relationship to be deemed robust. If this level is changed, making it easier to find robust relationships, then we can expect more to be found (Hoover and Perez 2003). Of course, depending upon practice, it would be possible to go the other way and find fewer robust relationships than Levine and Zervos. The point then is to accept that we are coping with practices associated with beliefs (Winch 1958), which appear to be unstable.

We now consider other examples of how these empirical issues have been addressed. This comparison can be very useful: coping with facts is not always easy, but then neither is it always hard. We start with what appears to be a stark example of the latter.

Examples of Literature Assuming Known Cause-Effect Relationships

Continued Belief in the "Known to be False"

Financing Gaps

Easterly (1999) examined the reliability of so-called gap models in predicting the capital required for short-run growth, that is "so many $100s million for GDP to rise 'x' per cent next year." This is worth revisiting. Contemporary economic teaching usually says that such models are not worth much. Easterly argued that this framework occurs in almost all International Monetary Fund (IMF) and World Bank (WB) country studies, used to compute requirements for external assistance. He reports that some 80 percent of bank staff members continued to use this simple model and have done since the 1960s. According to him, because the bank remained a lending institution, the model responded simply to a need to calculate how much to lend. Trillions of dollars had been lent based upon this model, but he found no relationship between capital and growth in the short run: "There is no theoretical or empirical justification for the assumption that filling a 'financing gap' determined by 'investment requirements' will raise investment or growth in the short-run" (Easterly 1999, 437). Yet the practice continued. It is clearly inconsistent with a wide range of criteria. Some may find this funny.

Capital Flows and Economics 101

An IMF economist (Zebregs 1998) reported his inability to find *any* clear relationship between what commonly taught economic models predicted and flows of foreign direct investment (FDI). The data led him to argue that most FDI was going to a small number of middle-income countries rather than to the poorest (where wages were lowest).[ii] This again tends to suggest that much assumed knowledge is best approached as not likely to be robust. Doctrines, as I have shown many times, change over time and vary between authorities.

It should now be obvious to the reader that significant risks accompany the ideas of knowable cause-effect relations that underpin classic views of policy. But what if experts disagree?

Disputes between Experts

Consider these two articles. Booth (then a professor of economics at the School of Oriental and African Studies, London University) explains differences between Southeast and Northeast Asian growth patterns as having to do with levels of education, technology, degree of industrialization, different government intervention, and the distribution of assets and skills (1999).

Her data places economies of East Asia into four groups. The first, "low per capita GDP after WWII, slow growth since," includes Cambodia, Myanmar, Laos, and Vietnam (although according to the Booth the last two had shown signs of growth acceleration); the second, "better per capita GDP after WWII, slow growth since," includes Brunei and the Philippines; the third, "low per capita GDP after WWII, rapid growth since," includes Indonesia, South Korea, and Thailand; and the fourth,

---

[ii]For a discussion of this issue in greater depth, see Chapters 3 and 4 of Ray 1998.

"better per capita GDP after WWII, fast growth since," includes Taiwan, Malaysia, and Singapore.

To compare North and Southeast Asia, Booth argues that there is "widespread agreement" on explanations for fast growth (302–308). She gives a list of factors—the importance of human and physical capital and good initial conditions; income and wealth distribution; the significant role of government and insulated bureaucracies; high levels of physical investment; and rapid export growth, although she remarks that the link to GDP growth of the latter was not clear (in terms of causality) because the export boom perhaps preceded investment gains.

One way to assess this is to look at competitors. Contrast Booth's views with Dowling and Summers (1998), who also look at factors influencing growth in Asia. They report (like Booth), "General agreement on factors responsible for rapid growth" (170): rapid growth in savings and investment; trading regimes which promoted exports; sound macroeconomic and broad sectoral policies; and, according to some, good initial conditions regarding education and skills.

Now both of these papers offer reasonable discussions, but they present the reader with different sets of factors to be taken as central and agreed upon in explaining differences between the two regions. The reader then must cope with the disagreement. How? Neither offer empirical reference to what they say their colleagues agree on. Both papers were published in refereed journals.

Globalization

The Failure to Secure Predictability

The issue of universalism is of particular importance in discussions of globalization. Statements about the general value of EOG (export-oriented growth) policies, construed in universalistic terms, and in particular the idea that free trade is a correct policy, appear rather clearly as good examples. What is said about this, given that the gains from openness may not simply be asserted (recall Levine and Zervos) as robustly supported by the data? What do literatures based upon their "facts" argue to be the benefits of trade and foreign investment?

Valuably, there are detailed critiques of how certain results were obtained (for example, Rodriguez and Rodrik 1999). These critiques suggest that readers of such work should proceed with extreme caution. Yet there is strong and widespread belief in the value of economic openness. The paper just cited is strongly critical of work by Dollar, Sachs, and others and provides an accessible object lesson in the value of skepticism and just how little we can expect from disciplinary self-policing.[iii] Let us now look at economists' arguments for international trade and investment.

Using the notion of comparative advantage, Rodriguez and Rodrik (1999) discusses how economic theory argues that countries benefit from producing and trading things that are relatively cheaper for them to produce, given the relative prices of inputs in their economies (that is, labor intensive goods, if labor is relatively cheap compared with capital, by comparison with countries they trade with). But these ideas are not well accepted because they are essentially static (see the section "The exotic origins of development as an idea: economics as an example" in Chapter 4, and Ray 1998 Chapters 16 and 17).

Standard economic analysis of the effects of a tariff (taxes on imports) has to include ways of comparing the net costs—the impact upon consumers, upon government, and upon producers. This involves not only agreeing on how to compare, say, the loss of $1 of spending power for two people, one rich, the other poor, but also agreeing on the value of, say, exposing a company to overseas competition. Getting agreement is not guaranteed, because these all involve judgments about how to compare people's welfare across time and place.

Economists' arguments, Rodrik says, commonly conclude that freer trade benefits the poor. These arguments are expressed in algebra. For example, Stolper-Samuelson (a dominant economic theory) argues that abundant factors of production gain from trade liberalization (such as workers in labor-abundant economies). But this is the model, not reality, and may not lead to stable facts.

This leads us back to two central issues: First, can dominant doctrine be said to be predictive? The WC asserted that capital *would* flow, with competition, to benefit those whose resources were priced comparatively low. Yet we have contradictory evidence suggesting that this is hard to support empirically (Zebregs 1998). The balance of evidence seems to suggest that dominant doctrine is not predictive and so best seen as explanatory. Second, if dominant doctrine is not predictive but explanatory, how can it cope? What happens next? Let us quickly examine a dispute that is central to the politics of EOG.

The Distributional Effects of Globalization

By the late 1990s, debates on the measurable effects of openness showed rather clear moves away from WC doctrine. Strong critiques of globalization are not hard to find, for example Smith (1997), Esteva (1992),

---

[iii]Readers may research for themselves the positions of Dollar (Dollar 1992) and Sachs (Sachs and Warner 1992) in their professions.

and Sachs (1992). As examples of moderate positions, see Wood and Ridao-Cano (1999) and Wood (1997). Great enthusiasm for the positive effects of globalization is also very accessible.

Wood and Ridao-Cano cite strong opinions from the mid-1990s, which argue that:

> Openness to trade is a necessary condition for poor countries to catch up, and that the widening income gap between rich countries and most poor countries over the past few decades . . . is due largely to the restrictions which the latter have imposed upon trade and other economic contacts with the rest of the world. (1999, 89)

They cite counterarguments with a reportedly long history that argue to the contrary, that "trade shifts the structure of production . . . away from (for the poorer partner) sectors of greater growth potential" (Wood and Ridao-Cano 1999, 89).

They add theory that focuses upon differences in skill to this position and report results that argue that:

> greater openness to trade tends to widen initial inter-country differences in skill endowment. . . .[T]he main message is that free trade . . . retards . . . accumulation of skills by causing [poor countries] to specialise in goods of low skill intensity. (1999, 113, 114)

Elsewhere, Wood concludes that:

> [a] substantial amount of empirical evidence supports the conventional wisdom that increased openness to trade in developing countries tends to raise the demand for unskilled, relative to skilled, labor and thus to reduce wage inequality. However, some recent evidence contradicts [this]. . . . [in] Latin America in the late 1980s and early 1990s . . . increased openness appears to have widened rather than narrowed skills differentials in wages. (Wood 1997, 55)

This contrasts with East Asia in the 1960s and 1970s. Wood concludes that the reasons are not related to the differences between the two regions but more because of the differences between the two periods.

> The entry of China and other large low-income countries into the world market for labor-intensive manufactures in the

1980s shifted the comparative advantage of middle-income countries into goods of medium skill intensity. As a result, increased openness in middle-income countries reduced the relative demand for unskilled workers by causing sectors of low skill intensity to contract . . . [whilst] . . . technical progress between the 1960s and the 1980s was biased against unskilled workers. (Wood 1997, 55)

In general, Wood stresses the weak empirical basis of the conclusions. The reader may note that the conclusions are as much to do with observation as with arguments about cause and effect. Openness is seen as problematic rather than a universal solution.

Classic Policy Logics and Globalization: The Trilemma

Recall my arguments in Chapter 4 that confidence in poor country governments as developers has tended to fall. With retained belief in trusteeship, this lack of confidence may be related to alleged characteristics of globalization and its effects upon countries' capacities to implement policies, and so the wider issue of sovereignty. According to Summers (1999) this reflects an integration trilemma. Countries often resist integration because the many are yet to benefit, and the losers are there to complain about it (recall Rodrik 1996, discussed in the section "Introduction" in Chapter 2). A big difference between present-day and nineteenth-century international economic integration is that governments' roles have greatly increased (taxing and regulating, maintaining macroeconomic stability).

According to Summers, the broad task of international political economy is reconciling three goals (the integration trilemma): greater economic integration, proper public economic management, and national sovereignty. Thus, a country wishing to manage its domestic economy and maintain sovereignty would have to insulate itself from the rest of the world: that is, reduce the extent of economic integration. By contrast, if little weight is given to the third, then it is easy, a position that may suit antistatists. By contrast, modern protectionists emphasize sovereignty and domestic economic management, and internationalist utopians advocate world government.

Summers argues that extremes that attempt to avoid the trilemma have not usually been followed. Instead, Summers sees continued efforts to work with and through *national* interests, thus securing maintenance of the nation-state with a stress on its legitimate roles in regulation and transparency, combined with a strengthening of international institutions to improve their capacity to regulate, especially international financial markets. Fundamental to this view is that the indispensable nation is the basic unit of the world system (compare to the discussion of Glassman 1999 in the section "Geographers and space" in Chapter 6). Agency, thus, remains founded upon the nation-state and *shared* between poor and rich countries, with the latter operating bilaterally through aid and other relationships as well as through multilateral institutions.

Doctrine in Limbo? The IMF and the Liberalization of Capital Flows

Prior to the 1997 crisis, many studies, often contested, reported that liberalization of capital markets was associated with good economic performance. Chapter 10 discusses perspectives on the characteristics of capital markets, and the liberalization of international capital flows. Assessment of policy shows shifts in IMF doctrine, in the 1950s willing to argue for controls on capital flows but by the 1980s, in keeping with WC thinking, strongly opposed.

Prasad et al. (2003) took a new position (one of the coauthors was the IMF chief economist). They argued that while countries with a high degree of financial integration had indeed grown faster than those without (a simple correlation), a detailed examination of the data failed to identify a robust causal relationship between the degree of financial integration and growth performance. Viewing this in terms of a doctrinal shift makes it easier to understand what then happened, for the authors felt obliged publicly to explain their report. While they argued that countries

> do enjoy the benefits of financial integration, in terms of both higher growth and lower instability, once they have crossed a certain threshold in terms of the soundness of their domestic monetary and fiscal policies and the quality of the social and economic institutions. (Prasad and Rogoff 2003, no page number)

They *also* argued that

> Economic theory leaves a number of complex and crucial questions unanswered. For instance, in order to control the risks associated with opening up to capital inflows, it seems necessary for countries to have strong institutions. On the other hand, inflows of capital, especially foreign direct investment, may bring technological know-how and knowledge of best practices in other countries that can improve domestic institutions. So should a country postpone opening its capital markets until it has good institutions? Or should it use financial integration as a tool to improve its institutions? Unfortunately, there are *no definitive answers to these issues, which are best approached by each*

country depending upon its circumstances. (Prasad and Rogoff 2003, no page number, italics added for emphasis)

Doctrine had thus gone through three basic options regarding the relative importance of the state: for, against, and "it depends" (Lindauer and Pritchett 2002). The past did not alter; rather the interpretation of it changed. The reader may recall Cowen and Shenton's discussion of the influence of dichotomous categories and the origins of development theory in doctrine as causing cyclicality in policy positions. Readers are then likely to ask, "What happens next?" I discuss this in Chapter 13.

Empirics—More Puzzles?

Readers thus advisedly treat confident statements about what we know with caution. Examples of such statements are not hard to find. In the rest of the chapter I look at some particularly interesting illustrations.

Human Capital, Human Capacity, and Social Capability

We have seen problems in confident explanations of economic change that look at increases in measurable inputs such as capital and labor. At the root of much of this thinking is the application of frameworks that involve use of aggregate production functions, whose algebra links inputs through set formulae to outputs. This appears predictive, naturally enough. See Ray (1998) Chapters 3 and 4, and recall Easterly (1999).

Such practices link categories of thought to purported empirics. Caution is needed—Abramovitz (1995) offers a discussion put entirely in terms of a measurable concept of social capability without providing a way to do so (compare to Dunn's comments on the state as "sociological fact"; see the section "Development as a global issue," in Chapter 2). Two examples are ideas of human capital and social capital. Empirical definition tends to be problematic, if attempted. Note the common idea that many categories refer to things like electricity—more gives you more—and recall Hindess' discussion of problems in treating power as a simple measurable quantity.

Human capital is a relevant example. People are encouraged to think that it has empirical reference. But Gundlach (1999) argues that economic theory was well ahead of measurement in reaching assessments of the role of human capital in development. As in other cases, it is felt and argued to be important, but Gundlach reports that authors offer little empirical grounds for doing so: the results of regression analyses, he says, range from unimportant to twice as important as capital in explaining growth. Such variation in published results suggests that they are likely to be spurious, because underlying assumptions are awry. Recall also Booth (1999) and Dowling and Summers (1998) about reporting a known importance of changes in human capital, and Wood's (1997) more nuanced position.

Gendered Humanity

If categories such as human capital pose problems, then gender—perhaps a universal par excellence—does also. Gender may be considered as a clear example of the power of ideas and dominant discourses in influencing development interventions and the actions of developers. See Marchand (1996) for a useful introduction. Gender-blindness may be viewed as a tendency to not see issues because they are hidden by categories and words that we see (or the discourse sees) as being undifferentiated, such as farmers. The literature here is rich—an example is Seidel and Vidal (1997), who argue that gender-blindness has led to major problems in the treatment of HIV and AIDS sufferers in Africa.

In many accounts, by the mid-1990s considerable resources and efforts had been put into addressing the exclusion of women's issues from development through activities such as Women in Development (WID) and the institutionalization of gender issues by aid donors and many other agencies. Much of this literature self-presents as challenging dominant discourses (for example, Escobar 1995). Yet Gender and Development (GAD) and WID did not, many argue, adequately problematize Western development models or address issues of culture and difference or tendencies to adopt a North-South dichotomy. It is possible to see tensions between the categorical thinking required by mainstream development and resistance to the external construction of identity discussed in the queer and third-wave feminist literatures. For a gentle dig in this direction, see Sylvester (1999).

Here Cowen and Shenton's reference to the effects of the corruption of the intention to develop echoes strongly. What, we are led to ask, is the intentionality, where is it sited, and how is the issue of trusteeship addressed? Classic views of policy seem so often to lead to entanglements.

Conclusions

This chapter has examined various empirics meant to underpin hopes of predictability. These are fundamental to the assumptions of classic policy approaches, giving particular meanings to the search for evidentially based cause-effect relationships.

Paradoxically, on examination, literature often shows theory running ahead of evidence, poor policing of empirical results (Fforde 2005a, 82), and a lack of willingness to critically examine literature as disputable theories develop. Theory as explanation is developed and then deployed very quickly to support statements about the correctness or otherwise of particular policies, and this may encourage skepticism. The literature, I conclude, is not on the whole about the production of agreed knowledge of cause-effect relationships but rather relies upon dispute to generate what is publishable and teachable, but yet unstable. And what is publishable and teachable is largely self-policed. In the framework offered by Shore and Wright, this is the way in which classic policy ideologies are part of practices of social organization.

At the level of global policy doctrines, the internal evidence strongly suggests two things: first, that predictability is absent; second, that practices tend to suggest that the tensions this creates are not particularly powerful. What we find is a combination in the literature of rather strong arguments that explain the situation, with evidence that these arguments are ignored. Fforde (2005a) looked at citations of Levine and Zervos (1993) and found that the response of the majority was to disregard the central result. This matches what Easterly found in looking at lending practices, the confident but contradictory assertions by experts of just what experts agree upon, and the example of how some analysts treated human capital. The chapter also points to ways in which the social practices associated with the search for knowable cause-effect relations tend to make it easier to report success than to report failure: to say that discoveries have been made rather than to report ignorance.

But beside these conclusions are others; although apparently not powerful, the tensions are tangible. The work on the distributional effects of globalization cited tends to report observed regularities rather than support for theory. In terms of the politics of development, IMF doctrine seems to be in an "it depends" position, with Summers' thoughts on the changing nature of sovereignty perhaps pointing toward ideas of shared intentionality, which would appear facilitated by preventing the IMF from telling everybody to do the same thing.

To return to Lao Tzu, it perhaps thus appears that fewer people (but not many) find it easy to think that music is the "five notes." We now turn to Part II, which examines the local fates of exotic doctrine in SEA.

Chapter 7 Questions

1. What—if any—are the likely consequences of the internal problems that development economics faces, as shown by the failure to get robust relationships between policy and growth? What does this imply for how alternative policy proposals are assessed?

2. Global issues matter globally, and so are "read into" local events, but may not matter locally. Just what may be happening?

3. How would you advise somebody on how to cope with the doctrinal, rather than scientific, nature of much development policy thinking?

PART II

Exotic Doctrine—Its Local Fates

CHAPTER 8

Comparing Development Policies

The Argument So Far

The main lesson to be drawn from the previous chapters is that a skeptical stance is advisable to cope with comparisons of development policies. Exotic doctrine assumes much: knowability, ontological and epistemological universalism, and, fundamentally, predictive success. Yet it is unstable. Part I has shown that there are good reasons for treating these assumptions with skepticism. This forms the basis for the discussion of development policies in the three country case studies. In working through my arguments, the reader will usefully have acquired some familiarity with the following:

- Different notions of the problem of development (specifically, Grindle and Thomas versus Cowen and Shenton) and the existence and nature of problems with basic ideas (Chapters 2 and 3).

- Histories of development thinking (Chapters 4 and 5).

- Issues concerning the basic building blocks of contemporary thinking about development policy (Chapters 6 and 7).

This should allow readers to pose fundamental questions with some confidence. First, is the notion of development under consideration a concept of a known or knowable process, and/or of something possessing intentionality? That is, *is development said to be process and/or product?* Second, if development is said to be something that is done, to be "transitive," *is there intentionality?* Who or what can persuasively be said to intentionally produce development? Is the view one that argues that intentionality actually exists, or that it should, and then discusses how and why? In other words, what is the status of the purported intention to develop? What is its nature? What is that intention? Third, *what agency hosts this intentionality?* Fourth, does agency actually exist, or, if it does not, why not? Fifth, what is the intervention logic: *how is the combination of intentionality and agency understood to "do" development?* This is related to cause-effect metaphors associated with assuming knowability.

These are a useful line of approach for the following reasons. Here I return to my own agnostic-cum-realist position. Change is far from *necessarily* best seen as a result of policy. But it may be. If we choose to focus upon a development-underdevelopment dialectic, policy may be seen as situated *within* rather than outside development, but we can remain open to the argument that it is not always, or necessarily. This means that, for analytical as well as practical reasons, the implementability of policy should be a central issue, not just a peripheral one.

To cope with, or even to form a view about, development policy, the reader should consider arguing for its inseparability from the issue of rationalities—rationalities of rule and the ordering of society; rationalities of social science and policy, which accompany state rule; and other rationalities that confront these, perhaps to ensure their implementation, perhaps to negotiate alternatives, or perhaps to nullify them. One way of doing this is to state the argument in terms of discourses and their logics. There are others.

Much literature on development policy, however, argues from the perspective of a single correct rationality; this inevitably stresses implementation issues, partly in self-defense. Usually, this single correct rationality is identified as correct, juxtaposed with other rationalities said to be wrong, and is best seen as doctrine. This is perhaps why international organizations, such as the World Bank (WB), in their roles as global developers, have had to keep trying to find ways of ensuring that good policy gets adopted. This has tended to fail. In the end, though, if policy is construed in a classic manner and thought to matter, it must (at least) be believed implementable. Yet constructing arguments based on the belief that policy is knowably correct and implementable leads to a wide range of tensions, not least those that compare muddle with model and tend to create arguments within which the stated outcomes of correct policies may never actually be attained, because they are idealized.

Given all this, then the main map of approaches to comparing development policies is usefully structured around doctrines. This is to do with the fundamental question of intentionality in mainstream development thinking, the search for agency upon which to site it, and the role of and nature of assumptions of knowability.

Why is there no knowledge? The reader is by now aware of the importance of Levine and Zervos' results to my arguments. This is for some an intriguing question, which sits beside the evident confidence and self-positioning of many who hold to the contrary view, that "We know now . . ." I can offer some possible answers:

- Because of the nature of regularities (so very few are reliably found). Here we can recall that Levine and Zervos did find some robust relationships between policy and outcomes, but very few. This may be related to the tensions between the implicit universalism, both ontological and epistemological, of much social science language and modeling, which leads, at root, to assumptions that sampling is from single populations, leading to spurious empirical results and so a series of inconsistent research results. The implication is that the stuff of much social science is far more varied than it appears. The five notes indeed make us deaf.

- Because of the importance of politics and issues to do with rule and the role of certainty in social order. There are strong pressures to believe, and this has become habit. Organizations organize based on shared beliefs, perhaps contested and negotiated (Shore and Wright 1997).

- Because of the nature of many development practices. Here the argument of Cowen and Shenton is that the problem of development, that it is both product and process, encourages recourse to the Newman solution: that those in authority will tell us what to believe. Much then gets thrown out the window.

- Because of the nature of policy. Policy is not, it seems, best thought of as being about cause-effect relations, but rather the politics and organization of group action. The issue of knowability may be thought of as the issue of the possibility of shared belief (Chapter 13).

- Because the nature of knowledge production seems so often to require "disputable theory." If core content is not internally predictive but explanatory, then the literature will be a series of accounts. Yet their value and scholarly authority will be influenced by a wide range of criteria, few if any of which offer a wise basis for believing in cause-effect logics, driving interventions upon which the well-being of many is thus thought to depend.

Meanwhile, the world keeps on turning, which is of more than casual interest.

The Case Studies: Intention, Agency, and Intervention Logics

The discussion of the case studies will show that much of the literature is tied up with the fundamental issues discussed in Part I. These, as discussed already in this chapter, can be looked at in terms of intention, agency, and intervention logic.

The Philippines is a country that many analysts, as we shall see, treat as being a failure in developmental terms. This means that two problems arise for those working within approaches that adopt what Cowen and

Shenton present as the Newman solution to the problem of development: first, to define correct development in some way, and second, to discuss how this has not come about.

An intention to develop has then to be related to some (typically exotic) standard or set of standards. Because these are assumed to be objective and because development is usually assumed to have failed, there must then be a search for agency—who or what could or should have embodied the presumed intention to develop (in terms associated with whatever authority the text refers to) and failed to do so. In simpler English, this often seems to come down to a simple blame game that, given the common statism of many approaches, focuses upon the Philippine state. I therefore call Chapter 11 "Intention without success, and the search for agency." Intervention logics may then be seen both in terms of assessments of why the assumed good policies were not adopted and in terms of resistance by the population.

Thailand, however, is generally seen as a success. Yet, for many, assessments that use standard frameworks seem lacking in persuasive power. The literature then appears to generate *pragmatic* approaches. Put this in a different way and consider the two alternatives that Cowen and Shenton reported as historical solutions to the problem of development: those of Marx and of Newman. The former implies that there is no real intentionality to development, as what appears as such simply reflects the immanent process of capitalist development. We can see this view reflected in some parts of the literature. For others, however, the natural problem is how to explain success in terms that in some way permit a projection of intentionality into the historical process (that can then, in Cowen and Shenton terms, be seen to be "done"). I therefore entitle Chapter 10 "Success without intention, and the search for cause."

Compared with Thailand, an ongoing element of Vietnamese development history from 1954, since the beginnings of development in the North under the current regime, has been the high levels of external assistance. Quite apart from the effects this may have had domestically, this assistance has meant that much of the Western literature has been under strong pressure to assess change in terms that support the classic model, in which correct development is attributed to correct and implemented policy. Like Thailand, development (since the emergence of a market economy in the early 1990s) has been widely reported as a success. Unlike Thailand, however, literature has been far more concerned—not to find cause—but to stress intentionality and the role of the aid recipient—formal structures largely dominated by the Communist Party—as the main agency articulating that intentionality. Because a part of the literature presents persuasive arguments to the contrary, to the effect that development has been largely driven by social and economic forces rather than policy, this presents striking tensions. As a result, I title Chapter 9 "Success without intention, and a theater of agency." This sense of theatre I owe both to Leninist practice, where the ruling party hides behind various facades, such as the state and mass organizations, and also to a paper by John Kleinen (2001).

A step back from the literature shows how these perspectives may shift the reader's attention to various issues that are valuable to the tempering of coping strategies, especially if the mind's focus is moved from development and toward change.

First, just what values and intentions drive and explain the behavior of various actors? If it is hard to see why the existing oligarchic families in the Philippines seem happy to restrict their realms of economic enjoyment to areas that seem to doom the country to increasingly backward status, then for Vietnam just what are the political strategies of dominant families and groups in the party? Such questions suggest that issues of intentionality and agency go far beyond what can be found in the existing literature. Second, what are the possible consequences of the ways in which success comes up against the persuasive shortcomings of much of the literature? What tensions are created by the juxtaposition of "intention without success" and "success without intention" that the development literature seems to confront in these parts of Southeast Asia (SEA)?

If one answer is the tension between exotic doctrine and its local fates, then what may happen when fate confronts doctrines? If we can increasingly see pragmatic approaches becoming more persuasive, then what does this suggest about the changing nature of our beliefs, and so of the ways in which we act and organize socially in this world? I will return to these issues after the case studies.

CHAPTER 9

Vietnam—"Success without Intention, and a Theater of Agency"

Introduction

We come now to Vietnam. The country is in many ways a source of surprises. It is not hard to argue that a series of predictions for what would happen in Vietnam, despite turning out correct, would at the time have been dismissed as incredible. Here are some examples:

- In the mid-1960s, as the heavy costs of the Vietnam War started to bite, most North Vietnamese farmers would succeed in subverting Communist Party norms for their agricultural cooperatives at little cost.

- In the mid-1970s, the reunited country, granted access to the Mekong Delta rice bowl, would nevertheless fail to implement neo-Stalinist industrialization.

- In the late 1970s, when a market economy started to emerge, a process of transition would be put in place that would result in its acceptance by the Vietnamese Communist Party (VCP) in 1986.

- Through the 1990s, after the emergence of a market economy, Vietnam would experience a *rising* state share of GDP, macroeconomic stability, and increasing globalization.

Yet research has shown that these things came to pass (Fforde 1989; Fforde and Paine 1987; de Vylder and Fforde 1996; Fforde 2007). The main reason why these predictions would have been dismissed is that, in the eyes of many, they amount to anomalies. They do not fit with what is meant to happen: Communist parties rule over strong states, they use Soviet institutions to develop, they view markets with great hostility and are powerful enough to eradicate them, and market economies with large state sectors incur heavy economic inefficiencies and grow slowly.

Further, there is considerable energy behind the idea that policy has played a major role in Vietnam's development. This means that the task of coping with the literature is both easier—because policy is given great stress—and harder—because that stress tends to overplay its hand, arguing its case in a wide range of authoritative sources. As for why this is a characteristic of the literature, persuasive elements of an explanation include the very high levels of foreign resource inflows, which affect how Vietnam is presented (this may be seen both during the period when the Soviet Bloc was the main source and after); the politics of the ruling Vietnamese Communist Party, which has allocated rather high levels of resources to presenting itself and its legitimacy in ways that involve claiming a major role in development; and the need common throughout development literature to assert the role of the state. We encounter both foreigners sympathetic to the regime in various ways as well as donor groups keen to base wider arguments on Vietnam's apparent experience.

By contrast, histories that stress major turning points as not primarily involved with policy therefore appear to be anomalies. A key marker is whether the emergence of a market economy is dated to the 1986 VIth Party Congress or to other factors, such as the late 1970s aid cuts. We start with an overview of recent history.

An Overview of Development and Development Policy[i]

North Vietnam Prior to 1975

1945:   Declaration of Independence by Ho Chi Minh; general and probably uncoordinated uprising against French. Armed struggle with French starts.

Late 1940s: Chinese Communist victory leads to increased access to military materiel by Vietminh over northern border.

1950–54:   With good control over northern border provinces and much of the countryside, Vietminh seek out opportunities to engage large-scale French forces and succeed. Dien Bien Phu victory leads to Geneva Conference and division of Vietnam. Democratic Republic of Vietnam establishes itself in North; Communists increasingly in control. Land reform distributes land, attempts and fails to establish secure "cadre" for party in rural areas; with "correction of errors" old leadership released from prison; class basis for socialist change in rural areas thus not secured.

1954–65:   Attempt to establish "classic" socialism. Development model combines Soviet institutions and assumes that lack of capital goods is the main cause of underdevelopment. Collectivization of agriculture, establishment of central planning, and

---

[i] I base this, and the judgments in it, upon my own work cited in this chapter. The reader should note how, as expert, I now assert positions to be more or less correct.

control of trade. Aim is to force resources into state industry through price and distributional controls. In practice, system is "softened" and adapted as macroeconomic imbalances lead to the rise of free market prices and shift to aid dependency.

The political system that arises as Ho Chi Minh's authority fades is one in which power is not concentrated at the peak. This introduces possibilities for political activity and change that are impossible in true Stalinist systems, where (as constructed by Stalin) party, security, and state power structures are concentrated at the peak in one individual. Situation discourages top-down change and predisposes the polity to bottom-up incremental processes in which peripheral bodies creatively violate norms.

1965–75:   Two bouts of air war ending in Christmas bombings, Paris talks, and agreement that US troops will leave. Unexpected fall of South in 1975. From around 1972, attempts to reform the Democratic Republic of Vietnam (DRV) economic system in conservative direction (party accepts that there is a problem). Throughout the period, the northern economy maintains a balance between high-price, outside economy (*kinh te ngoai*) and state-controlled, planned economy; balance depends upon wartime sentiments, high aid flows, and lack of pressure to accumulate and save.

1975:   Fall of the southern regime.

1976 on

1976:   Establishment of Socialist Republic and decision to extend DRV methods to whole country; no alternative for the South. Renewed pressure to increase accumulation and develop economy.

1977–79:   Failure of Second Five-Year Plan. Increasing tensions as free market prices rise and consumer goods rations become less reliable. Collectivization of Mekong Delta and state control of rice trade lead to falls in supplies of rice to cities. International events lead to loss of Chinese and Western aid, forcing state-owned enterprises (SOEs) to seek supplies elsewhere, precipitating "spontaneous" breakdown of socialist economy (fence-breaking) and beginnings of ad hoc decollectivization. The Sixth Plenum of the Central Committee of the Vietnamese Communist Party, VCP, (August–September 1979) sees acceptance of markets de facto (not yet in ideological terms)—production should "explode" (*bung ra*). Abandonment of collectivization of Mekong.

1979–80:   Intense political debate, leading to legalization of "partial reforms" in early 1980: output contracts in agriculture and the three-plan system in SOEs; attempts to reform domestic trade lead to inflation as price rises do not stick; attempts to permit localities (especially Ho Chi Minh City) to trade internationally also introduced. Transitional political economy now clears, driven by commercializing SOEs, building up capital and with important political influence.

1981–84:   Increased marketization of the economy based upon SOEs. Farmers in cooperatives see slight rise in incomes, not sustained; urban population living conditions improve marginally. Soviet aid increases in volume, replacing Chinese and Western. Various policy changes attempt to rein in liberalization: reductions in SOEs' legal freedoms, attacks on free market, closure of Ho Chi Minh City's export-import corporations. Rather rapid economic growth starts to slow around 1984.

1985:   Final attempt at conservative reform: combination of renewed attack on southern rice trade with price-wage reforms aims to establish state-controlled prices that are sustainable—thus, the *anti*-market. Fails and introduces a period of hyperinflation.

1986:   Death of Le Duan, party general secretary, responsible for leading the country against the US, for the conservative reforms of 1972–78, for the partial reforms of 1979–85. VIth Party Congress introduces "renovation" as slogan and opens way (ideologically) to market economy.

1987–88:   Liberalizing partial reforms to SOEs and cooperatives. Cooperative reforms destroy many rural cadres' jobs. Opening up of domestic trade (interprovincial); foreign investment encouraged; some liberalization of exports. Continuing hyperinflation. Maintenance of central-planning "core" of system and no mention of decollectivization. Market-oriented reformers full of confidence, drawing upon Central European ideas and (for some) heading toward multiparty system. Minor gestures to encourage private sector, which remains very cautious. De-Stalinization of everyday life under party General Secretary Nguyen Van Linh.

1989:   Soviet aid collapses; macroeconomic measures taken to attack inflation (big increases in interest rates for deposits). Opening of international borders floods domestic markets with goods. Removal of most price controls introduces market economy without dealing with central issues: land, labor, and capital all remain highly subject to state control. Also, main commercial force is the state sector, which has been accustomed to securing economic rents and remains close to the party at all levels. Private trade reemerges, and streets start to look normal by SEA standards—shops, food stalls, and so forth.

1990–91:   Vietnamese economy recovers, to great surprise, and SOEs' output grows. IMF and World Bank greet Vietnam as example of effective top-down reform implementing IMF methods. Western aid starts to come in, as do foreign businesses. No positive position taken in favor of the private sector. Political atmosphere continues to ease, but party sacks politburo member accused of supporting multiparty system. No political reforms. Population somewhat surprised that all this has happened.

1992–95:   Rapid economic growth. Vast inflow of foreign direct investment (FDI) and aid. Commoditization of land leads to real estate boom and, with emergence of labor market, creates premises for capitalism in markets for key factors of production. SOEs continue to dominate the economy and foreign trade. Government continues to view them as having a leading role in economy. Talk of Vietnam as a "coming tiger." Rapid growth of exports. Transformation of middle-class lifestyles and significant increases in rural incomes. Very limited growth of private sector.

1996:   Post-boom. Rural unrest as farmers object to corrupt local officials' exactions, in some areas effectively removing local administration. Increasing corruption and signs that officialdom has been acting in its own interests in many areas (for example, infrastructure). Foreign investors increasingly tire of red tape and evidence that goalposts will be moved against them to preserve local interests. FDI falls before regional economic crisis. Many SOEs are bankrupt, with credit and tax decisions in their favor now showing the irrationality of decisions and the particular interests they favored. There is gathering popular sense that the government is neither very competent nor honest, but it remains in power.

Attempt to establish and reestablish rural cooperatives of a new type, perhaps in response to rural unrest and sense that a civil society is emerging in the rural areas. Minor reforms to enhance local democracy in rural communes.

1997:	Regional crisis sees Vietnam maintain positive GDP growth. Favorable prices and efforts to increase SOE efficiency combine with a stream of FDI projects to boost exports. No concessions are made to the private sector, but it starts to grow significantly. Foreign-invested companies (joint ventures, JVs, and 100 percent foreign-owned) start to become near 50 percent of industrial output.
1999:	Enterprise Law marks acceptance of emerging private sector. Actively setting up businesses, SOE managers are now joined by private businesspersons as the main elements of Vietnamese capitalists. Strong signs that with this change some form of capitalism exists in Vietnam, with classes based upon markets in land, labor, and capital.
2000s:	Continued rapid growth. No major political changes. Vietnam joins the World Trade Organization (WTO) in 2006.

Transition—The Context of Debates

In my opinion, Vietnamese experiences tell us much about the pace and resource costs of institutional change.[ii] Much of their experience suggests that rapid transformation is extremely hard. The Vietnamese transition from plan to market took around a decade (1979–1989/90), with some form of capitalism and its associated classes and markets then emerging clearly to view about a decade after that (1999–2000). At a micro level, changing from a plan-oriented organization to one that is market-oriented (in the North) could take a few years: marketing, accounting, labor hiring, and so on all require knowledge and resourcing of institutions (Fforde 2007). In terms of markets, structural change to permit the emergence of stable exchange patterns also takes time and resources (Fforde 2002). Finally, ideas also take time to change. Local accounts of reform focus upon *tu duy* ("thought"), in part reflecting the ongoing power of conservatives but also the extent to which people were risk-averse and unwilling to move too quickly into the unknown.

These views depend upon an approach to explaining change in Vietnam that greatly underplays any role played by agency in any simple categorical sense. De Vylder and Fforde (1996) articulate this and emphasize the value of looking at what is going on independently of policy shifts (policy does not necessarily matter), so as to assess impact and the detail of policy.

[ii] Again, the reader should note here my willingness as expert to assert in ways that this book questions.

In combination, therefore, de Vylder and Fforde pressured political scientists to refine their analysis, which is what Vasavakul (1993) and others did. Note that de Vylder and Fforde were rather well translated into Vietnamese and published by one of the party's publishing houses as de Vylder and Fforde (1997). This was in part because of a strand in Vietnamese opinion that also focused upon process, downplaying the role of policy change.

The context of debates was therefore one in which heterodox positions were taken rather early, in ways that confronted many classic assumptions, centrally the importance of policy in change and the associated notions of agency and intentionality. The question of knowability remained, of course. I now turn to the question of intentionality.

Politics and Policy

Introduction

A range of political analyses exist to provide examples of different approaches to the politics and the political economy of Vietnam after 1975. Most are either Marxist or pluralist, and nearly all focus on the problem of explaining policy and why it changed in the way it did. This method tends to assume that policy is important; in their different ways, both main types of explanation assume a classic view of policy. The views I have selected are chosen primarily to illustrate my arguments about development.

Vasavakul (1993) stands out, in that she places the classic political question of the creation and maintenance of order centrally. She thus explains the attempts to secure emergence of a new order in the late 1990s, arguing that these came forward as a conscious political response to the gathering emergence of a societal order (business networks) that was thought to threaten the regime.

Let us start by examining Marxist views and how they resolve the issues of the classic view of policy: what is intentionality, how is it sited, and how is the assumption of knowability addressed?

Marxist Views: Party or State as the Agent of Development?

Beresford (1993, 1997) is one of the best political economists working on contemporary Vietnam. Beresford employs Marxist approaches, and we can observe how the treatment of agency changed between the 1993 and the 1997 analyses. Beresford's 1993 analysis is sympathetic to the party. Greenfield (1993) is also Marxist, but hostile. Reform, Beresford argues in 1993, was introduced to address political problems in the rural areas, because resource extraction failed as farm output stagnated and also because the regime's basic rationale, industrialization, was in jeopardy. Her analysis of change centers upon policy shifts resulting from the political consequences of failure. As a committed analysis, it is necessary to assume that the party has legitimacy, and this fits with an account in which policy is part of a history of attempts to implement traditional socialism, leading to problems, and so to reform. Maintaining a classic view of policy, she dislikes: "political interference in economic decision-making" (231).

The approach can be seen as similar to those pluralists who seek an insulated elite bureaucracy to implement economic reforms and then find that implementation is confounded. Beresford attempts to get around this by the assertion that the VCP has tended to operate in a decentralized manner and with a certain but varying flexibility—and is thus close to the people. We are given a picture of a ruling party actively responding to the situation in which it finds itself. In terms of classic views of policy, this analysis therefore asserts knowability (in particular, by elites) and sites intentionality upon the party as the prime agency of development. It is fair to say that the party, in this view, is most certainly in trusteeship, though this is camouflaged by ideas that it is representative in some way.

Beresford develops these ideas in 1997, changing them most importantly by placing the state rather than the party as the prime agent of development, playing a necessary role as the mediator between evolving social interests. This change avoids too much discussion of VCP politics. It means that Beresford sees policy in terms of different tendencies among top leaders and also links VCP activities to societal interests (workers and poor peasants). In passing, I will add my view that the VCP has ruled in classic Leninist fashion, directly controlling all levels of the state and the mass organizations, so that treating the state as a prime category of analysis is problematic (Fforde 2008). The shift between these two analyses shows how writers may select, in their search for agency, different sites: first the party and then the state.

Greenfield (1993) writes from an antiparty Trotskyite position. He sees a major ideological shift in Vietnam and the rapid emergence of capitalism. He takes issue with Beresford, reversing her argument. The economic crisis is not something to be solved by reform, such as of SOEs, but is caused by interests associated with the SOEs and their relationship with the regime. Policy, in this view, supports the emergence of capitalism rather than preserving the interests of the masses. A process of state-supported privatization (or appropriation) is for Greenfield at the core of what was happening, a process by which a capitalist class is created, through state action, based on the private acquisition and control of SOEs.

Greenfield argues that this process requires disciplining of labor and farmers through market forces and reducing the tendency to democratize through the concentration of power on reformists close to central state power. He links these debates not simply to ideas but also to interests.

Non-Marxist Views of the Emergence of Agency

If the question of agency arises clearly in these Marxist studies and is dealt with in now familiar ways, then it is confronted with some subtlety by Vasavakul She addresses the issue in two very different works. In Vasavakul 1993, she focuses upon the *internal* dynamics of structures established by the VCP: the party, the state, and institutions such as SOEs, cooperatives, and so on. Thus the crisis of the administrative state under central planning was precipitated by conflict among socioeconomic sectors *within* the socialized sectors: cooperative farmers, state farm workers, enterprise managers, workers, and technocrats. These sectors were not synonymous with or constituted society; neither were these sectors synonymous with interest groups or classes as understood in the context of capitalism. Conflict and disagreements among party leaders interpreted as signs of personal struggle were, in fact, not divorced from the fundamental question of sectoral conflict within the state. Here though the very existence of the state as developmental agency is not yet problematical or placed center stage:

> The shift to a market economy gave rise to new forms of conflict within the state apparatus as the old socio-economic sectors tried to reposition themselves . . . The arrival of the market also gave rise to new forms of conflict between the government bureaucracy and different sections of Vietnamese "society" as the administrative and legal void was not filled. (Vasavakul 1993, 82)

This analysis appears mechanistic and unsatisfying to the author herself. This seems to be because she does not yet treat these categories as problematic per se; that is, she accepts the existence of a state as a sociological fact. Yet this assumption, in effect that the state *exists* as source of policy and developmental agency, leads to problems. What, for instance, are the relationships between these structures and the rest of Vietnam? The answer is not clear, suggesting that the problem may center upon the attempt to apply a state-civil society model. That is the perhaps inherent problem in conceiving of the party/state apparatus as having some boundary. A questioning of the very *existence* of a state as conventionally thought lurks here.

An alternative is to treat politics in terms of the creation and maintenance of order. Thus in her 1996 study, analysis shifts to focus upon political responses to perceptions of a threat to the VCP from changes in Vietnamese society as a whole. This response is then construed as the emergence of a coherent state with agency. Policy could then come to have a classic meaning, where it did not before. Thus, "Under central planning, the political power of the state rested mainly on its ability to claim property rights, control and allocate economic resources, and attain output targets. . . . At the level of state bureaucracy, politics tended to be vertically confined" (Vasavakul 1996, 45).

But, under the new market economy-based order, "With diminishing resources coming from the centre and with the relaxation of some aspects of administrative control over production activities, the existing vertical . . . ties disintegrated" (Vasavakul 1996, 46). Her innovation is to stress that power moved down as economic freedom at the base increased (that is, greater independence from the plan). This threatened the regime, but previously this had not been seen to matter, as a *need* for classic policy was not yet appreciated. It also means that her concept of power shifts with what she is analyzing:

> New forms of conflict [arose] between government agencies and society. This problematic relationship was characterised foremost by a lack of adequate administrative and legal ties between the state and various sectors of society. . . . The market-based, multisectoral economy . . . brought with it new practices . . . that generated and reinforced . . . networks. (Vasavakul 50, 53)

In her account it was these changes that provoked a new order, involving state regulation both of society and itself. The analysis remains focused upon the state and its role in creating order, but now in competition with societal sources of order to create a new state-society relationship under party leadership, with the state emerging as a new sociological fact, a site for developmental agency.

The central reason this happened was to address a perceived threat to regime legitimacy and political power. One overt policy response was public administration reform. But this was preceded by the drive to establish the state as sociological fact in a form that allowed it to be attributed with agency. This implies that prior to this point agency did not exist. Note, though, that while creation of agency was intended, Vasavakul's argument leaves open the question of just how successful this was.[iii]

[iii]Fforde 2004 and 2005 discuss the view that this project, by the mid-2000s, had still failed. The search for agency continued. Gainsborough (2007) threw open the question of agency, arguing that there was far more money-making than policymaking going on among state officials.

This approach reveals basic questions about the sources of order and places them into a dynamic context. Note, however, that it does not go into the issue of where state reform ideas came from. An idea of conscious responses to perceived problems is central.

Confident Economists: A Classic View of Policy

Because of the extensive involvement of aid agencies in knowledge production, a wide range of materials can be found to illustrate the contrasting approaches of various economists. Most of these materials are predictably classic in their views of policy and its importance. Here I limit the discussion to two. Others are easy to find. Kokko and Sjoholm (2000) is a straightforward analysis, attributing change to reform, that called for more reform because of economic problems. The authors recount a litany of incorrect policies, including a shift toward ISI, also slow privatization of SOEs, poor support for the private sector, and so on. They sidestep many questions, not least of which why policies are as they are, and what is possible. The analysis facilitates this by assuming that policymakers are relatively insulated from politics (and so hopefully susceptible to good advice).

Riedel and Turley (1999) is a joint work by an economist (Riedel) and a political scientist (Turley) with experience in Vietnam dating back to well before 1975. The two authors have quite different perspectives, and this can be seen in the study. Riedel supports WC views. The analysis is therefore driven by the classic views of policy that the WC shares with other positions, and the implementation issue is then addressed by bringing in political analysis. The paper poses its core questions in a classic manner:

> 1. What are the policies Viet Nam must adopt to sustain growth at or near present rates? 2. What are the political variables and trends shaping the choice of policies? And 3. What has been the impact of the Asian financial crisis on Viet Nam's reform process? (Riedel and Turley 1999, 1)

Important questions, such as where these policies come from and how they may be implemented, are not really posed. The state is assumed to be a site for intentionality, and so policy drives change, dated to the 1986 VIth Party Congress. Reform is a: "process of discovery, the hard way, that the alternative to a mixed economy does not work" (Riedel and Turley 1999, 4). And the issue of whether the local agent of development is worthy of trusteeship presents clearly: "Whether or not Viet Nam's political leaders and institutions have the qualities needed to adopt good policies and to implement them is very much open to question" (23).

Again, familiar from much analysis epitomizing Rodrik's view of the *inherent* problems, in terms of the associated interests political analysis suggests inhibit securing implementation of correct policies, Riedel and Turley identify interests and link them to power. Interest groups are identified: farmers, SOEs, managers, officials, and so forth. They are said to have vested interests in delaying further reform. This meant that the effects of reform within the VCP were differentiated. An economics bloc gained as the political, ideological, and mobilization bloc lost out—the former allegedly controlled central and some local state management bodies.[iv] "Doi moi [reform] itself thus generated impediments to reform" (1999, 13).

This key question followed: has policy implementability improved? This is revealing of the assumptions of classic views of policy, stressing the implementation issue while assuming that correct policies are knowable. Riedel and Turley can be contrasted with Vasavakul (1996) and her concern to establish whether the assumptions of classic views of policy yet hold. For those holding classic views, any idea that intentionality lacked a viable site was anathema, and reform and policy change were the clear duty of the party.

Reflections

Although space is limited, in two areas the Vietnamese case study poses questions about exotic doctrine. As far as the party was concerned, the most important external doctrines relating to development policy up until the early 1990s came from the USSR. These were exotic, but not capitalist. They failed, and histories exist that analyze this (de Vylder and Fforde 1996; Fforde 2007). Here we can point to development of an autonomous history evoked by Smail (1972) perhaps comparable in some ways to Bello's (1982) arguments about the resistance of the Philippines to development doctrine, also Western but in that case capitalist.

I have also argued elsewhere (de Vylder and Fforde 1996) that during the 1980s Vietnamese thinkers and policy-advisers created a set of ideas to explain what was happening around them. This was a local rather than an exotic development doctrine; it was doctrine in the sense that it was taught and—like WC ideas as they were pushed into the World Bank in the early 1980s—bitterly resented by bearers of old ideas. There is little evidence that Soviet experts who also set out to create a transition doctrine of their own in the mid-1980s had had any contact with these processes. Accounts suggest that their own experience led

---

[iv]There are other accounts. See Fforde 2007, arguing that central economic bodies at times strongly opposed the apparent interests of SOEs.

them to conclude, like their Vietnamese colleagues, that a conservative transition was possible and could leave their own party in power, as in China. This did not come to pass (Ellman and Kontorovich 1998; Fforde 2009).

It seems hard to imagine that the puzzles proposed by Vasavakul (1993) and de Vylder and Fforde (1996) would matter so much if Vietnam were not so widely proposed as an example of success. These anomalies are related to a questioning of the validity of classic views of policy. Specifically, they cast doubt on the persuasiveness of arguments that *assume* change is policy-driven, and they do this by mounting various arguments that deny agency and intentionality to the VCP. But these positions do not adopt Marxist approaches that subject agency to the requirements of capitalism, whether from pro- or antiparty stances. Whether their accounts are persuasive remains to be seen, but to the extent that they are accepted they point toward wider ways of thinking about intentionality *within* change processes that do not require assessing policies as correct in the terms used by classic views of policy. This points to thinking of development studies as studies of intentionality in social change, rather than—classically—as judgments of whether policies are correct and examination of conditions for their implementation.

CHAPTER 10

Thailand—"Success without Intention, and the Search for Cause"

Introduction

The literature on Thailand is well developed, and the apparent success of the country contrasts with a frequent sense of puzzlement, related to a search for cause—how can there be success *without* intentionality expressed in development policy? Is the success no more than a "subsequent event"? If the Philippine literature, dealing with apparent failure, looks for agency and hoped-for intentionality, then the Thai literature, dealing with apparent success, looks for cause: if not policy, clear ex ante, then what? How did it happen?

Two puzzles in particular challenge many assumptions: first, the coincidence of massive corruption with rapid economic growth, and, second, the blurred or weak developmental state, with little sign of intended development beyond maintenance of macroeconomic stability. Both of these appear to be anomalies.

A clear example of a specific approach dealing with the first puzzle is the theory of competitive clientelism advanced by Doner and Ramsay (1997). It is useful to start with a short discussion. What is clientelism, and why is it an issue? Businesspersons and others seek out patrons within the state to gain support under various forms. They seek to become clients of political leaders. This, however, may kill the goose that lays the golden eggs and stifle growth as levels of corrupt extraction rise. Why might this not happen? If clientelism is competitive, Doner and Ramsay argue, this does not necessarily curb development, for patrons may compete for clients, preventing any single patron, or patron clique, from gouging at excessively high levels. Their comparison of Thailand with the Philippines drives this home:

> Separated from land ownership, the interests of Sino-Thai firms were profoundly commercial and export-oriented. Moreover, they needed the backing of Thai political patrons, even as the latter relied on Sino-Thai entrepreneurs both to generate revenues for the state and to provide them with personal finances necessary for a soft landing in the case of political adversity. (275)

147

Philippine state officials, Doner and Ramsay argue, had to contend with an oligarchy both landed and politically organized. This had sufficient leverage to undermine institutional and economic reforms. So they argue that the *competitive* nature of Thai clientelism is a possible explanation for why clientelism may accompany good economic performance. Doner and Ramsay search for, and so identify for their theory, *causes* of Thai development success. One cause of Thailand's anomalous capacity to grow fast while remaining deeply corrupt is that policy is not needed to correct corruption because aspects of Thai society mute its effects. Cause is then found, solving the problem of development, in specific aspects of Thai life. One may note in passing that this assumes that corruption is a problem for development. Evidence from, say, the late nineteenth-century US or from eighteenth-century Britain would suggest otherwise, reminding us of the odd conclusions that universalistic assumptions lead to. Before going further into the literature, it is useful to outline recent development history.

An Outline of Postwar History

1911:   Nationality Act permits the taking of Thai nationality regardless of ethnic background.

1930s: Politicians set up SOEs and invite leading Chinese businesspersons to run them.

Early 1940s: War curtails imports, and foreign businesses are largely wiped out; various entrepreneurs, most born in Thailand of Chinese parentage, seize opportunities, often founding leading businesses. War also closes the foreign banks that had financed trade until then. Founding of Bangkok Bank by Chinese.

1947:   Coup places generals in power.

1950s: Growth averages 5 percent. US advisers argue against "state socialism" implied by SOEs, which in any case are performing badly. Sell-off of SOEs favors certain businesspersons, who acquire factories and monopolies; negotiation of textile deals with Japan also favors certain future tycoons.

1950s: Migrants' remittances stopped (early in decade). Initiation of state-supported agricultural-export-led growth (compare with East Asia) (late in decade).

1953:   Generals invest state funds in Bangkok Bank, cementing relations and creating politico-financial axis that lasted until the mid-1970s.

1960s: Thai developmentalism diverges from East Asia with stress upon agriculture; agriculture drives exports for next three decades. ISI weak and partly driven by revenue-seeking by the minister of finance on the back of successful agricultural exports. Growth averages 8 percent; US infrastructure investments (security-driven) put in roads to open up rural areas.

Government tariffs encourage import substitution (but not greatly); urban businesses move into manufacture from bases in crop trading, agribusiness, and import trade. Urban economy comes to be dominated by a small number of large conglomerates (in the 1960s and 70s), often based upon families that emerged with Thai banks in the 1940s. Bangkok Bank group most prominent. Japanese joint ventures (JVs) in textiles.

1960:   Establishment, under US assistance, of then-orthodox developmental institutions: the Board of Investment (BOI), the National Economic and Social Development Board (NESDB); and Budget Bureau. Teak, rubber, and rice are 2/3 of exports.

1962:   Changes in bank laws make banks more attractive than pawnshops; Chinese traders' savings generally channeled into banks, and deposits grow 20 percent a year for the next two decades. Government promises that banks will not be nationalized. Technocrats concerned about limits to agricultural-export-led growth.

1975:   Stock market founded. Government starts to borrow overseas.

By late 1970s: Thailand has 30 key conglomerates: 6 based upon banks, 9 in agribusiness, 6 based upon consumer goods, 2 in textiles, and the rest in basic process industries (building materials, chemicals, steel and glass). These business groups linked together through dense and complex links of business and family connections. Agriculture-based export growth starts to falter; business pressures the government to switch to East Asian export-oriented growth model. The government resists until 1984–85.

1978–81:   Oil imports triple in value in wake of second oil price shock.

1980:   Main exports are still rice and cassava chips.

Early 1980s: World Bank takes advantage of Thai need for money in wake of oil crisis by pushing a package of export reforms. Thai government continues with ISI and agricultural export focus.

1983–85:	Slump, and the finance sector is under great pressure. Urban sector starts to share deflationary burden with rural areas.
1985:	Start of large-scale foreign investment—driven by restructuring in East Asia.
Late 1980s:	Rapid growth in manufactures exports (30 percent yearly) shows policymakers that economy was moving in this direction before the policy had really shifted. Rapid gains in real incomes skewed toward middle classes and nouveau rich, feeding consumer and property development booms (property, finance, media and telecommunications, and suburban growth around Bangkok).
Very late 1980s:	Main exports now textiles and cheap-labor manufactures. Medium-tech exports start to increase sharply.
1988–89:	First round of tariff reductions accompanied introduction of the Value Added Tax (VAT), introduced once export push was clear to policymakers and pushed by business interests.
1990:	Peak of foreign direct investment (FDI) at 3 percent of GDP. Thai corporate investment at this time around 25 percent of GDP. Foreign stockbroking firms rush to gain access to Bangkok stock market and disseminate knowledge on how to access global funds.
1991:	Further tariff cuts; trade controls removed, and corporate and income tax structures reformed.
Early 1990s:	Developmental policies introduced to support manufactured-exports orientation: foreign policy, education, labor, finance, as boom pushed up revenues. Macroeconomic management techniques also changed to adapt to new situation. Main exports now computer parts and other electronics; semiconductor exports grow sharply (by mid-1990s, twice the value of rice). Financial sector changes qualitatively (starts in late 1980s) as traditional banking, with its basis in personal relationships between established groups, well linked through kin, friendship, and so forth and is replaced by exploitation of new forms of financial intermediary (stock market, takeovers, etc.).
1990s:	Domestic businesses spurred on by FDI boom; most investments financed by retained earnings but assisted by foreign inflows as well as financing through the new financial institutions. While existing conglomerates are

important, rapid growth sees many new companies successful, emerging from the existing, huge base of small trading, service, and manufacturing companies. Often US-trained, the FDI "third wave" of relocation in which technology is again higher than before—chemicals, petrochemicals, electronics, and machinery.

1992: The start of financial reforms and break of traditional banks' monopolies: legalization of offshore banking and issuing of licenses both to new Thai banks and foreign banks (former results in accelerated overseas borrowing).

1993: Launch of Thailand's first satellite by the Thaksin Shinawatra group. Extreme increase in inward investments into Bangkok stock market.

1994: Further tariff cuts.

Mid-1990s: Thai capital exports now considered "normal." Baht becomes even more competitive—to 388 yen by 1995.

1996: Economy starts to slow—the end of the property boom, declining export growth, and signs of weaknesses in financial institutions.

1997: Economic crisis as massive capital outflows occur, and Baht and Thai stock markets collapse.

2000s: Ongoing political problems after recovery from 1997 crisis. Major political changes, including a new constitution and the temporary rise to dominance of Thaksin as prime minister, toppled by a coup in 2006 and elections in 2008.

Analyses of Development Policy

Overview

Significant issues in Thailand's development are related to the central positions and interests that we have already encountered in Chapter 1 concerning intentionality, agency, and the identification of cause-effect relationships, which may be explored through the issue of what caused change. For those following classic views of policy, questioning the role of policy confronts the tendency of classic views to assume a central position for development policy.

We find arguments that policy was incoherent and ineffective, linking this to the lack of regulation that led to the 1997 crisis. This is a familiar realization argument, premised on the idea of knowable correct policy. But it confronts the evidence for developmental success rather than failure: without correct policy how may development occur?

Answers to this anomaly come, apart from Doner and Ramsay's (1997) treatment of competitive clientelism, from Unger (1998), who uses ideas of social capital to explain unintended success. In both cases we may see reinterpretations of what these scholars understand as conventional views of state policy and debates about the extent to which state policy existed and mattered. I find these usefully labeled as searches for cause. By contrast, Marxists such as Hewison (1997) argue that policy was *inevitably* supportive of capitalism. This should by now be familiar. Pragmatists, writers whose avoidance of universalistic frameworks make them hard to categorize, exemplified here by Pasuk and Baker (1996), take policy as having been important but treat the topic as atheoretical. They provide an example of a way in which classic views of policy are avoided.

Development Policy and Practice: Explanations of Intentionality and Change

The rich literature provides great detail about state actions. While the analyses are very different, they usually report various phases: SOEs, ISI, EOG, but disagree as to whether these were development models (that is, what happened) or development strategies in the sense of an intentional policy-set.

Pasuk and Baker

Pasuk and Baker (1996) deal with this with some subtlety. The issue here is the jump from identification of certain stereotypical attributes of policy to assuming that this shows the presence of intentionality and a state as agency, and what happens when this is avoided. For Pasuk and Baker, the core question is why Thailand came to play such a large role in the relocation of production. Their basic answer is that Thailand became a good place to do business. Government was pro-business, and there were few racial complications. Thai companies had built good relations with overseas companies over a generation (since the 1960s). It turned out that Thai firms could compete and so did not press for protection; the government knew this and so did not restrict capital flows. Why? Their answer is in terms of a multiplicity of causes.

> Because Thailand already had a strong momentum of growth over the four previous decades. Because this growth was based upon an expansive private sector which operated relatively free of political and social restrictions. Because this private sector was oriented outwards, and responded nimbly to the new opportunities of the globalizing decade. (Pasuk and Baker 1996, 54)

For Pasuk and Baker, the meaning of policy emerges from their historical discussion. Yet was the government just an observer? They think not. They point to effective macroeconomic management in making observers start to rethink the role of the state in Thai development, for previously the view had often been that it was soft and passive compared with successful East Asian countries. Yet the argument is clearly heading to a nuanced sense of the meaning of development policy. Their argument is consistently historical, arguing that the difference between Thailand and the East Asian Tigers has more to do with sequence and timing than with differences in intent. Thailand also made development a national crusade, with a technocracy and an institutional base to make this happen. Official visions were permeated by the idea that Thailand was a trading nation. Core to this was the Bank of Thailand, whose self-view was developmentally and politically independent. It had been set up in the early 1940s to fend off Japanese deprivations.

Also, the 1960s had seen US assistance in establishing then-orthodox developmental institutions—but these were used quite differently from their intentions. This happened, Pasuk and Baker state, for three reasons: first, Thailand was land- and resource-rich, so agriculture export-based development was feasible; second, ideas came from the US, rather than the French or German statism studied by Taiwan and Korea; third, the banks were neither nationalized nor used as developmental mechanisms. Instead, they were left alone to spot winners.

Thus the developmental toolkit in Thailand simply had a different makeup from that in East Asia. "'Policy as implemented' was different from 'policy-as-written' . . . and evolved from a subtle mixture of government vision and business ambition" (Pasuk and Baker 1996, 60). Thus, for Pasuk and Baker, the important policy shift to support manufactured exports that presaged the 1990s boom was due to pressure from the business lobby *after* this direction had started and was seen to be feasible by both business and government. The technocrats needed to be convinced. Thus, intentionality can be presented as noticeably reactive and post hoc, similar to pragmatic analyses of Vietnam and similarly not identifying any clear ex ante blueprint.

As the shift to a push for manufactures exports came through, Pasuk and Baker stress that policy changes came *after* practice had shown this strategy feasible. These included tariff reductions, as well as developmental/institutional changes across a range of fields: foreign policy, education, labor, and finance.

It is useful to treat the approach as pragmatic. A stress, consistent with Cowen and Shenton, upon the values and subjectivity underlying policy, without giving policy excessive status by introducing the idea that it may be correct, produces a nuanced and textured description. The argument therefore has a local flavor, and much of this argument derives from the focus upon subjectivity, as specific meanings of policy and policymaking are presented contextually. They thereby avoid classic views of policy by ignoring the issue of whether policy can be said to be correct. I now turn to an examination of contrasting approaches that do judge policy in such terms.

Hewison

Hewison (1997) focuses upon the multiple changes required for a society to become capitalist—the establishment of classes, of private property, of wage-commodity relations, and so forth. This is a normal and powerful Marxist perspective, asserting that capitalism requires institutions of certain types to support its basic logic. Hewison's treatment of agency, and more importantly the question of correct development, reflects the Marxist solution to the problem of development discussed by Cowen and Shenton.

The focus is upon the role of the state in Thailand's capitalist development. Hewison argues that the WB East Asian Miracle study advanced the idea that the state had been neither minimalist nor activist and that Thailand was a case in which the market had compensated for government failures and in which the state had been ineffective at interventions. Marxist approaches (see also Ungpakorn 2002), Hewison argues, by contrast look for links to explain how and why the state acts to support capital, but without any obvious *personal* links in terms of direct interests (for example, through the need to maintain the country's international position, while supporting private investment). This involves protecting private property and the interests of capital over labor—the relation of domination of labor by capital.

Hewison concludes that the question as to whether the Thai state supported business or not is sterile and narrow, for, of course it has: what may appear as choice is no such thing. Correct policy and correct development are determined by the requirements of capitalism. Agency has no true discretion in selecting between policies for that which is correct in terms of known cause-effect relations. This is a clear analysis of development as *immanent*, in which choice is an illusion.

Warr

By contrast, Warr adopts an approach that assumes that correct policy may be known and chosen based on knowledge of cause-effect relationships. Warr (1994) is a useful example of economic thinking that assumes that correct policy can be discovered through the application of economic methodology. Yet he starts by pointing out that the literature contains three elements:

- Writings by Thai, in Thai, that focus upon economic change and the dire social consequences as material improvement failed to be enjoyed by all social groups.

- A group of foreigners who casually attribute Thai economic success to neoliberal policies and ignore most of the problems the Thai focus upon.

- A second group of foreigners who find little positive in Thai economic growth and seem not very keen to find workable solutions to the big problems that exist.

This characterization of the literature reveals aspects of Warr's approach. Central, however, is an assumption that policy can be known to be correct and that the main problems with the existing literature are related to the lack of suitable effort to find out what real effects policy has been having, and with the need to develop better policies to cope with existing real problems. In his discussion of development policy, Warr examines sectoral interventions in preparation for a discussion of what could be done better.

Agriculture. Warr discusses the rice export tax, suspended in 1986. He argues simply that it reduced farmers' incomes and impeded technological change by changing the price-cost ratio. Other interventions are dealt with in similar manner. He argues that these policies introduce monopolistic elements, reducing efficiency.

Industry. Mainly, policy here is reported as related to the promotion of private investment by the Board of Investment. Other parts of the state also intervene but play a minor role (compare Rock 1995 in the section "The World Bank and Its Challengers" in this chapter).

Protection policy. Warr notes the existence of tariffs and controls on imports and exports. He reports that studies show that the protective system had been biased against agri-industries and the manufacturing sectors over the past three decades. The new export-oriented sectors were usually not protected, and in general protected industries tended to perform badly.

Warr confirms my earlier argument that positions that assume policy can be said to be correct or incorrect often provide little analysis of the overall process of change and the relative importance of policy in that process (because the latter is assumed). Policy is thus made to matter. This happens here. There is, despite the underlying view of the importance of policy, little that situates Warr's points in a discussion of just why Thailand grew so fast. If we compare Warr with Pasuk and Baker, we note that the latter are far less interested in identifying correct policy and spend far more time analyzing change.

Unger

We turn now to a perspective that assumes that correct development and development policy can be known and which copes with apparent anomalies by introducing contextual explanation. Unger (1998) has as its central argument the idea that a relative absence of cohesive groups within the Thai polity worked against policy deliberations, consensus formation, and the mobilization of broad political support. The paucity of social capital in Thailand had the effect of weakening efforts by Thais to cooperate in pursuit of shared goals (2).

Unger's main focus is the idea that policymakers must operate in a vacuum in the absence of social capital. They are autonomous, and this cuts any link between policymaking and associated interests. According to Unger, a Thai lack of associational culture thus explains why policy was not embedded. How, then, could Thailand develop? Central to his answer to this question is Chinese abilities to associate, which then explains developmental success in an absence of state agency by finding as a cause particular characteristics of Chinese Thai.

Unger examines two big projects—the Bangkok Mass Transit (MT) System and the Eastern Seaboard Project—that aimed to develop a second large city in the south of the country to reduce problems caused by Bangkok's primacy. In the case of the Bangkok MT System, Unger argues that social capital proved too weak, concerned interests could not associate, state practice was therefore poor, and the problem was not solved. Collective interests remained unmet, in a classic expression of the collective action problem. Traffic jams continued.

In the case of the Eastern Seaboard project, however, businesses showed that they could associate to improve state practice in their collective interests. The problem was thus solved. Thus Unger's focus upon policy as state practice, ex post rather than ex ante, helps his analysis.

The World Bank and Its Challengers

It is useful to look at approaches that take a strong view of the importance of implementing correct policies. Again, note that I am selecting texts to examine roles policy plays in different approaches. The literature is not seeking to create convergence to agreement, so that writers' conclusions and interests are relatively easy to predict given their approaches. It is interesting to look at the Thailand country study produced for the WB East Asian Miracle study and referenced within it as the predominant support for the study's conclusions. It argues that development happens if governments get out of the way of the market.

Rock (1995) argues that the bank's position is based upon weak data, and he calls for more research. His position may be thought of as the common one that argues (like Baer et al. 1999) that cause-effect relations are known, but the posited ones are in error. He starts with an exposition and critique of what he calls the standard view that Thai policy intervention was too limited and incoherent to have significant effect. He argues that the neoliberal position is based upon the inability of those particular parts of the Thai state charged with industrial support to act coherently. The Bank of Thailand, a key player, was thus said to have had only very limited influence over sectoral policy. Similar arguments, he says, are applied to trade policy, for facilitation of permits by one agency would be blocked by others. He points out, however, that *existence of incoherence does not prove that policy did not matter.*

Rock argues that in the 1980s, policies that had supported agricultural exports shifted to support nontraditional manufactures. He says that the combination of rising effective rates of protection and export subsidies was reminiscent of South Korea in its early stages. It is clear where this is heading: intentionality is being pushed upon the state and space created to discuss correct policy. Cause is found in an assertion of the existence of intentionality.

The Thai Health Sector—Two Approaches to Policy Analysis

Finally, it is useful to look at two contrasting approaches to policy in an important sector: health. These approaches both bring out different treatments of the issue of state capacity, as well as give informative access to different approaches.

Bennet and Tangcharoensathien (1994) work with an underlying assumption that actual performance is suboptimal; Thailand could get better morbidity results with less spending if health-care provision were organized differently. This is, therefore, usefully treated as classic policy analysis. It explains that state policy and actions have not led to better outcomes and can usefully be understood as statist. Bennet and Tangcharoensathien position this argument within a historical analysis that largely explains state actions in terms of mistakes (doctrinally determined) and the wider political context.

Problems resulting from rapid growth of private sector providers led, they say, to reactions from the early 1990s. Possible solutions were then resisted by entrenched interests. There was no plan; measures were taken to open up the ground, reduce regulation, and support private expansion. But there was no regulation of the expanding private sector until problems arose.

Fundamental to this approach, as we saw from Grindle and Thomas, is the notion that entrenched interests are central to understanding change. What do they identify under this heading? First, they point to officials and others running the insurance schemes; second, private suppliers; third, the lack of voice of those who would gain from public supply—farmers and workers. The authors also note a lack of strong voice from within the public health sector.

It is worth questioning the empirical basis for the position taken, specifically that these interests had significant influence; how believable is this? This approach tends to assume and/or assert that such forces exist to explain policy development and take-up. This can then be viewed (and coped with) as an example of classic policy analysis.

By contrast, Green (2000) argues that rational policy is a myth and that any policy debate has to be seen politically. Policymakers are part of that political economy, not outside it. For him policy issues are simply what people are discussing, not what "real problems" are said by some analysts to be. Green identifies these issues as lack of private sector supply to rural areas, relative quality of care (public vs. private), the effects of unregulated private sector growth on choice of technology, and leakages of (state-trained) staff to the private sector.

To what extent are these related to any plan designed to secure certain morbidity patterns at a certain cost? Not much. Note here again my concern about empirics, which are very different. For example, how persuasive are arguments that what people are discussing does indeed reflect their political concerns? This article tends to see data in terms of discourse, linked to the subjective concerns of various groups. Bennet and Tangcharoensathien (1994) tended to read various interests into the situation.

This is a revealing example of method. We may note that Green takes no position on the rationality of current global concerns and discussions about health policy, simply noting them. Unlike Bennet and Tangcharoensathien, however, Green points to substantial inputs to rational policy discussion (various technical assistance and research activities) and also to three occasions when state practice changed significantly (the integration of preventive/curative service provision in the 1960s, free rural health care, and primary health care, PHC, in the 1970s). Perhaps this shows how a relaxation of the knowability assumption permits greater interest in local policy discussions and state practices that are now harder to dismiss as simply wrong.

Green concludes that state intervention is an important part of the political economy of health. He refers to various decisions: to support the private sector from the 1980s, to carry out public initiatives deemed important (for example, rural health care in the wake of the 1970s). Within this, he concludes that the ebb and flow of interest groups is both proactive (attacking regulation, creating space for private sector growth) and reactive (creating agencies to respond to saturation, securing additional funding for Social Security). And he stresses his conclusion that among Thai commentators and policymakers, there has been a clear learning process within the ebb and flow of wider global doctrines. But he clearly does not view state intervention through any assumption that it can be thought of as correct. In this way he finds cause in his discussion of process, clear to him and in his way *after* the event (Pressman and Wildavsky 1973).

Reflections

It is useful to examine how different approaches deal with the combination of apparent development success without clear development policy. For writers for whom development is immanent process, this is unimportant, as issues of intentionality and agency are subsumed under the overall assumption that policy essentially acts to support capitalism and therefore the analytical task is to explicate this in a particular context. For others, for whom development is (or should be) intentional product, various aspects of Thai experience create tensions, as policy is defined and its impact discussed. If this cannot easily be done, as in the case of Unger, then, as for Doner and Ramsay, local analytical frameworks push against common universalistic views, though tending to stay within a wider discourse.

The approaches of Unger (1998) and Doner and Ramsay (1997) thus create tensions with assertions of universalism and may provoke reflection, such as on the assumptions behind them. But, as Fforde (2005a) reported regarding the effects of Levine and Zervos, this need not have any major negative impact on core assumptions. But this is not the end of the story. Pasuk and Baker show a pragmatic approach, pointing toward localized analytical frameworks that do not fit and are not self-consciously fitted into some wider system.

This suggests that those adopting classic views of policy may again be pushed, this time by the Thai case study, away from the classic view that correct policy is central, associated with a siting of intentionality upon an agency and underpinned by knowably correct intervention logics. What they would seem to be pushed toward, as with the Vietnamese case, is to view intentionality in terms of discussions about the acceptability of "subsequent events," abandoning the belief in knowable cause-effect relations. But the review here suggests that the extent to which this happens may well be rather limited.

CHAPTER 11

The Philippines—"Intention without Success, and the Search for Agency"

Introduction

Prisms and Kaleidoscopes—The Blame Game

In some ways, the Philippines presents clear support for the methodological approach of this book: we can learn much from learning to cope with the frameworks through which study of the development of the country has to be approached. Central to coping with these are the issues of intentionality, agency, and intervention logic.

The literature in the Philippines shows this clearly, with much energy focused upon aspects of failure discussed in precisely these terms—lack of intentionality, lack of agency, and adoption of intervention logics assessed to be incorrect. And just why and how this could be leads to discussion about how intentionality and agency could or should be created (and, of course, why so far this has not happened, as is often argued[i]).

If, as is rather clear, the Philippines stands in stark contrast to Vietnam and Thailand as a picture of "intention without success," then certain questions arise. First, what, if anything, was the developmental intention, and what values drove it? It will become clear that developmental intentionality is hard to relate to local politics, and so such intentions fast appear as lacking articulation with the local; rather, they are perhaps too easily presented as exotic, alien to many Philippine concerns. Therefore, development failure may be reinterpreted as a successful resistance to alien intentions. This leads us to a second question: what values and preconceptions are the foundations to the evaluation of "subsequent events"? And this will return us to a discussion of just how and by whom "subsequent events" of development are judged to be correct.

Fundamental to much of the relevant literature seems to be the colonial experience. The Vietnamese fought long and hard for political independence, and the Thai never lost theirs—at least formally, ignoring debates about neo-imperialism. Related arguments, though, seem to me

---

[i]The famous poem by Kipling quoted in Chapter 1 referred to the Philippines.

to have great force for the Philippines, and to act as a strong undercurrent to much of the literature.

History—Of Whom, By Whom?

Philippine histories, like those of many if not most countries, are complicated and contentious. Largely populated by the first waves of Malay immigrants from the north, who were then apparently leapfrogged by later groups heading south, the people of the area now subject to the Philippine government are said to be unusual, in a Southeast Asian (SEA) perspective. Common arguments emphasize that they were long-colonized by the first wave of European projection of power far from Europe, the Spanish, and were subsequently an American colony until gaining full independence, de jure, after World War II. As is often said in introductory courses on the making of SEA, for this latter reason they were initially excluded from the American geopolitical definition of the region that emerged during WWII.

To cope with current development policy stances, I look in some detail at the twentieth-century history of the Philippines, which follows in the next sections. Ideas arguing for programs of marginal or partial reforms are illuminated by themes in the academic literature that emphasize relative immobility and unhappy results from models derived from exotic doctrine, including developmental ones. Thus, Kerkvliet (1980) argues that the failed Huk risings after WWII happened in part because of changes in the self-identity of landlords who had obtained new ideas, often derived from the US, of what it meant to be a landlord. They were far less enthusiastic about meeting traditional obligations to those dependent upon them—who objected. Arguments about the implementability of Philippine development policy refer to political unrest. Erickson et al. (2003) and Sidel (1998) provide accessible accounts, as does Rutten (2000).

According to many indicators, the Philippines is a developmental failure. This is argued in many ways, varying from issues such as economic growth rates to lack of convergence with perceived objects of emulation. It can be argued that many writings focus strongly upon mismatches between what is and what could and should be.

This arguably has strong roots in how histories have been written and read. The 1898 revolution notwithstanding, narratives argue that US colonial reforms were a top-down modernization that created a constitutional framework reliant upon rule by law, leading to what is presented as chronic tension between ideals of legal texts and realities of state practice. For some writers this amounts to a state that has botched the task of becoming a motor of development (for example, Woodiwiss 1998, 142) and is an example of failed trusteeship.

Before examining the discussion, let us look at a chronology.

An Outline of Events

1898:	US replaces Spain as colonial power.
1935:	US Tydings-McDuffie Act commits to Philippine independence "in ten years," brings in universal suffrage for the literate, and creates Philippine Commonwealth. Constitutionally powerful president in practice subject to powerful congress.
1939–45:	The Philippines suffers severe physical damage from World War II.
1946:	Independence from US; Bell Trade Act attempts to impose free trade upon the Philippines.
	From independence, pattern of unstable patronage networks behind electoral process established and survives through to present day.
1947:	Military Bases Agreement signed with US (Subic Bay).
Late 1940s:	Direct controls upon imports and foreign exchange imposed in response to drain of foreign exchange—a result of a surge of imports of manufactures.
1950s:	State-backed import-substituting industrialization (ISI) and rapid manufacturing growth. Anti-Chinese policies push Chinese out of retailing and into manufacturing. Rapid politicization of public service with temporary appointments, although most remained well-trained. High proportion of domestic investment funded from overseas. Very large payments to Filipino veterans.
1951:	Security Treaty signed with US.
1957:	Tariff protection introduced.
Early 1960s:	Economy fails to respond to reduction in protectionism, with little restructuring. Beginnings of steep fall in prices of Philippine exports compared with imports—especially sugar—and of a shift away from agricultural exports to garments and electronics.
1960s:	Gross domestic product (GDP) growth in 1960s slower than in 1950s. Growth of private banks. Stagnation in manufacturing employment leads to debate over what should replace ISI. "Nationalist" industrialization group advocated tighter controls on foreign investment, nationalization, extension of ISI to capital goods, and massive

income redistribution with land reform. Conservatives advocate liberalization by reducing protection and attracting foreign capital. Local entrepreneurs do not support "nationalist" position because of its redistributionist elements.

1962:   Macapagal elected, moves against ISI without clear economic success. Further shift from direct import controls to tariffs. Partial removal of protection in favor of export agriculture, under pressure from International Monetary Fund (backed by US). Hundred percent devaluation of peso. Severe deflation; many businesses taken over by foreign interests.

1965–66:   Marcos becomes president and recruits technocrats to set up export-oriented growth (EOG) institutions.

1967:   Investment Incentives Act and 1970 Exports Incentives Act reserve crowded consumer goods sectors for Filipinos even as exports and capital goods for foreign direct investment (FDI) are granted important incentives.

1969:   Mariveles export processing zone (EPZ) legislation passed (modeled on Kaohsiung in Taiwan).

Late 1960s: Rising pressure from WB/IMF to liberalize and shift to EOG; models cited were Brazil and South Korea.

1969:   Marcos runs down foreign exchange reserves in buying second election success.

1970s: Marcos development program emphasizes EOG, New International Division of Labor, free-trade zones. Rapid growth of manufactured exports. Philippines revealed as less popular destination for FDI, especially Japanese. Tariff protection remains high until late 1970s. Weak investment in infrastructure and other assistance. Rural economy grows, helped by Green Revolution and agribusiness, without emergence of new rich in rural areas.

Early 1970s: WB forces implementation of 1970 Export Incentives Act (subsidies to exports mount). WB pushes for duty-free imports for exporters, plus other incentives. Push to subsidize EPZs. Strikes banned, and free trade unions pressured by establishment of industrial labor federations and deregistration. Cuts made to minimum wage.

Early 1970s: EOG leads to changes in labor regime, with new export industries—electronics, garments—often employing women, with very weak or nonexistent unions. Working conditions deteriorate.

Early 1970:	Foreign exchange reserves reach very low levels. IMF/WB push for peso devaluation (60 percent) and get it. Again (as in 1962), severe deflation and many business bankruptcies, but protectionist system remains in place. US seen as fearful of rising political power of Filipino business interests hostile to US domination.
1970:	Constitutional Convention meets. Political calls for "nationalist" development from business interests. Foreign investment outflow. Street protests from nationalist left. Left and right allied in anti-US feelings.
1972:	Supreme Court "Quasha" decision decrees that lands acquired by Americans since 1946 had been acquired illegally.
1972 Sept.:	Declaration of martial law. New central political actors—Marcos' cronies and the opposition—largely *not* from old landed oligarchy or urban bourgeoisie. Assets of some old families confiscated, but majority depoliticized.
1975:	Change in citizenship requirements permits Chinese to own property legitimately.
1975:	Labor unrest comes to the surface.
Late 1970s:	Very rapid growth in exports (garments and electronics). Steep drops in real wages.
Late 1970s:	Renewed pressure from WB for removal of protection, resisted by pressure from national consumer goods producers. Policy debate between WB and some Filipino economists about whether ISI should continue in capital and intermediate goods sectors.
1978:	WB position on full-scale liberalization (100 percent end to ISI) established; resisted by Filipino technocrats, by now not so happy with EOG. Certain local businesspeople want to carry out large-scale joint ventures (JVs) with foreigners in capital and intermediate goods sectors.
1979:	Government announces plan to implement eleven big industrial projects; opposed by WB. Government argues these are export-oriented and not nationalist because financed by overseas private sector. Plan vetoed by WB and so failed.
1979:	Labor problems—invasion of EPZs with strike at Ford plant in Bataan EPZ.
Very late 1970s:	Problems with EOG.
1981 Jan.:	Cosmetic lifting of martial law. Worker unrest forces Marcos to promise to lift ban on strikes.

1983:	Default on international loans; Central Bank switches to targeting monetary aggregates.

1983–84:   GDP collapses.

1986:   Fall of Marcos regime, driven by the middle class. Political power thereafter tends to devolve to moderate liberal leadership, supported by the Catholic church and corporate interests damaged by martial law.

Late 1980s: Dismantling of sugar and coconut monopolies; creation of Presidential Commission on Good Government (PCGG). Privatization of Philippine Airlines and Petron. Rather rapid GDP growth. Very rapid real estate development.

1990s: Old oligarchy under increasing pressure as bourgeoisie widens and becomes more variegated. Regional investments tending to replace US investments, and focus of development increasingly regional. Philippine elites increasingly focused upon Asian Miracle as source of values and goals. Gradual political stabilization of the state; economic liberalization. Aquino and Ramos both committed to free-market capitalism, defined as privatization and deregulation of trade and investment. Manufacturing output growth slow by comparison with other countries in the region, often based upon small and medium enterprises (SMEs)—larger groups tending to stay in real estate, etc. Strong trend to professionalization of management—non-family—employed by family owners. Rapid improvement in housing, car ownership, etc., for these groups, and also for families of overseas contract workers. Rapid growth of NGOs as middle-class phenomenon.

Economy: rather fast export growth, especially in 1998–99, primarily in electronics. Macroeconomic balance maintained through crisis as Philippines benefits from longstanding banking sector reforms and lack of real estate boom prior to crisis.

Early 1990s: GDP growth slows temporarily.

1992:   Closure of US bases. US aid cuts. Ramos elected—strongly supported by large section of urban business community and military officers known for their resentment of the old landed oligarchy. Ramos economic policy designed to increase competition through breaking up private monopolies. Breakup of telecommunications monopoly.

Late 1990s: Growing sense of political stability. Expectations for reductions in import tariffs, removal of restrictions on foreign investment, and deregulation of banking and oil industries. Major problems with electricity supply.

1998:   Election of Estrada. Reforms slow.

2001:   Departure of Estrada, new president, from technocratic and oligarchic background. Few signs of an energetic reform agenda.

Issues in the Literature: Model and Muddle

Introduction

We find a strong tendency in this literature toward comparison of "model with muddle." Granted that the Philippines has been so often classed as a failure, the issue of success means that fundamental change must be identified or denied, and *attributed*. For us, then, a central issue in approaching comparative analyses is the framework used to cope with intentionality. Success is often predicated upon reform capacity—the ability to implement or hinder the implementation of doctrine that remains exotic.

What, then, would a major change be? How would we know whether things had changed? We can note the relevance here of different approaches to political economy:

- Statists look for ways of securing a platform in state power for neoliberal reforms.

- Marxists look for changing economic structures and interests linked to them.

- Pluralists look for changing social organization and political action.

For example, one author takes the common position that because of a lack of state autonomy, the Philippine state cannot pursue goals that are not simply reflective of the demands or interests of social groups, classes, or society. This is a nice articulation of a transcendentally rooted correct development doctrine, a statement of the impossibility of solving the realization problem. This he attributes to four enduring social features:

> A resilient oligarchy rooted in land and export agriculture; tradition of authoritarian-clientelistic political leadership in a politically fractured polity; history of significant popular opposition movements erupting at critical conjunctures; and continuing marked dependence on foreign external resources. (Villacorta 1994, 68, quoting Temario Rivera, *Class, the state and foreign*

capital: the politics of Philippine industrialization, 1950–1986, PhD
University of Wisconsin 1991, 190.)

How, then, could there ever be progress?

The 1990s and the Politics of Executive Power

We will see that, at least until the Estrada period, it seemed possible to
view the 1990s as a period of fundamental change. Strikingly, after the closure of Subic Bay in 1991–92 there were no US bases in the Philippines.

Economic growth in the 1990s indeed saw indicators of a shift to
greater outward orientation, with rapid growth of manufactured exports,
helped by Japanese and other regional investors' decisions to locate in
the country. The WB praised the Philippines for orthodox reforms. (See
also praise from the Australian government in the section "The 1990s and
the politics of executive power," in this chapter). The effects of the 1997
Asian crisis were muted by the lack of excessive lending to Philippine
companies beforehand, and the lack of a boom. This was praised and
taken to imply capacity to implement policies to secure macroeconomic
stability.

> . . . this paper takes the latter view, namely, that recent structural
> changes in the Philippines do stand some chance of being sus-
> tained, since they have come to correspond with a changed per-
> ception of national interest and purpose, especially amongst the
> elite. These changes were occasioned by a deep sense of national
> crisis, a reconstructed strategy for emulating the success of the
> newly industrializing countries, and no less important, some real
> opportunities to accommodate incumbent interests in a liberal-
> izing environment. (de Dios 1999a)

The Philippines possesses, on paper, a formal constitution derived from
that of the US. If developmental agency—so far thought to be lacking—
is to be found, then the obvious questions to ask are: *Is the executive powerful and relatively autonomous?* and *If not, why not?*

Statist developmentalism accompanies both the desire and the view
that politics should support economic reform—seen as the implementation of correct policies. Consistent with this, as we have seen many times,
is the search for an answer to the question: what are the political forces
acting to determine state policy and practice? We can note, yet again, that
this involves a wide range of assumptions. At its root is the search for effective agency to embrace intentionality as a vehicle for what is presented as
correct development and development policy. So long as this remains no

more than a search, we are on familiar ground, where discussion focuses upon *implementation*, because correct policies are assumed to exist.

We find positions that present evidence for widespread illegality, as non-enforcement of labor laws and commercial laws is commonplace (Woodiwiss 1998; Erickson et al. 2003). Such arguments encourage readers to believe that state sovereignty, or the relative power of the state in the state-society relationship, is a central issue.

Thus, what sorts of analysis does the literature present to explain the forces that determine state policy and practice in the Philippines? In developed versions, these forces are seen as interests linked to past overseas domination by the Spanish and Americans. Such oligarchic families, moving from land and politics to the exploitation of business opportunities in ISI-protected sectors as their power bases, are identified as the source of political opposition to reform. And such interests may also be linked to arguments about patron-client structures, used by politicians to gain and retain support. In another variant, similar groups can be argued to be the basis for crony capitalism. This ends up presenting the reader with a powerful pathology: a weak state dominated by conservative forces that can and will block both laws and their implementation.

De Dios vs. Hutchcroft

Let us look at two contrasting expressions of these approaches: those of de Dios (1999b) and Hutchcroft (1998). We will start with the latter, written by an American political scientist. Hutchcroft is deeply pessimistic about state developmentalism in the Philippines, and it is not surprising that practitioners such as de Dios and others argue that he overemphasizes the role played by the oligarchs and patron-client relations in preventing the state from acting developmentally. Hutchcroft seeks to explain why the country's large development assets have failed to produce sustained developmental success.

What are the political prerequisites of economic success? The Philippines, Hutchcroft argues, is hindered by

- Patrimonial features that hinder the development of more advanced forms of capitalist accumulation. By this he means that officials' actions are not predictable but arbitrary, based upon their particular interests rather than their position in a rational bureaucracy.

- Important particular aspects of Philippine patrimonial politics. Here Hutchcroft contrasts situations in which rent beneficiaries are primarily *within* the state (bureaucratic capitalism) to those in which they are mainly *outside* it (booty capitalism). The latter, he argues, holds in the Philippines.

Thus the Philippines presents particularly strong barriers to a rational-legal state, mainly because of pressures *against* the emergence of new social forces able to encourage change. The oligarchs are in charge, and there is little incentive for them to do anything to change things.

Central to Hutchcroft's analysis is his view of the state and oligarchy in the Philippine banking sector. This is evocative of other discussions about the potential for banks to play a role as developers. In a nice argument *against* those who seek progress through structural change, he points to the use of the banking sector as a source of plunder for oligarchs moving out from old economic bases (that is, into ISI and then on into exports), and the importance of the use of private commercial banks as a way of doing this. Conservative forces, once politically entrenched, translate themselves into new forms as the situation changes. This is, of course, a firm foundation for profound if not tautological pessimism.

Hutchcroft's argument identifies sources *within* the Philippines that corrupt not only the essential value of US-inspired institutions but also those particular latent opportunities that should embody the drive to develop. Hutchcroft's particular focus is upon the roles of the banks, meant to act as intermediaries for savings and agents of change but, according to his analysis, too often diverted from this role by the interests of entrenched oligarchic families.

Hutchcroft examines Ramos' reforms and concludes that these remain limited, because cartels remain. The main push for reform has come, Hutchcroft says, from a committed core of reformers within the administration; and he asserts that the diversified conglomerates of oligarchic families remain dominant. This view is shared by a World Bank report (2000) that nevertheless contrasts with Hutchcroft's pessimism, asserting the possibility of progressive change. Such optimistic arguments refer to wider social changes, such as an emergent middle class (for example, Pinches 1996), but these tend to deny developmental agency.

Thus it is useful to examine an analysis of ways in which insulated technocrats were able to use state power when they had high-level political support. This is provided by de Dios (1999a), in an assertion of the power of classic views of policy.

At the time of his writing, de Dios was a professor of economics at the University of the Philippines. He creates space for classic policy action in the *indeterminate* nature of his analytical framework: the future is not clear, and options are open. The state offers itself (to whom?) as a site for agency. This can be compared with Hutchcroft, who emphasizes the *unchanging* nature of patron-client relations, the implied weak executive, and the associated assumed importance of de-linking executive decisions from popular pressures. De Dios is practical and pragmatic. Recall that he is discussing a constitution modeled on that of the US, with its ideas of the importance of a separation of powers so as to limit the powers of the executive.[ii]

In developing his position, de Dios argues that the executive branch tends *by its very nature* to articulate national concerns, in comparison with the particularism of the legislature. Thus, in his view, the Marcos period amounted to an attempt to link "civil society" anew to the executive, thus explaining Marcos' attack on the old oligarchies as asserting the powers of the executive. De Dios thus builds up his position: Changes since 1987 did not merely return things to the way they had been; rather, martial law had increased opportunities for a classic siting of developmental agency in the state.

Further improving the chances of success, de Dios argues, were ways in which traditional patron-client relations had been undermined by new sources of wealth, by urbanization, and by incomplete rural reform. He also refers—as do others—to a growing middle class and mass organizations, such the widespread popularity of NGOs.

In formal political terms, constitutional change since Marcos had strengthened the executive. Single-term presidents with six years in office, de Dios argues, gained in relation to congressmen, who were subject to re-election every three years. The end of the old two-party system improved opportunities to use the presidency as a vehicle for development. Pork-barrel politics also granted political opportunities to an executive trying to push reform—value-added tax (VAT) and oil deregulation were pushed through by bribing congressmen behind closed doors.

De Dios concludes, in stark contrast to Hutchcroft, that there was political space for reform and economic liberalization driven by policy, and that this centered upon building up executive authority and power.

I find this a valuable analysis. Note certain elements: first, the notion of an underlying process of social and ideological change both acting as the object of policy and conditioning the extent to which the state can act as an agent of change. De Dios thinks in terms of the importance of the

---

[ii]The possibilities that this offers for sectarian capture of the executive with a constitution modeled on that of the US seem to me to be obvious and inherent in the politics that de Dios (here) and Rodrik (elsewhere) discuss. This certainly influences my own views of the Vietnam War. For the views of a practitioner, see Acheson (1969) passim, especially pp. 99 et seq. For the views of an academic, see Roberts (2008). Both emphasize the issue of the lack of domestic sovereignty created by the US Constitution—in the terms used in this book, the problems facing Americans in creating developmental agency that has adequate, perhaps democratically derived, authority, and thus political power. This problem arguably also faced the VCP in the first years of the twenty-first century (Fforde 2004 and 2005b): international sovereignty is not domestic hegemony—interestingly, a point made by Acheson about the US.

Rules of the Game, both in the formal constitutional sense and in how these regulations and laws are used.

De Dios' analysis reads well beside the discussion of Grindle and Thomas in Chapter 3. Like them, he does not ask how correct policies are known to be correct, simply assuming that they are.

De Dios and Hutchcroft can therefore be understood in terms of the different ways in which they cope with the notion of development as product. Hutchcroft is deeply pessimistic about the possibility of the state's acting as site of intentional development; de Dios disagrees. This brings out their differences as well as their shared classic view of policy.

But there remains the issue of predictability: Will "what works there work here"? From a mainstream neoclassical quarter, we can observe an official Australian study (EAAU 1998) that focuses upon bad policy as the central explanation for poor economic performance. By contrast, Bello (1982) also focuses upon the idea of bad policy, but this time from the opposite direction, founded upon his hostility toward what he calls the neoclassical development model. The contrast between the two is informative.

Agency Assumed? Official Analyses from Australia

The approach of the Australian government's East Asian Analytical Unit (1998) is close to that of the WC. Economic disaster happened as a result of bad policies, and change came because this realization convinced the government and business elite to undertake major reforms. Policies of export-led growth and private-sector development, it is asserted, are the reliable cause of better economic performance.

Stark use of cause-and-effect metaphors is abundant: improved trade performance is attributed to reform (seen as increased openness); FDI increased because of liberalization of the investment regime; the business environment had improved but remained subject to incomplete architecture. And across a wide range, the study sees reforms following the contemporary approved model (WC) being put into place (for example, privatized power generation) but disapproves of attempts to implement land reform (inefficient) and encourage rice self-sufficiency (crop diversification is advised, with major state support under various channels, all market-supporting). The text is a familiar example of strong belief in known cause-and-effect relationships.

Thus—keeping in mind that the text was written in 1998—the outlook was said to be good, because the external environment for trade and investment was now more open, and the country committed to reform, with clear outward orientation. It was expected that whoever won the 1998 elections would remain committed to the reform program. This did not come to pass, as we now know.

This issue of the potential of the state as a subject for development, a site for the embrace of intentionality by agency, is also explored by Mackie and Villegas (1993) in a thoughtful analysis that we will examine after we contrast the EAAU with Bello.

A Radical Perspective

For thinking about comparative development policy, Bello (1982) is very useful. Bello is hostile to orthodoxy. He sets up his argument in terms of an account of what he portrays as the attempt by the WB and IMF to impose upon the Philippines—granted Marcos' martial law—similar policies to the East Asian newly industrializing countries (NICs). He uses this to point to flaws in the economic and political assumptions of the EOG model as he defines it.

Note elements of his historical framework: that policy debates prior to Marcos saw the left and the national bourgeoisie united in supporting protectionism, with free-trade forces seen as pro-US and therefore politically weak. Furthermore, ISI was less politically attractive because many protected companies were American. Yet the economy was not doing well, and the partial dismantling of ISI in 1962 was followed by poor economic results. Note here an apparent failure of *partial* liberalization.

Exotic doctrine came in hard and strong under Marcos' team of technocrats recruited from the US: EPZs were set up, ISI was partially dismantled, and significant IMF support was gained. But political struggles meant that ISI was not fully dismantled, with the result of labor unrest as nationalist forces mobilized. The incentives scheme for exporters, combined with the need to finance infrastructure for the EPZs, was too much for the macroeconomy, leading to balance-of-payments problems and inflation. The WB was satisfied with the export-incentives system but unsatisfied with the slow dismantling of ISI. By the end of the 1970s, EOI seemed not to have generated much in the way of exports or employment. Failure to attract much FDI was also a factor. A central unanswered question here is just why exports growth was limited, and at the end of the day, I feel this is not clear.

The WB's policies at the time, according to Bello, were basically political and intended to defuse social unrest. Yet the opposite occurred—in Bello's opinion, largely because in the urban areas the Bank tried to destroy barriers to imports and forestall nationalist controls over investment. Labor unrest and poor export performance meant that these barriers could not be overcome.

Bello thus presents a pattern of severe implementation problems. These result in part from domestic resistance, and in part from the failure of policy to generate the economic changes expected. Assumed known cause-and-effect relationships did not, it appears, turn out as predicted.

So once again we are in a world of classic views of policy: with correct policy assumed to exist, failure is explained through the notion of problems in implementation. Recall the tensions between de Dios and Hutchcroft. The difference is that Bello does not believe in these policies.

Pragmatism?

Mackie and Villegas (1993) center their argument upon politics and note the failure of the successful anti-Marcos forces to introduce fundamental political change. Instead, they see

> the restoration of older democratic institutions (with some modifications) that had been abolished under the Marcos regime. (Mackie and Villegas 1993, 143)

Their central puzzle, then, is

> Why is it that the Philippines seems so attached to formal democracy and yet accepts a rather incomplete and patrimonial form of that polity? (Mackie and Villegas 1993, 143)

Their answer comes in terms of so-called unique features of Philippine history and its socioeconomic system, which emphasizes the old oligarchy with its dispersed and coherent family groups that arose during the US period and controlled the congress—and thus the executive—by manipulating the democratic system. This, Mackie and Villegas argue, was unique in SEA. The state-society balance thus favored the latter, whereas elsewhere the former dominated. This helps explain, for Mackie and Villegas, why an educated middle class is so much more developed in the Philippines. For us, it points to how the search for agency is so common in the development policy literature.

Mackie and Villegas view political conditions pre-Marcos as relatively good, a view they also take of the situation under US rule: orderly, progressive. In terms of development policy, the weakness of the executive was the main problem prior to Marcos. The "two hundred families" dominated the congress, and presidents did not exert themselves. Thus the crisis of the late 1960s had major political implications. Business resisted attempts to remove ISI as growth slowed. The ensuing development debate (already mentioned by Bello) was ideological, for the first time since independence. The economic breakdown was largely the result of Marcos' use of state funds to buy re-election, and the political consequences were solved through martial law.

Thus the new and central issue was national development and the political change necessary to attain it. The oligarchs had been blamed, opening the way for Marcos. Martial law was thus a triumph for the state over social forces. Why, Mackie and Villegas ask, did the Marcos experiment collapse? State power eroded underneath him. Mackie and Villegas seem somewhat unclear as to exactly why; something happened around 1976 when Marcos moved away from reform and a rural focus, and his wife Imelda gained at the expense of the technocrats. But Mackie and Villegas conclude that by shifting away from a developmental basis for state power,

> The Marcos regime ended up behaving as a patronage machine . . . (Mackie and Villegas 1993, 150)

Reflections

Because Mackie and Villegas focus upon political reform, mainly as a means to develop and use state power as executive authority, for us they have very relevant observations. Reading this text beside those of de Dios, Bello, and Hutchcroft is illuminating.

Mackie and Villegas sidestep the economists' call for reforms by arguing that executive power is needed for any such reform, as it entails the coherent and sustained exercise of state power: the issue is not fundamentally economic but is, in this sense, political. Without a site for agency and intentionality, any discussion of development policy is somewhat empty. This is true by definition for a classic view of policy.

But this assumes—indeed, de Dios argues—that if that intentionality and agency were attained, correct policy *would* cause changes through exploitation of known intervention logics. In this sense, it should work. But why did exports respond so weakly to the early devaluations and later EOI efforts under Marcos?

What is striking here is that Thai and Vietnamese successes appear linkable to ways of dealing with intentionality that move away from classic views of policy, and (by changing the way in which developmental acts are viewed) that they allow for a sense that the absence of classic agency accompanies narratives in terms of partial reforms—or rather, the view that cause-and-effect relations are accessible in and through practice, rather than as blueprints. "Subsequent events" may then be assessed in terms of experienced reals, as Rodrick reminds us, rather than through discussions about the unknowable and—more important—unexperienced future.

We have seen that the literature focuses strongly upon fates of exotic doctrine: various ways in which the Philippines appears to fail to realize sets of ideas and intentions that are profoundly Western and thus deeply exotic.

The ways in which constraints come into various arguments are noteworthy. Many authors agree that state policy and practice need to be seen in a historical perspective. And this is taken to suggest the presence of deep social and economic legacies that will take time to correct; so if securing development is largely the task of economic policy, then a longer-term perspective seems to be required. An important element of this position is its skepticism in the face of reformist arguments.

Recall the view of Mackie and Villegas: that failed political reform led to problems in sustained and coherent use of state power. This could be seen as failed authoritarianism under Marcos, as well as failed political reform after his fall. Marcos failed to produce a strong state based upon a business-state alliance with strong backing from the technocrats, the army, and foreign capital. He had such support initially, including support from oligarchs, but subsequently lost it. Ramos sought to gain authority through good management, rather than political reform. Again and again, the discussion comes back to the corruption of an intention to develop by a failure to secure its premises.

We can note also that this literature does not turn up much heterodox thinking about the content of policy. This is not to say that it does not exist and may simply reveal my own ignorance. What I find is a series of stories composed predominantly of unchallenged exotic ideas. There is little of what I referred to earlier as pragmatic analysis, moving away from dominant exotic doctrines and toward the local approaches evident in the cases of Vietnam and Thailand. This suggests that such approaches may become visible when their sites are presentable as successes. The very failure (in orthodox terms) of the Philippines may therefore hide local frameworks from view.

The case studies thus highlight the basic conclusions from the discussion in Part I, and also point toward how the tensions arising from the ways in which the problem of development has been addressed, in Cowen and Shenton's analysis, are manifest. I have shown how the literature both articulates and challenges these positions. But these tensions are also as much manifest as cognitive: inconsistencies generate anomalies, and these intersect with two striking conclusions from Thailand and Vietnam, which is that what we are perhaps persuasively observing are neither immanent processes nor developmental acts associated with authoritative statements about purportedly known-to-be-correct policies, but rather creative learning purposes. In the following chapter, calling these *heuristics*, I explore aspects of such original learning by doing. Like aspects of the case study discussion, these illuminate possible future directions, in that they appear to move beyond classic policy ideologies.

PART III

Conclusions

CHAPTER 12

Exotic Doctrine and Its Local Fates— Failures, Facts, and Creative Learning

Introduction

The issue of knowability may be thought of as the issue of the possibility of shared belief: the significance of a category such as "mass" to Newtonian physics is that, through a combination of theory and observation, there is an experience of shared belief. Views associated with a category such as mass are experienced as sufficiently stable to allow people to organize around them. This does not seem to be the same with categories of development and their associated cause-effect intervention logics, which we have seen are unstable.

The instability of development categories is highlighted in different ways by different people. Cowen and Shenton argue that this instability poses a problem of development that is answered in ways that involve considerable tension, associated with the importance attached to doing a historical process in ways that need to resolve the question of prediction. Strikingly, Cowen and Shenton argue that existing ways of solving this problem seem to set up the problem in ways that ensure that belief may not easily be shared. The very instability of beliefs based upon cause-effect relations accompanies the sectarianism of "disputable theory"; this is all very well if we are dealing with intriguing narratives and accounts but may be pathological if associated with cause-effect relations intended to form a basis for organizing social action such as aid projects—not least because it may inhibit discussion and agreement. Unstable beliefs make creative learning harder.

Policy studies tends to argue about similar contradictions, to do with those between visions of practice that on the one hand tell practitioners to search for cause-effect relationships, yet on the other present narratives in which such relationships are created as part of politics rather than some reality. Dunn (2000) argued that the state was usually seen as both sociological fact and normative political proposition, with little guidance as to whether it was one or the other, or perhaps both.

I have argued that the assumption of knowability is fundamental to classic policy ideologies, and, because these dominate, by understanding this we may better understand both what tends to happen and what the future may hold. I make the latter point because shared belief does not seem to have to depend upon ideas about knowability that may be delusions, in that they are thought to access some objective, evidentially-based set of cause-effect relations that turn out to be unstable in time and across organizations. Knowability is classically understood in terms of cause-effect relations, and these are, in the internal of classic policy logics, not reliably and robustly known and largely absent in predictive terms. We must therefore expect both pathology, as spurious cause-effect relations are produced and abandoned (To suit whose interests?), and, in the face of this, change. Change, we should expect, will take the form of shifts in what should be believed for things to make sense. Some things can be said about this "here and now," but I believe these matters will come about through practice: that is, that we do our best to look and see, rather than sit and think, if we want to find out what people may turn to or come up with. I return to this final issue in the closing chapter.

Cowen and Shenton (1996) argue that the problem of development was mainly resolved by founding an idea of true development upon notions of trusteeship and by defining correct development in reference to authority. Many texts in development studies do not discuss questions as to the origins or validity of such authority in any depth. This is understandable in that the knowability assumption implies that authority should derive from objective knowledge, and so it is natural to assume that this is what authority has to offer. This is not a very wise assumption. Yet it is, rather clearly, an energizer of action and organization.

The case studies of Part II highlight various important ideas. Developmental acts were present, as were partial reforms and what was called *post hoc* policy. Pressman and Wildavsky's (1973) ideas that policy has reliable meaning only in implementation shifted the realization problem away from the classic focus upon implementation of policy believed correct ex ante to something different. The focus shifted to process, to pragmatic approaches within which cognition could be thought of as something evolving in ways that reflected process, and not as something correct or incorrect. Further, this new focus would naturally be seen as something, perhaps good, perhaps bad, that involved learning. What was learned was not given ex ante but could still perhaps reflect general lessons. One metaphor I once heard to describe this focus upon orderly but unpredictable practice was that of football: common rules and different ways of playing, with no preordained outcome.[i] This is what is called a *heuristic:* a "learning by doing." I am aware of cultural arguments related to this: that Thai and Vietnamese culture may tend to treat knowledge in ways that

---

[i] Che Viet Tan, a conservative Vietnamese economist.

encourage such behavior.[ii] But here the inclusion of the Philippines is useful, for clearly the country is not necessarily excluded from learning processes by having different cultural heritages. Space prevents me giving these issues more attention here, but they stress the subjective.

I turn now to discuss aspects of what seems to be learned from coping with "subsequent events"—what has been said about the problems "coping with facts" have led to. This adds some space to the discussion of development and policy. If we think of development as to do with issues of intentionality in change, then we may access a far wider literature than simply development studies.

I start by looking at approaches to learning about markets that can be found in the work of Polanyi (1975) and Zysman (1983). I then look at interpretations of the 1997 Asian crisis, and after that I look at accounts of the "lost decades"—the idea that the implementation of policy-sets of the Washington Consensus set back development in many parts of the world as the 1980s and 1990s saw major problems.

Coping with "Subsequent Events"—Three Examples

Historical Accounts of the Emergence of Capitalism: Heuristics

Many of the arguments in this book are very old ones (perhaps only the econometrics is entirely new). A range of studies point to heuristics— processes of learning—and how these need not be seen as right or wrong. An account of the emergence of capitalism in Western Europe and interactions between intentionality and immanent process can be found in Polanyi (1975; also North 1996), a study dating from before WWII. Polanyi argues that the growth of markets and the exercise of state power were historically inseparable. Development was not the natural outcome of market development but a result of the exercise of state power. The question is, how and why was this done? What was the intentionality? Where did it come from?

Central to Polyani's account is the chaos caused by the three "fictitious commodities" (land, labor, and capital), which led to state intervention to permit their development. He argues that, in the rise of national markets, historically, such markets could be competitive and related to market production in ways that long-term international trade, by itself, could not be. This is because, historically, production for markets had to arise in towns

---

[ii]It is argued that for Thai and Vietnamese, whose cultures are deeply influenced by Buddhism, the mainstream epistemological and ethical habits of monotheists are frequently rather strange—specifically, the idea that we can and should think of ourselves as separate from whatever we are trying to understand and judge (John Powers, personal communication). Interestingly, the Vietnamese expression usually translated as "in reality" is literally "on reality" (*tren thuc te*).

or in concentrated locations, obtaining food and other inputs from a hinterland. Thus, local and long-distance trade were very different. Towns tended to oppose the establishment of national markets, because for them the controllability of local markets offset the uncontrollability of their profitable long-distance trade. State intervention had to be used to break down these local trade barriers. Note that Polyani's argument relies upon an analysis that *concludes* that intentionality was necessary: this is close to Cowen and Shenton's interpretation of the Marxist view that intention is simply part of the logic of capitalist development.

The *requirements* of the three fictitious markets (land, labor, and capital) forced major changes upon society: separation of economics from politics to prevent the interference in factor markets that historically was so great (through guilds, feudal landholding practices, and usury laws). But these very changes, without state action to control and moderate them, were extremely dangerous. People were thrown off the land, populations were enriched and impoverished, and financial markets moved chaotically. Thus, regulation arose to deal with these consequences. And this was embedded in much history that saw large-scale social organization manifest in states as well as non-state organizations, many of which had arisen centuries earlier.[iii]

Polanyi's position shows the power of an argument that links an emergence of subjective action to the objective requirements of the situation. Yet this subjective action is not clearly intentional in a developmental sense; his account is rather different from modern discussions about how correct policy is known and implemented. This is mainly because his account is pragmatic and historical, reminiscent, for example, of Pasuk and Baker's (1996) explanation of what happened in Thailand.

Variants of this, which also stress a *heuristic*, or learning by doing, are common. Another example discusses the origins of East Asian state-driven development and focuses upon finance and the role of government.

Wade (1988) comes at this issue of heuristics from the point of view of state interventionary power in the East Asian Miracle debate. The book that the chapter comes from is a hymn to the WC, but his chapter dissents. A longer exposition of his ideas is in Wade's 1990 work. There he argues that East Asian newly industrialized countries (NICs) had an unusually developed capacity for selective intervention, based upon a powerful set of policy instruments (here he focuses upon finance among other things) and a certain kind of state organization. The question is, where did these come from?

Wade discusses policy, which is what concerns us here. He starts with Zysman's (1983) distinction between credit-based and capital market-based

---

[iii]Once again the literature here is vast and fascinating. Spruyt (1994) is an introduction.

financial systems. In the latter, typified by the US and the UK, securities (stocks and bonds) are the main sources of long-term finance. Financial institutions tend to have arms-length relations with particular firms and tend to compete with each other in terms of price and supply. Capital markets are important.

In credit-based financial systems, firms depend heavily upon rather short-term bank credit, and, because of their dependence, a cut-off in credit rapidly leads to business problems. Banks can be relatively independent of government (for example, Germany, early Thailand) or dependent on it, with interest rates set officially and credit allocation also influenced by the government.

Japan, Taiwan, and Korea were all countries with credit-based systems.[iv] All discouraged growth of capital markets. What advantages did this confer? Savings could be increased by raising deposit rates and protected from speculation and other wastage of capital. Credit-based systems encouraged rapid sectoral mobility and avoided short-term bias in decision-making. They also offered political advantages in granting powers to support *implementation* of industrial strategy.

But credit-based systems also had important implications for the government's role in the economy (this is the core of Zysman's argument): the government must learn to help socialize risk. That is, the governments must face the consequences of involvement in credit decisions: the need to find ways of assisting firms that are heavily credit-dependent and the need to deal with highly correlated risk—that is, risk to which large numbers of firms are simultaneously exposed.

This tends to lead governments operating with such credit systems to put in place a wide range of back-up measures: subsidies and so forth, and so become heavily involved in corporate finance—with obvious implications if things go wrong. They learned by doing.

I turn now to the 1997 Asian crisis, which also shows similar heuristic tensions. It also shows how readily criticism formed, based upon assumptions of knowability and notions of trusteeship.

Coping with Failure? The 1997 Asian Regional Crisis

The range of explanations is relevant to what I argue below. Many of the approaches should by now be familiar. Issues of knowability, intentionality, and the tensions created by classic views of policy all come into the discussions. Johnson (1998) is a useful pragmatic approach. He argues that the reasons for the crisis remain unclear, but arguments so far have tended to support the revisionists, and not the Anglo-American economic orthodoxy.

[iv]See also Johnson (1982) for his seminal study of MITI and heuristics.

However, there is not one simple revisionist argument. Johnson's position is that the Asian development picture cannot be understood outside of the global and cultural context. He asserts that the focused and effective drive to export and grow shown by Japan and South Korea relied upon various factors, including access to US markets. This was predicated upon their subordination to US geopolitical interests, with major political consequences in terms of countries' abilities to change.

By contrast, but also referring to powerful historical processes, Hiley uses as his central metaphor the so-called geese pattern (Yamazawa 1992). This is a paradigm of changing international economic relations. Foreign direct investment (FDI) and domestic adaptation takes place in response to changing international patterns of comparative advantage.

Both of these approaches stress the relative unimportance of policy—the absence of feasible intentionality. Naturally, official views of the crisis saw things from the other side of the coin, stressing what could have been done. For example, the WB (1998) argues once again that there are correct policies. Economic success in SEA is attributed to low inflation and competitive exchange rates; high investments in human capital; encouraging high levels of savings by avoiding financial repression; limiting price distortions; encouraged absorption of foreign technology; and avoided biases against agriculture (WB 1998, 3).

Thus, rapid growth without proper capital markets due to failure of institutional design and poor regulation meant that firms relied heavily upon short-term finance. At the same time economic growth was undermining traditional safety nets and natural resource exploitation was running up against limits. "East Asia's crisis is best seen as a story of rapid growth built upon an incomplete foundation" (WB 1998, 16).

Central to this is the problem of development as posed by Cowen and Shenton—how to "do" a historical process. Much of this depends upon the ways in which authority makes statements about cause-effect relationships, and what basis we use for judging these statements. Given what has been said about the nature of financial markets, it is clear that a powerful view, which underpins the position of central banks (Nukul Commission 1998), is that institutions such as central banks and the IMF exist to cope with the instability of financial markets.

It is worth finishing with a text from Pomerleano (1998). The author was a senior official at the World Bank. His findings, he says, support the view advanced by Paul Krugman in a number of influential newspaper articles that crony capitalism enabled by weak policies related to implicit guarantees and poor banking supervision led to poor credit decisions in the banking system.

What, we may ask, was being discussed in relation to these problems *before* the crisis? Pomerleano argues that there is (and was) evidence for widespread imprudent practices. What is most striking about this text is his view that, usually, little was known about such things. Macroeconomic stability told little about the realities behind the veil of finance: what funds were used for, and on what terms. This seems to reveal a lack of attention in the belief-sets of institutions such as the World Bank to what was presumably commonly known among businesspeople, informed journalists, and commercial bankers.

To some extent, many of these analyses seem to miss a fundamental point, which is that the beliefs that help organize institutions such as central banks are not fixed but arise and change. It is likely that almost all countries that now have well-functioning central banks have past experience of mistakes and the costs imposed by them, from which lessons were drawn that in many ways come down to the value of granting central banks and what they are meant to do a certain authority.[v] Deregulation of the British (in the early 1970s), American (in the 1980s), and Australian (in the 1990s) financial markets all led to problems, from which lessons were learned; whether they will be forgotten is another matter. This is to say that beliefs in Asia about the roles of central banks were very different after 1997 from what they had been before.

Coping with Failure? The "Lost Decades"

It is hard to avoid strong feelings when comparing the great confidence of WC positions with subsequent events. We cannot link these too readily to the specifics of WC policy, because the Levine and Zervos results suggest that almost nothing is reasonably said to work—to have reliable and knowable consequences—in terms of universalistic categories of policy and performance. But we may feel that reckless confidence is blameworthy. The case studies suggest that heuristic processes may well accompany positive "subsequent events" and encourage caution and a pragmatic step-by-step attitude. Most accounts suggest that, like earlier advocacy of ISI itself, the drive to replace it with EOG was associated with great confidence, although we can perhaps judge that belief was not based upon much more than authority: these were doctrines.

Easterly (2001) shows an economist's confidence in known cause-effect relations confronting "facts." The paper argues that from around the early 1980s many poor countries started implementing market-friendly policies, and then shifted from per cap GDP growth of 2.5 percent in 1960–79 to 0.0 percent in 1980–99. According to Easterly, this happened

---

[v]Note that the Nukul Commission (1998) largely concludes, not that the formal constitution of the Bank of Thailand was wrong, but that the way it was used (or not used) was wrong.

despite two things: strong evidence from research on the period before the 1980s that growth was determined by various policy settings; second, evidence that policy then moved in a positive direction after 1980. This is the standard argument that "we knew what worked," but it did not, so the question here is why.

Easterly gives only two possible explanations. The first is that the research before the 1980s was spurious, and second that there were other things happening to offset the favorable policy shifts. He looks for and finds correlations that point to such other things, mainly the Organization for Economic Cooperation and Development (OECD) slowdown and common shocks slowing both OECD and poor countries. Is this persuasive? For me, it is not, but is likely for others. What seems to be happening here is the attempt to preserve the assumption of knowability by ignoring the possibility that the earlier research had not identified robust causes of growth. He does not consider this. The reader may readily find a vast range of studies that, like Easterly (2001), cope with facts largely by not challenging the basic assumption of knowability. These come, in the case of the lost decades, from both those trying to defend as well as those trying to attack.

But we should not forget the option of "it depends," which we found exemplified in the doctrinal position of the IMF regarding the issue of liberalization of the capital account of the balance of payments. This is clearly brought out by the simple account in Lindauer and Pritchett (2002), who contrast the great confidence felt by mainstream economists in 1962 and 1982 with the hesitancies of 2002. Yet reflection on the reliability of their judgments, and simply noting the lack of cited empirical support for them, shows just how facts are so often coped with: the importance of belief to the ways in which humans organize themselves. Many of these beliefs have clearly been shaken by incidents such as the 1997 Asian crisis and the lost decades. But the fate of the work of Levine and Zervos (1993), who suggested that the main issue was not belief in specific global policy-sets but the wider one of their reliable existence, is another matter.

Conclusions

The great advantage of heuristics is that it moves us away from classic policy approaches. So long as learning is understood not to be an immanent process but rather an unpredictable one, then we may be in less danger from assumptions of knowability. In these senses the historical accounts suggest that we can discuss and appreciate others' learning processes and think of them in terms of creative responses to situations to which we too can relate. In that they are creative, they encourage skepticism, as indeed does my general argument.

It is with this sense of the possibilities of discussion, perhaps about "subsequent events," that I now turn to finish this book by presenting some ideas about what may happen. Central to this is the perhaps obvious fact that those who study development have little else to study other than what we have been examining. There is no other set of texts to be discovered in a cave, and, with contemporary information technology and the predominance of English, the tensions that I have been identifying are inescapable. They are expressions of powerful trends, not least the declining authority of statements about "the development process" and "known solutions." If words are used to govern, then the meanings of those words are not entirely predictable, or, rather, as any teacher knows, whether a student believes it or not is, at the end of the day, unpredictable.

What Now?

Introduction

The question "what now" is intriguing. My arguments in this book about the tensions created by the assumptions of classic policy ideologies suggest that an answer should refer to rather more than armchair reasoning. In this final chapter I gather reflections to point to what may be happening, for what I have been discussing so far is not simply a critique of solutions to the problem of development, but observations of what these solutions have tended to be and how they relate to common criteria of what an acceptable solution is.

My view is that many answers are inconsistent with what their authors suggest an acceptable answer is, and so there are pressures and tensions, even if they may not be enough to push for major change. But these pressures, which come down in many ways to the authority of positions taken, do seem to be significant. The world of the early 2000s showed interesting trends, in part associated with the further evolution of processes already discussed above. Central to these trends were the declining authority of mainstream development doctrines and a related tendency for a reduction in the respect accorded to the sovereignty of poor country governments.

These trends have two very different aspects to them. First, consider what could be called the "internal" of development thinking, which asserts the possibility of knowable cause-effect relations and embodies a search for them. Practice, as we have seen, often continues when facts suggest that they have not been found. Yet the issue of implementation frequently explains away failure, while resources continue to be devoted to further research. As we have seen, however, the weakness of the assumption of universalism supports this quest, because it generates spurious statistical results that can be valorized, published, and projected into development activities. Tensions arise in the contradictions among the practices of different groups and in the instability of the practices of particular groups over time. One obvious way of coping with this is to embrace sectarianism even more strongly and to shoulder aside obstacles, one of which is the state, now labeled perhaps as failed. It might work, but will it ever be reliably clear just why? I doubt it. And so lessons will not *reliably* work elsewhere. Furthermore, under such situations, other interests appear to be given greater scope, benefiting some and not others.

Second, consider possible consequences for intellectual development and social meanings. I find it intriguing that, while unpalatable to many, the facts I have discussed can be widely accessed. Fforde (2005a) is able to track the citations of Levine and Zervos (1993) and conclude that, although not the main effect, there were signs that skepticism had increased. Works like Lindauer and Pritchett (2002) seem consistent with this, whereas Craig and Porter (2006) point to a "new consensus" beyond neoliberalism. Something seems to be going on.

Practice and the Value of Experiences with Exotic Doctrine

It is not just Cowen and Shenton who stress the notion that too much of what policymakers "do" obscures their values. In some sense, this is not really too much to get worried about. And belief in cause-effect relations as an underpinning to collective action does not seem a priori to be necessarily a bad thing either. Further, it does not seem at all odd that people differ in the extent to which they focus upon issues of the creation of mythology as opposed to belief in mythology. As Disraeli put it and Clinton implied, if truth cannot be known, then something else must directly govern us. Yet classic views of policy assume far more. This creates inconsistency and may lead to tensions. But these may ease by a shift in focus to acceptable "subsequent events."

Consider the following. Think of two agencies, each charged with using resources to meet certain "subsequent events," whose performance is managed through the degree to which they use the resources allocated to them to produce various outputs. Assume two things: first, that each is deemed successful, and second, that each has its own view of the world that contradicts that of the other. A concrete example could be two agencies producing educational outputs (for example, language training) deemed to be successful, yet one assumes that gender differences are profound and the other that they are negligible. It seems reasonable that this could happen.

Does it matter that they have contradictory worldviews? It depends on how truth is organized. Deng Xiao Ping put it that the color of the cat does not matter so long as it catches mice. To those who argue that it does matter, a fair question is why. I am tempted to remind the reader that Socrates was given hemlock to drink because his extreme skepticism was seen as corrupting the young.

So there is a choice, and we may organize to accept that the cause-effect relationships that each agency is so concerned with are no more significant than the particular ways to "skin cats." But of course there are wider concerns associated here with differing views of gender equality.

Here I have broached the issue of the views taken of "subsequent events." But the central issues are best viewed empirically: what can be found happening as populations for whom truth is relative interact with processes that allocate resources through structures usually called states? So far as I can see, increasingly little attention will be paid to whether intervention logics are true, if the question is increasingly thought meaningless and so replies to it spurious and rather uninformative. This, it seems to me, is what the development literature now suggests. People move on.

Histories of development, of exotic doctrines, show that policy fetishism turns too easily into a corruption of the intention of development, as Cowen and Shenton argue, and turns policy toward being an instrument of rule, and no more. But not all of us live in situations in which unwanted "subsequent events" lead to political change, and belief in known cause-effect relations may be politically powerful.

To return to issues raised at the start of the book, recall that both Lao Tzu and Marx, in their different ways, were radicals, opposed to the very different rulers of their days. And both their radicalisms, though different, confronted ideas that certain things are knowable, linking this to questions of power. To argue *pace* Lao Tzu that "history is not history," that writing may obscure, is to argue about issues of perception. And to argue *pace* Marx that the very nature of capitalism prevents, through the nature of commodities, things being seen as they really are, is to argue that social intentionality based upon facts related to predictability is impossible. Yet, for each, there remains the question: what is the point of saying such things? Lao Tzu's work is itself written; Marx certainly believed that political action by the working class was meaningful, though he also argued that Communism would only come when capitalism had developed to its own limits. Because they were human like us, we may sympathize with their limitations.

Pragmatism?

People may and do still query whether reasonable actions may be taken in a development context, that is, one in which there are discussions about "interventions"—actions taken based upon a belief in cause-effect relations. This is a strong point, and this book has tried to show what is sacrificed by thinking that such discussions are reasonable. To do so is to deny the lack of much in the way of a reliable basis for knowledge of cause-effect relations when these are expressed in a classic language of ontological and epistemological universalism. While I have made reference to a number of pragmatic approaches to the creation of analyses of change, or development, it cannot persuasively be said that these are robust, as by contrast are approaches to building bridges. In part, this can be attributed to the wide range of perspectives that are inherent to the political nature of much human activity (Dunn 2000). But that does not solve the problem. So how might things change and the problem appear solved?

Another approach is to ask a different question, which is to ask about practice—what do reasonable people who are aware of the shortcomings of knowledge but yet still work in development actually do when they form judgments about the value of interventions? This is a question that can be posed and answered within an agnostic, realist framework. That is, what are people doing when they form judgments about actions, after they have established a reasonable skepticism about the value of belief in cause-effect relations? Further, what do they think actions are? Recall the argument that actions are what humans associate with attributions of responsibility, and that all this discussion of cause and effect is not much more than that (Box 3.1—*The metaphor of the king and his courtiers*). So what are they up to?

This suggests a research agenda. I referred in Chapter 1 to "pragmatic approaches that avoid blueprints and similar predictive ex ante positions." In my own experience, such apparently clear expressions of classic policy logic as the aid project "log frame" can be treated not as such, but simply as a framework for discussion; I also have experience of situations in which organizational beliefs are such as to treat such suggestions as anathema and totally and absolutely wrong, in my opinion then leading to an aid politics not entirely in the interests of the donor. Organizational beliefs are not monolithic, and from changing contemporary practice I think much can probably be learned. Consultants, for example, have to manage interactions between their self-identity and the differences in beliefs between organizations in which they work, not to mention the same organization over time. This is the stuff of research.

Intentionality—Simple or Complex?

Let us return to the discussion in Chapter 1, which stressed the problems that arise in thinking about policy as an attribute of certain actions, entailing an intention, an agency as a site for it, and a knowability assumption to underpin an intervention logic expressed in cause-effect terms. Much of the rest of the book has explored these problems, treating them primarily, not as philosophical in nature but explored through the tensions they create in various parts of the development literature. These assumptions drive the major contradiction in much of what is taught in policy studies: that the search for a known cause-effect relation upon which to construct policy, because it is futile, rubs up against the contingency and theater that is the practical politics that uses policy. What, so it seems, may happen when these assumptions, and ways of thinking are not present?

Let us start with the knowability assumption. If, for whatever reason, people start to assume that some action may not consistently be based upon known cause-effect relations, then one thing that would seem necessarily to follow is far greater tolerance of disagreement. This requires some form of organized recognition of how difference is to be negotiated, and this may be done through recourse to a hierarchy of order: rules about rules. So we would expect to find differentiation between arguments about the acceptability of statements about cause-effect relationships and arguments about what should then be agreed on. These may be related to a requirement that proposals include reference to data, be consistent in some way, and so on, yet mark a boundary beyond which consistency is not required. In this way there are organized ways to agree to disagree. Can this happen? It can, in some areas.

Let me refer to three examples of practices that I have come across. First, consider the UNCDF RIDEF project referred to and think about the basic ideas underlying its practice. What is required for a small-scale infrastructure proposal to be approved? We observed procedures that prevented disbursement unless certain criteria were met, such as participatory methods of project selection identified by certain norms, the commune's presence on a list of "poor" communes, and so on. But in terms of classic views of policy, there is no requirement for each proposal to articulate a correct intervention logic: what the bridge, culvert, or road upgrade would do. This is bypassed by the shift in focus to the *acceptability* of the proposal to various parties, including local officials, and a formalized—organized—recognition of this.

But the usual political questions still arise: is it what everybody wanted? And what is meant by "want"? Yet at the time of evaluation the formal system did *not* include provision for an ex post participatory evaluation of the project. This does not seem to have been deliberate, and the absence may be seen as an unrealized opportunity for further organization of agreement.

A second practice comes from a very different area, the use of output-based disbursement targets by ministries and departments of finance, or treasuries. This remains rare but can be found in jurisdictions such as the state of Victoria (Australia). In these systems, so far as I can see, we find a metaphor of the government as purchaser, on behalf of the population, of goods and services. Suppliers may be government agencies (such as education departments) or private (such as construction companies). Following this approach, contracts are agreed upon that define what will be supplied, bearing in mind price, quality, and delivery schedule, and payments are made when and as those contracts are implemented. It may happen that suppliers deliver at a cost below the amount they calculated when the agreement was made, and in that case they may, even if they are a government agency, retain the difference as profit. These systems appear to offer combinations of greater efficiency and greater effectiveness as agencies align to generate outputs rather than directly financed activities. An education department, in this way of thinking, is not paid to hire teachers but to produce education services. Payment is not made for doing things but for producing outputs.

Such systems are interesting in what they suggest about the problem of development. As in the case of the thinking associated with RIDEF, these systems differentiate between what will be agreed on and what will not be. One way of expressing this is a distinction between "outputs" and "outcomes." For example, in discussions among the wider community, agreement can be reached relatively easily on "outputs," *but their relationships with "outcomes" are then open to debate.* There is then no need to generate agreement about relationships between outputs and outcomes, because formalized procedures (needed by the bureaucracies) are limited in scope.

A second implication of such systems relates to how they deal with agency intervention logics. In that the main power of treasuries is that of the purse, disbursement against output means that there is less interest in intervention logics. Indeed, it is possible that, if two spending agencies have inconsistent logics, no attention may be paid to this. One may assume that the sky is green and another that it is purple, but if they both meet their agreed output contacts then they both should be paid. This can be understood as a formal system that permits—and organizes consistently with—the view that cause-effect relations are either not knowable, or that it is not worth assuming that they are.

It then may be seen as "unusual" if intervention logics are subject to criteria that look like a requirement for consistency and organized to inhibit "vertical" inconsistency. Deng Xiao Ping's position on the color of cats may now be recalled. It is striking that modern views of the subjectivity of truth should be dealt with through such methods by a bureaucracy in a rich region. I have no idea what drove the creation of this system and the role within it of the tolerance of differences between agency intervention logics. I have a strong suspicion that one driver was the need to gain control, as "paying for outcomes" may avoid the treasury being dragged into negotiations for additional payments attributed to problems in implementation.

A third practice was reported to me in discussing the organizing of conditionality terms in a multilateral loan. It appeared that deliberate attempts had been made to deal with the issues raised by Levine and Zervos regarding whether "what works there, works here." This was done by agreeing to a dualistic approach. Some intervention logics were agreed to be "universalistic"; others were not. The former included arguments similar to the arguement "we all agree that it is always unwise to allow an institution such as a stock market to develop spontaneously and without regulation." The latter simply said that, for local reasons, "what works there does not work here," and so "what works here is what works here." This can be seen as a way of organizing agreement to disagree (here with global certainties).

These examples suggest that Cowen and Shenton's view of solutions to the problem of development, being limited to those they link to Marx and Newman, reflects not what is necessarily possible, but where things had got to when they wrote their book. In these instances, we can see organizational and belief adaptation that reflects the central problems posed by classic views of policy. In all three cases there is a focus upon dealing with the knowability assumption. For me, each also says something about the value of heuristics and avoiding the idea that what is learned is preordained or imminent. This in turn suggests that issues of intentionality and agency are secondary. What does this imply for matters of governance?

This seems to have two main implications: first, profound forces are pushing for fundamental change as many supports for classic views of policy erode. These are not strong enough to generate rapid change, but they are there. Recall that it is not hard to find contemporary policy handbooks that avoid the assumption of knowability (for example, Bridgman and Davis 1998). Second, there is no fundamental difficulty in constructing rationalities and procedures that cope with this. These procedures involve shifting attention and resources toward the acceptability of "subsequent events"; in various ways; that is, they fundamentally change the position in organized social actions of the troubled search for reliable and stable cause-effect relations.

One final implication of the ideas in this book is that any assertion that it is feasible to "think globally" is probably misplaced; human perspectives are too varied to avoid recourse to doctrine and authority, and so instability and unreliable agreement. The sorry saga of the cross-country growth literature shows what happens when working to the assumption that we can all think together. One implication of the weaknesses of ontological and epistemological universalism is that it may be better to "think locally." Yet it seems that we may with less risk act globally, in the sense developed here that actions may be associated with acceptable "subsequent events," acceptable in likely different ways to different people. Perhaps, then, it should be, "Think locally, act globally." For, as has been said before, "Understanding is limited and misunderstanding limitless."[i] And, in contemporary postindustrial societies, that limitless misunderstanding seems

---

[i] I owe this quote to the Vietnamese economist Hoang Kim Giao, who never asserted to me that it was originally his.

increasingly experienced as a fondness for, rather than a fear of, noncategorical meaning. But, for obvious reasons, capitalism and power politics remain powerful, and if "spin" and inconsistency are what it takes to maintain the structure of the food chain, then what appears to follow is likely to be all too familiar.

Melbourne 2008

Bibliography

Abramovitz, Moses. 1995. The elements of social capability. In Ed. Bon Ho Koo and Dwight H. Perkins, *Social capability and long-term economic growth*. London: St Martin's Press.

Acheson, Dean. 1969. *Present at the creation*. London: Hamish Hamilton.

Agenor, Pierre-Richard and Peter J. Montiel. 1999. *Development macroeconomics*, 2nd edition. Princeton, NJ Princeton University Press.

Almond, Gabriel A. 1988. The return to the state. *American Political Science Review* 82 no. 3 (Sept): 853–74.

Amsden, Alice. 1997. Bringing production back in: Understanding government's economic role in late industrialization. *World Development* April 25:4.

Anderson, Benedict R.O.G. 1983. Old state, new society: Indonesia's new order in comparative historical perspective. *Journal of Asian Studies* 42 no. 3 (May): 477–98.

Armstrong, Karen. 1993. *A history of God: The 4,000 year quest of Judaism, Christianity and Islam*. New York: Ballantine Books.

Arndt, H.W. 1981. Economic development: A semantic history. *Economic Development and Cultural Change* 29 no. 3 (Apr.): 457–66.

Arndt, H.W. 1987. *Economic development: The history of an idea*. Chicago: University of Chicago Press.

Ashdown, Paddy. 2007. *Swords and ploughshares—Bringing peace to the 21st century*. London: Weidenfeld & Nicholson.

Baer, Werner, William R. Miles and Allen B. Moran. 1999. The end of the Asian myth: Why were the experts fooled? *World Development* 27 no. 4: 1735–47.

Baker, Judy L. 2000. *Evaluating the impact of development projects on poverty—A handbook for practitioners*. Washington DC: The World Bank.

Bardhan, Pranab and Christopher Udry. 1999. *Development microeconomics*. Oxford: Oxford University Press.

Bardhan, Pranab. 1993. Economics of development and the development of economics. *The Journal of Economic Perspectives* 7 no. 2 (Spring): 129–42.

Bates, Robert H. 1995. Social dilemmas and rational individuals: An assessment of the new institutionalism. In Ed. John Harriss et al., *The New Institutional Economics and Third World Development.* London: Routledge.

Bello, W. 1982. Export-oriented industrialization: The short-lived illusion. In Ed. W. Bello et al., *Development debacle: The World Bank in the Philippines.* San Francisco: Institute of Food and Development Policy.

Bennett, Sara and Viroj Tangcharoensathien. 1994. A shrinking state? Politics, economics and private health care in Thailand. *Public Administration and Development* 14: 1–17.

Beresford, Melanie. 1993. The political economy of dismantling the 'bureaucratic centralism and subsidy system' in Vietnam. In Ed. Kevin Hewison et al., *Southeast Asia in the 1990s: Authoritarianism, democracy, and capitalism.* Sydney: Allen and Unwin.

Beresford, Melanie. 1997. Vietnam: The transition from central planning. In Ed. Gerry Rodan et al., *The political economy of South-East Asia.* Oxford: Oxford University Press.

Bimber, B. and David H. Guston. 1997. Introduction: The end of OTA and the future of technological assessment. *Technological Forecasting and Social Change* 54: 125–30.

Blomstrom, Magnus and P. Meller, Eds. 1991. *Divergent paths: Comparing a century of Scandinavian and Latin American economic development.* Baltimore: Johns Hopkins Press.

Booth, Anne. 1999. Initial conditions and miraculous growth; why is South East Asia different from Taiwan and South Korea? *World Development* 27 no. 2: 301–22.

Bray, F. 1983. Patterns of evolution in rice-growing societies. *Journal of Peasant Studies* 11: 3–33.

Bridgman, P. and Gavin Davis. 1998. *Australian policy handbook.* Sydney: Allen and Unwin.

Campbell, Tom D. 1997. Legal positivism and political power. In Ed. Andrew Vincent. *Political theory: Tradition and diversity.* Cambridge: Cambridge University Press.

Carpenter, Christine. 1997. *The Wars of the Roses: Politics and the constitution in England, C. 1437–1509.* Cambridge: Cambridge University Press.

Carroll, Lewis. 1895. What the tortoise said to Achilles. *Mind* no. 4: 278–80.

Caute, David. 1988. *Sixty-eight: The year of the barricades.* London: Hamilton.

Chambers, Robert. 1983. *Rural development: Putting the last first.* London: Longman.

Chambers, Robert. 1997. *Whose reality counts? Putting the first last.* Bath: Intermediate Technology Publications.

Chang, Ha-Joon. 2000. The hazard of moral hazard: Untangling the Asian crisis. *World Development* 28 no. 4: 775–88.

Chang, Ha-Joon. 2003. *Kicking away the ladder: Development strategy in historical perspective.* London: Anthem Press.

Chenery, Hollis, et al. 1974. *Redistribution with growth: Policies to improve income distribution in developing countries in the context of economic growth: A joint study (commissioned) by the World Bank's Development Research Center and the Institute of Development Studies.* University of Sussex, London: Published for the World Bank and the Institute of Development Studies, University of Sussex (by) Oxford University Press.

Churchill, Winston S. 1943. The price of greatness is responsibility. First printed in *Finest Hour* 80, Third Quarter, 1993.

Clinton, Bill. 2004. *My life.* London: Hutchinson.

Cohen, J. 1994. The earth is round (p<0.5). *American Psychologist* 49 no. 12: 997–1003.

Cowen, Michael and Robert Shenton. 1996. *Doctrines of development.* London: Routledge.

Craig, David and Doug Porter. 2006. *Development beyond neoliberalism? Governance, poverty reduction and political economy.* Abingdon: Routledge.

de Dios, Emmanuel S. 1999a. *Philippine economic growth: Can it last?* Asia Society, Internet download. http://www.asiasociety.org/publications/philippines/economic.html.

de Dios, Emmanuel S. 1999b. Executive-legislative relations in the Philippines: Continuity and change. In Ed. Colin Barlow, *Institutions and economic change in SEA: The context of development from the 1960s to the 1990s.* Northampton, MA: Edward Elgar Publishing.

de Vylder, Stefan and Adam Fforde. 1996. *From plan to market: The economic transition in Vietnam.* Boulder CO: Westview.

de Vylder, Stefan and Adam Fforde. 1997. *Tu ke hoach den thi truong: su chuyen bien kinh te tai Viet Nam.* Hanoi: Nha xuat ban Chinh tri quoc gia (translation of *From plan to market . . . 1996*).

Disraeli, Benjamin. 1932. *Contarini Fleming: A psychological romance; The rise of Iskander*, Part 1, ch xxi 33, first published 1832. London: P. Davies, 1926–1927.

Dollar, David. 1992. Outward-oriented developing economies really do grow more rapidly: Evidence from 95 LDCs, 1976–85. *Economic Development and Cultural Change* 40, no. 3 (April): 523–44.

Doner, Richard F. and Ansil Ramsay. 1997. Competitive clientelism and economic governance: The case of Thailand. In Ed. Sylvia Maxfield and Ben Ross Schneider, *Business and the state in developing countries*. Ithaca: Cornell University Press.

Doshi, Tilak and Peter Coclanis. 1999. The economic architect: Goh Keng Swee. In Ed. Lam Peng and Kevin Y.L. Tan, *Lee's lieutenants: Singapore's Old Guard*. Sydney: Allen and Unwin.

Dowling, Malcolm and Peter M. Summers. 1998. Total factor productivity and economic growth: Some issues for Asia. *The Economic Record* 74 no. 225 (June): 170–85.

Dunn, John. 2000. *The cunning of unreason: Making sense of politics*. New York, Basic Books.

EAAU—East Asian Analytical Unit (Australian Dept. of Foreign Affairs and Trade). 1998. *The Philippines: Beyond the crisis*. Canberra: DFAT.

Easterly, William. 1999. The ghost of financing gap: Testing the growth model used in the international financial institutions. *Journal of Development Economics* 60: 423–38.

Easterly, William. 2001. The lost decade: Developing countries' stagnation in spite of policy reforms 1980–1998. *Journal of Economic Growth* 6: 135–57.

Easterly, William., Norman Loayza and Peter Montiel. 1997. Has Latin America's post-reform growth been disappointing? *Journal of International Economics* 43: 287–311.

Eatwell, John and Joan Robinson. 1973. *An introduction to modern economics*. London: McGraw Hill.

Edwards, Michael. 1999. NGO performance—What breeds success? New evidence from South Asia. *World Development* 27 no. 2: 361–74.

Ellman, Michael and Vladimir Kontorovich. 1998. *The destruction of the Soviet economic system—An insiders' history*. Armonk, NY: M.E. Sharpe.

Erickson, Christopher L., Sarosh Kuruvilla, Rene E. Ofreno and Maria Asuncion Ortiz. 2003. From core to periphery? Recent developments in employment relations in the Philippines. *Industrial Relations* 42: 368–95.

Escobar, Arturo. 1995. *Encountering development: The making and unmaking of the Third World*. Princeton, NJ: Princeton University Press, Princeton Studies in Culture/Power/History.

Esteva, G. 1992. Development. In Ed. W. Sachs, *The development dictionary: A guide to knowledge as power*. London: Zed Books.

Fairclough, Norman. 1992. *Discourse and social change*. Cambridge: Polity Press.

Ferguson, James. 1997. Development and bureaucratic power in Lesotho. In Ed. Majid Rahnema and Victoria Bawtree, *The post-development reader*. London: Zed Books.

Fforde, Adam and S.H. Paine. 1987. *The limits of national liberation—Problems of economic management in the Democratic Republic of Vietnam, with a statistical appendix*. London: Croom-Helm.

———. 1989. *The agrarian question in North Vietnam 1974–79: A study of cooperator resistance to state policy*. New York: M.E. Sharpe.

———. 2002. Resourcing conservative transition in Vietnam: Rent-switching and resource appropriation. *Post-Communist Economies* 14 no. 2 (June): 203–26.

———. 2004. Vietnam in 2003: The road to un-governability? *Asian Survey* 44 no. 1 (January/February): 121–29.

———. 2005a. Persuasion: Reflections on economics, data and the "homogeneity assumption." *Journal of Economic Methodology* 12 no. 1 (March): 63–91.

———. 2005b. Vietnam in 2004: Popular authority seeking power. *Asian Survey* 45 no. 1 (January/February): 146–52.

———. 2007. *Vietnamese state industry and the political economy of commercial renaissance: Dragon's tooth or curate's egg?* Oxford: Chandos.

———. 2008. Vietnam's informal farmers' groups: Narratives and policy implications. *Suedostasien aktuell—Journal of Current Southeast Asian Affairs* no. 1: 3–37.

———. 2009. Policy ethnography and conservative transition from plan to market—The construction of policy rationalities and the "intellectual limitations of leading comrades." *International Journal of Social Economics* 36 no 7, forthcoming.

Fforde, John S. 1995. Comments on Johan de Vries' presentation. In Ed. Martin M.G. Fase, *How to write the history of a bank*. Aldershot, England: Scolar Press.

Fine, Ben. 1999. The development state is dead: Long live social capital. *Development and Change* 30 no. 1 (January): 1–19.

Frank, Andre Gunder. 1966. The development of underdevelopment. *Monthly Review* 18 no. 4: 17–31.

Friedman, M. 1953. The methodology of positive economics. Reprinted in Milton Friedman, *Essays in positive economics*. Chicago: University of Chicago Press.

Gainsborough, Martin. 2007. From patronage to "outcomes": Vietnam's Communist Party Congresses reconsidered. *Journal of Vietnam Studies* 2 no. 1 (Winter): 3–26.

Glassman, Jim. 1999. State power beyond the "territorial trap": The internationalization of the state. *Political Geography* 18: 669–96.

Granger, C.W.J. 1990. Spurious regression. In Ed. John Eatwell, Murray Milgate and Peter Newman, *Econometrics*. London: W.W. Norton & Company.

Granger, C.W.J. and P. Newbold 1974. Spurious regressions in econometrics. *Journal of Econometrics* 2 no. 2 (July): 111–20.

Green, Andrew. 2000. Reforming the health sector in Thailand: The role of policy actors on the policy stage. *International Journal of Health Planning and Management* 15: 39–59.

Greenfield, Gerard. 1993. The emergence of capitalism in Vietnam. *Socialist Register* 29: 203–35.

Grindle, Merilee S. and John W. Thomas. 1991. *Public choices and policy change: The political economy of reform in developing countries*. London: Johns Hopkins Press.

Gundlach, Erich. 1999. The impact of human capital on economic development: Problems and perspectives. In Ed. Joseph L.H. Tan, *Human capital formation as an engine of growth*. Singapore: ISEAS.

Haggard, Stephen. 1990. *Pathways from the periphery: The politics of growth in the newly industrializing countries*. Ithaca, NY: Cornell University Press.

Haggard, Stephen. 1994. Politics and institutions in the World Bank's East Asia. In Ed. Albert Fishlow, Catherine Gwin, Stephan Haggard, Dani Rodrik and Robert Wade, *Miracle or design? Lessons from the East Asian experience*. Washington DC: Overseas Development Council.

Heidegger, M. 1977. *The question of technology and other essays*. Trans. William Lovitt. New York: Harper and Row.

Heryanto, Ariel. 1990. The making of language: Developmentalism in Indonesia. *Prisma* no. 50: 40–52.

Heryanto, Ariel. 1995. *Language of development and development of language: The case of Indonesia*. Canberra: Pacific Linguists.

Hewison, Kevin. 1997. Thailand: Capitalist development and the state. In Ed. Gerry Rodan, Kevin Hewison and Richard Robison, *The political economy of South-East Asia.* Oxford: Oxford University Press.

Hiley, Mark. 1999. Industrial restructuring in ASEA and the role of Japanese foreign investment. *European Business Review* 99 no. 2: 80–90.

Hill, Christopher T. 1997. The Congressional Office of Technological Assessment: A retrospective and prospects for the post-OTA world. *Technological Forecasting and Social Change* 54: 191–98.

Hindess, Barry. 1996. *Discourses of power; From Hobbes to Foucault.* Oxford: Blackwell.

Hoogvelt, Ankie M.M. 2001. *Globalization and the postcolonial world: The new political economy of development.* Basingstoke, Hampshire: Palgrave.

Hoos, I.R. 1999. From my perspective—The anatomy of a decision. *Technological Forecasting and Social Change* 60: 295–97.

Hoover, Kevin and Stephen Perez. 2003. Truth and robustness in cross-country growth regressions. *Oxford Bulletin of Economics and Statistics* 66: 765–98.

Hutchcroft, Paul D. 1998. *Booty capitalism: The politics of banking in the Philippines.* Ithaca NY: Cornell University Press.

Illich, Ivan. 1992. Needs. In Ed. W. Sachs, *The development dictionary: A guide to knowledge as power.* London: Zed Press.

Jehle, G.A. and P.J. Reny. 1998. *Advanced microeconomic theory.* New York: Addison-Wesley.

Johnson, Chalmers. 1982. *MITI and the Japanese miracle: The growth of industrial policy, 1925–1975.* Stanford CA: Stanford University Press.

Johnson, Chalmers. 1998. Economic crisis in East Asia: The clash of capitalisms. *Cambridge Journal of Economics* 22: 653–61.

Joll, James. 1965. *Three intellectuals in politics.* New York: Harper & Row.

Kipling, Rudyard. 1899. "The white man's burden." First published in *McClure's Magazine*, Feb. 1899.

Kenny, Charles and David Williams. 2001. What do we know about economic growth? Or, why don't we know very much? *World Development* 29 no. 1: 1–22.

Kerkvliet, Benedict J. Tria. 1980. *The Huk rebellion.* Berkeley: University of California Press.

Kerkvliet, Benedict J. Tria. 2005. *The power of everyday politics: How Vietnamese peasants transformed national policy.* Ithaca, NY: Cornell University Press.

Kleinen, John. 2001. La comédie de l'Etat-parti. Le Viêt Nam depuis la réunification. In Raisons Politiques. *Etudes de pensée politique.* Numéro spécial sur "Ce qui reste du Communisme" no. 3 (August): 37–64.

Kline, Morris. 1980. *Mathematics: The loss of certainty.* Oxford: Oxford University Press.

Kokko, Ari and Fredrik Sjoholm. 2000. Some alternative scenarios for the role of the state in Vietnam. *The Pacific Review* 13 no. 2 (June): 257–77.

Kuhn, Thomas. 1962. *The structure of scientific revolutions.* Chicago: Chicago University Press.

Lakatos, Imre and A. Musgrave, eds. 1970. *Criticism and the growth of knowledge.* Cambridge: Cambridge University Press.

Lao Tzu. 1963. *Tao Te Ching.* Transl. D.C. Lau. London: Penguin Books.

Levine, Ross and Sara J. Zervos. 1993. What have we learnt about policy and growth from cross-country regressions? *The American Economic Review* 82 no. 2 Papers and Proceedings (May): 426–30.

Lindauer, David L. and Lant Pritchett. 2002. What's the big idea? The third generation of policies for economic growth. *Economia* 3 no. 1 (Fall): 1–39.

Lindblom, Charles E. and Edward J. Woodhouse. 1993. *The policy-making process.* Englewood Cliffs NJ: Simon and Schuster.

Macintyre, Andrew. 1994. Business, government and development: Northeast and SEA comparisons. In Ed. Andrew MacIntyre, *Business and government in industrializing Asia.* Sydney: Allen and Unwin.

Mackie, James and Bernardo M. Villegas. 1993. The Philippines: Still an exceptional case. In Ed. James W. Morley, *Driven by growth: Political change in the Asia-Pacific Region.* New York: M.E. Sharpe.

Mallon, Raymond and Brian Van Arkadie. 2003. *Viet Nam—A transition tiger?* Canberra: Asia Pacific Press.

Marchand, Marianne. 1996. Reconceptualising "gender and development" in an era of globalization. *Millennium: Journal of International Studies* 25 no. 3: 577–603.

Marx, Karl. The fetishism of commodities and the secret thereof In *Das Kapital,* Vol 1, Section 4. http://www.marxists.org/archive/marx/works/1867-c1/ch01.htm

McCall, Elizabeth. 1998. Partnership with government: A realistic strategy for poverty focused NGOs. SOAS Mimeo July.

McLean, Ian, ed. 1996. *Oxford dictionary of politics*. Oxford: Oxford University Press.

Meier, G.M. 1976. *Leading issues in economic development*. New York: Oxford University Press.

Meier, G.M. 1984. The formative period. In Ed. G.M. Meier and D. Seers, *Pioneers in development*. New York: Oxford University Press.

Mitchell, Timothy. 1991. The limits of the state: Beyond statist approaches and their critics. *American Political Science Review* 85 no. 1 (March): 77–96.

Molund, Stefan and Goran Schill. 2004. *Looking backward, moving forward*. Stockholm: Sida. Downloaded from www.sida.se.

Moore, Bruce. 1996. *The Australian pocket Oxford dictionary*, 4th edition. Melbourne: Oxford University Press.

Morel, Edmund D. 1971. (Reprint of 1920 original.) *The black man's burden*. Northbrook, IL: Metro Books.

Morris, Christopher. 1955. *The Tudors*. London: Fontana/Collins.

Mulder, Niels. 1996. "This god-forsaken land": Filipino images of the nation. In Ed. Stein Tonnesson and Hans Antlov, *Asian forms of the nation*. Richmond, Surrey: Curzon.

Naughton, B. 1995. *Growing out of the plan: Chinese economic reform 1978–1993*. Cambridge: Cambridge University Press.

Newman, John Henry Cardinal. 1989 (1878). *An essay on the development of Christian doctrine*. Notre Dame, IN: University of Notre Dame Press.

North, Douglass C. 1995. The new institutional economics and Third World development. In Ed. John Harriss et al., *The new institutional economics and Third World development*. London: Routledge.

North, Douglass C. 1996. Markets and other allocation systems in history: The challenge of Karl Polanyi. In Ed. Richard Swedberg, *Economic sociology*. Cheltenham Glos: E. Elgar.

Norton, M. 1997. The UK Parliamentary Office of Science and Technology and its interaction with the OTA. *Technological Forecasting and Social Change* 54: 215–31.

Nukul Commission. 1998. *Analysis and evaluation on facts behind Thailand's economic crisis by the Commission tasked with making recommendations to improve the efficiency and management of Thailand's financial system*. Bangkok mimeo March 31.

Ohno, Kenichi. 1998. Overview: Creating the market economy. In Ed. Kenichi Ohno, and Izumi Ohno, *Japanese views on economic development*. London: Routledge.

Osborne, Milton. 1997. The European advance and challenge. In Ed. Milton Osborne, *Southeast Asia. An introductory history*, 7th edition. NSW, Australia: Allen and Unwin.

Panlilio, F. 1963. *Elementary theory of structural strength*. London: John Wiley and Sons.

Pasuk, Phongpaichit and Chris Baker. 1996. *Thailand's boom*. Sydney: Allen and Unwin.

Pieterse, Jan Nederveen. 1998. My paradigm or yours? Alternative development, post-development, reflexive development. *Development and Change* 29: 343–73.

Pinches, M. 1996. The Philippines' new rich: Capitalist transformation amidst economic gloom. In Ed. Richard Robison and David Goodman, *The new rich in Asia*. London: Routledge.

Polanyi, Karl. 1975. *The great transformation*. New York: Octagon Books.

Pomerleano, Michael. 1998. The East Asian crisis and corporate finances: The untold micro story. *Emerging Markets Quarterly* (Winter): 14–27.

Popper, Karl. 1977 (1959). *The logic of scientific discovery*. London: Hutchinson.

Prasad, Eswar and Kenneth Rogoff. 2003. The emerging truth of going global. London: *Financial Times*, September 1st.

Prasad, Eswar, Kenneth Rogoff, Shang-Jin Wei and M. Ayhan Kose. 2003. *Effects of financial market liberalization on developing countries: Some empirical evidence*. Washington DC: IMF. http://www.imf.org/external/pubs/nft/op/220/index.htm

Pressman, Jeffrey L. and Aaron Wildavsky. 1973. *Implementation: How great expectations in Washington are dashed in Oakland; or, why it's amazing that Federal programs work at all, this being a saga of the Economic Development Administration as told by two sympathetic observers who seek to build morals on a foundation of ruined hopes*. Berkeley: University of California Press.

Rahnema, Majid and Victoria Bawtree, ed. 1997. *The post-development reader*. London: Zed Books.

Ray, Debraj. 1998. *Development economics*. Princeton, NJ: Princeton University Press.

Riedel, James and William Turley. 1999. *Vietnam: Ordeals of transition*. Paris: OECD.

Rigg, Jonathan, Anna Allott, Rachel Harrison, and Ulrich Kratz. 1999. Understanding languages of modernization: A southeast Asian view. *Modern Asian Studies* 33 no. 3: 581–602.

Roberts, Alasdair. 2008. *The collapse of Fortress Bush—The crisis of authority in American government.* New York: New York University Press.

Rock, M. 1995. Thai industrial policy: How irrelevant was it to export success? *Journal of International Development* 7 no. 5: 759–73.

Rodan, Gerry, Kevin Hewison and Richard Robison. 1997. Introduction. In Ed. Gerry Rodan, Kevin Hewison and Richard Robison, *The political economy of South-East Asia.* Oxford: Oxford University Press.

Rodgers, Yana van der Meulen and Jane C. Cooley. 1999. Outstanding female economists in the analysis and practice of development economics. *World Development* 27 no. 4: 1397–1444.

Rodriguez, Francisco and Dani Rodrik. 1999. *Trade policy and economic growth: A skeptic's guide to the cross-national evidence.* NBER Working Paper 7081 April.

Rodrik, Dani. 1994. King Kong meets Godzilla: The World Bank and the East Asian Miracle. In Ed. Albert Fishlow, Catherine Gwin, Stephan Haggard, Dani Rodrik and Robert Wade, *Miracle or design? Lessons from the East Asian experience.* Washington DC: Overseas Development Council.

Rodrik, Dani. 1996. Understanding economic policy reform. *Journal of Economic Literature* XXXIV (March): 9–41.

Rodrik, Dani. 1998. Symposium on globalization in perspective: An introduction. *Journal of Economic Perspectives* 12 no. 4 (Fall): 3–8.

Rostow, W.W. 1971. *Politics and the stages of growth.* Cambridge: Cambridge University Press.

Rothschild, Michael and Joseph E. Stiglitz. 1976. Equilibrium in competitive insurance markets: An essay on the economics of imperfect information. *Quarterly Journal of Economics* 90 no. 4 (Nov): 629–49.

Rutten, Rosanne. 2000. High-cost activism and the worker household: Interests, commitments and the costs of revolutionary activism in a Philippine plantation region. *Theory and Society* 29: 215–52.

Sachs, Jeffrey and Andrew Warner. 1995. Economic reform and the process of global integration. *Brookings Papers on Economic Activity* 1: 1–118.

Sachs, Wolfgang. 1992. One world. In Ed. W. Sachs, *The development dictionary: A guide to knowledge as power.* London: Zed Press.

Scott, James C. 1998. *Seeing like a state: How certain schemes to improve the human condition have failed.* New Haven: Yale University Press.

Sears, Laurie J. 1972. The contingency of autonomous history. In Ed. Laurie J. Sears, *Autonomous histories, particular truths. Essays in honor of John W.R. Smail.* University of Wisconsin Center for SEA Studies Mono 11.

Seidel, Gill and Laurent Vidal. 1997. The implication of "medical," gender in "development" and "culturalist" discourses for HIV/AIDS policy in Africa. In Ed. Chris Shore and Susan Wright, *Anthropology of policy: Critical perspective on governance and power.* London: Routledge.

Sen, Amartya K. 1999. *Development as freedom.* Oxford: Oxford University Press.

Shonfield, Andrew. 1965. *Modern capitalism: The changing balance of public and private power.* London: Oxford University Press.

Shore, Chris and Susan Wright. 1997. Policy: A new field of anthropology. In Ed. Chris Shore and Susan Wright, *Anthropology of policy: Critical perspectives on governance and power.* London: Routledge.

Sidel, John T. 1998. The underside of progress: Land, labor and violence in two Philippine growth zones, 1985–1995. *Bulletin of Concerned Asia Scholars* 30 no. 1.

Simon, Herbert A. 1986. Rationality in psychology and economics. *Journal of Business* 59 no. 4 part 2 (Oct): S209–S224.

Smail, John W.R. 1972. On the possibility of an autonomous history of Southeast Asia. In Ed. Laurie J. Sears, *Autonomous histories, particular truths. Essays in honor of John W.R. Smail.* University of Wisconsin Center for SEA Studies Mono 11.

Smith, Neil. 1997. The Satanic geographies of globalization: Uneven development in the 1990s. *Public Culture* 10: 169–89.

Smith, T.C. 1959. *The agrarian origins of modern Japan.* Stanford, CA: Stanford University Press.

Spruyt, Hendrik. 1994. *The sovereign state and its competitors: An analysis of systems change.* Princeton, NJ: Princeton University Press.

Stern, N. 1989. The economics of development: A survey. *The Economic Journal* 99 no. 397 (Sept): 597–685.

Stigler, G.J. 1947. *The theory of price.* New York: The Macmillan Company.

Stiglitz, Joseph E. 1996. Some lessons from the East Asian Miracle. *World Bank Research Observer* 11 no. 2 (August): 157–78.

Stiglitz, Joseph E. 1998. More instruments and broader goals: Moving towards the post-Washington consensus. WIDER Annual Lecture: Helsinki.

Stiglitz, Joseph E. 2000. *Economics of the public sector.* New York: W.W. Norton and Company.

Stoecker, Ralf. 2007. Action and responsibility—A second look at ascriptivism. In Ed. Christopher Lumer and Sandro Nannini, *Intentionality, deliberation and autonomy*. Aldershot: Ashgate.

Summers, Lawrence H. 1999. Reflections on managing global integration. *Journal of Economic Perspectives* 13 no. 2 (Spring): 3–18.

Sun Yat Sen. 1928. *The international development of China.* London: Hutchinson, published on behalf of the London Office, Chinese Ministry of Information.

Sylvester, Christine. 1999. Development studies and postcolonial studies: Disparate tales of the Third World. *Third World Quarterly* 20 no. 4: 703–21.

The Economist. 2000. South-east Asia's problem trio and China and ASEA: The best things in life. Dec 2: 29–30.

Todaro, Michael P. and Stephen C. Smith. 2006. *Economic Development,* 9th edition. Boston: Pearson Addison Wesley.

Toye, J. 1983. The disparaging of development economics. *Journal of Development Studies* 20 no. 1: 87–108.

Toye, J. 1987. *Dilemmas of development: Reflections on the counter-revolution in development theory and practice.* Oxford: Blackwell.

Trocki, Carl A. 1999 (1992). Political structures in the nineteenth and early twentieth centuries. In Ed. Nicholas Tarling, *The Cambridge history of Southeast Asia*, Vol. Three. Cambridge: Cambridge University Press.

Turk, Carrie. 2001. Linking participatory poverty assessments to policy and policymaking: Experience from Vietnam. Policy Research Working Paper No 2526. Washington DC: World Bank.

Unger, Danny. 1998. *Building social capital in Thailand: Fibers, finance and infrastructure.* Cambridge: Cambridge University Press.

Ungpakorn, Ji Giles. 2002. From tragedy to comedy: Political reform in Thailand. *Journal of Contemporary Asia* 32 (2): 191–205.

Van Eijndhoven, Josee C.M. 1997. Technology assessment: product or process? *Technological Forecasting and Social Change* 54: 269–86.

Vasavakul, Thaveeporn. 1993. Vietnam: Sectors, classes and the transformation of a Leninist state. In Ed. James W. Morley, *Driven by growth: Political change in the Asia-Pacific Region.* New York: M.E. Sharpe.

Vasavakul, Thaveeporn. 1996. Politics of the reform of state institutions in post-socialist Vietnam. In Ed. Suiwah Leung, *Vietnam assessment: Creating a sound investment climate.* Singapore: ISEAS.

Vickerman, Andrew. 1986. *The fate of the peasantry—premature "transition to socialism" in the Democratic Republic of Vietnam.* Monograph Series no. 28, Yale University Southeast Asian Studies Centre for International and Area Studies.

Villacorta, Wilfrido V. 1994. The curse of the weak state: Leadership imperatives for the Ramos government. *Contemporary Southeast Asia* 16 no. 1: 67–92.

Wade, Robert. 1988. The role of government in overcoming market failure: Taiwan, Republic of Korea and Japan. In Ed. Helen Hughes, *Achieving industrialization in East Asia.* Cambridge: Cambridge University Press.

Wade, Robert. 1990. *Governing the market: Economic theory and the role of government in East Asian industrialization.* Princeton, NJ: Princeton University Press.

Warr, P. 1994. The Thai economy. In Ed. Peter Warr, *The Thai economy in transition.* Cambridge: Cambridge University Press.

Waterbury, John. 1999. The long gestation and brief triumph of import-substituting industrialization. *World Development* 27 no. 2: 323–41.

Williamson, John. 1990. *Latin American adjustment.* Washington DC: Institute of International Economics.

Williamson, John. 2000. What should the World Bank think about the Washington Consensus? *The World Bank Research Observer* 15 no. 2 (Aug): 251–64.

Winch, Peter. 1958. *The idea of a social science and its relation to philosophy.* London: Routledge.

Wood, Adrian. 1997. Openness and wage inequality in developing countries: The Latin American challenge to East Asian conventional wisdom. *The World Bank Economic Review* 11 no. 1: 33–57.

Wood, Adrian and Cristobal Ridao-Cano. 1999. Skill, trade and international inequality. *Oxford Economic Papers* 51: 89–119.

Woodiwiss, Anthony. 1998. *Globalisation, human rights and labour law in Pacific Asia.* Cambridge: Cambridge University Press.

World Bank. 1993. *The East Asian miracle: Economic growth and public policy.* Washington DC: World Bank.

World Bank. 1998. *East Asia: The road to recovery.* Washington DC: World Bank.

World Bank. 2000. *Philippines: Growth with equity—The remaining agenda—A World Bank social and structural review.* Washington DC: World Bank.

World Bank. 2007. *World Development Report 2007: Development and the next generation.* Washington DC: World Bank.

Yamazawa, I. 1992. On Pacific economic cooperation. *Economic Journal* 102 (November): 1519–29.

Yonay, Yuval P. 1998. *The struggle over the soul of economics.* Princeton, NJ: Princeton University Press.

Zebregs, Harm. 1998. Can the neo-classical model explain the distribution of foreign direct investment across developing countries? Washington DC: IMF Working Paper No 139 9/1998.

Zysman, John. 1983. *Governments, markets and growth: Financial systems and the politics of industrial change.* Ithaca, NY: Cornell University Press.

Index

About the Author

Adam Fforde is currently chairman of Adam Fforde and Associates p/l, and principal fellow at the Asia Institute, the University of Melbourne. He has spent about two-thirds of his career in development consultancy and the rest as an academic. He studied engineering and economics at Oxford and then worked as an economic consultant in London before taking master's and doctoral degrees in economics at Birkbeck College, London, and Cambridge, respectively. His PhD (1982) was about agricultural cooperatives in North Vietnam, and he was a student at Hanoi University from 1978 to 1979. From 1983 to 1987 he was a postdoctoral research fellow, and since then he has combined academic and consulting work related to Vietnam and to development issues more generally. He worked for the Swedish-Vietnamese cooperation from 1987 to 1992, and was a senior fellow at the SEA Studies Program, NUS, from 2000 to 2001. In Melbourne he has taught at Monash, La Trobe, and the University of Melbourne. His most recent book on Vietnam is *Vietnamese State Industry and the Political Economy of Commercial Renaissance: Dragon's Tooth or Curate's Egg?* (Oxford: Chandos 2007).

Also from Kumarian Press...

International Development:

The World Bank and the Gods of Lending
Steve Berkman

Rights-Based Approaches to Development: Exploring the Potentials and Pitfalls
Edited by Sam Hickey and Diana Mitlin

Human Rights and Development
Peter Uvin

New and Forthcoming:

Creating Credibility: Legitimacy and Accountability for Transnational Civil Society
L. David Brown

Reluctant Bedfellows: Feminism, Activism and Prostitution in the Philippines
Meredith Ralston and Edna Keeble

Humanitarianism Under Fire: The US and UN Intervention in Somalia
Kenneth R. Rutherford

Visit Kumarian Press at www.kpbooks.com or call toll-free 800.232.0223 for a complete catalog